THE POLITICS OF
THE PRESIDENT'S
WIFE

Joseph V. Hughes Jr. and Holly O. Hughes Series
on the Presidency and Leadership
JAMES P. PFIFFNER, GENERAL EDITOR

A list of titles in this series is available at the back of the book.

THE POLITICS OF
THE PRESIDENT'S

Wife

———————— ★ ————————

MaryAnne Borrelli

TEXAS A&M UNIVERSITY PRESS
College Station

This paper meets the requirements of ANSI/NISO Z39.48-1992
(Permanence of Paper).
Binding materials have been chosen for durability.
⊗ ♻

Library of Congress Cataloging-in-Publication Data

Borrelli, MaryAnne.
The politics of the president's wife / MaryAnne Borrelli. — 1st ed.
p. cm. — (Joseph V. Hughes Jr. and Holly O. Hughes series
on the presidency and leadership)
Includes bibliographical references and index.
ISBN-13: 978-1-60344-284-8 (cloth : alk. paper)
ISBN-10: 1-60344-284-7 (cloth : alk. paper)
ISBN-13: 978-1-60344-285-5 (pbk. : alk. paper)
ISBN-10: 1-60344-285-5 (pbk. : alk. paper)
[etc.]
1. Presidents' spouses—United States—History—20th century.
2. Presidents' spouses—United States—History—21st century.
3. Women—Political activity—United States. I. Title.
II. Series: Joseph V. Hughes, Jr. and Holly O. Hughes series
on the presidency and leadership.
E176.2.B67 2011
973.09′9—dc22
2010053056

To Mom and Dad,
my first and best teachers.
Thank you.

CONTENTS

ILLUSTRATIONS

TABLES

Acknowledgments

I am overwhelmed by the generosity of my colleagues, friends, and family, who have contributed so much of their time and their expertise to this book. These acknowledgments can only hint at the extent of my indebtedness and my appreciation.

My first thanks are extended to Mary Lenn Dixon, editor-in-chief at Texas A&M University Press, and to James P. Pfiffner, series editor and university professor at George Mason University. Their confidence and their patience were extraordinary. I can only hope to equal them as supportive and reflective mentors.

The data presented in this volume were gathered at a series of presidential archives, whose staffs did not even flinch at my constant requests for documents, photographs, and manuscripts. Thanks go to the archivists at the Herbert Hoover Library, the Harry S. Truman Library, the Dwight D. Eisenhower Library, the John F. Kennedy Library, the Lyndon B. Johnson Library, the Nixon Presidential Materials, the Gerald R. Ford Library, the Jimmy Carter Library, the Ronald Reagan Library, the George Bush Library, and the William J. Clinton Library. I am especially grateful for the help provided by Barbara Constable and Claudia Anderson at the Johnson Library, and Geir Gundersen at the Ford Library. No less critically important to my research were the librarians at Connecticut College, who were peerless in their thoughtful professionalism. Special thanks are extended to reference librarians Jim MacDonald, Kathy Gehring, Beth Hansen, Ashley Hanson, and Amanda Watson; to interlibrary loan librarian Emily Aylward; and to acquisitions librarians Melodie Hamilton and Lorraine McKinney.

Travel and research were supported through several generous grants. The Herbert Hoover Foundation, the Lyndon B. Johnson Foundation, and the Gerald R. Ford Foundation underwrote research conducted at their respective presidential libraries. The George H. W. Bush School of Government and Public Service provided a travel grant to a conference at Texas A&M University, which also facilitated research at the Bush archives. The Connecticut College R. F. Johnson Fund for Faculty Development helped to allay costs associated with obtaining documents from the Kennedy and Bush libraries.

In preparing the manuscript for publication, I benefited from the talents of several extraordinary individuals. At Connecticut College, Mike Dreimiller, Ruth Seeley, and Gary Tiller rescued me on innumerable occasions from my own computer inabilities. Frank Fulchiero and Janet Hayes provided critical support in preparing the illustrations. Nancy Lewandowski was a patient and cheerful voice of reason, providing guidance and confidence in response to every sort of difficulty. Anonymous reviewers contributed insight and wisdom. When Texas A&M University Press duly forwarded the manuscript to copyeditor Lona Dearmont, my good fortune continued. And then, the editors and designers in College Station created a book that is a joy to hold, a piece of art in its own right.

Finally, my family provided support and challenge—each in proper measure—throughout this entire project. Whether it was finding a place for boxes of documents or clearing the dining room table for writing, offering a late-night meal or listening to my complaints, getting me to the airport or celebrating my successes, they have contributed in every way to this book. The mistakes are mine. The accomplishment is ours. Thank you.

THE POLITICS OF
THE PRESIDENT'S
WIFE

INTRODUCTION

The wives of the modern presidents are complicated women. Their personalities defy easy categorization, their partisan and gender ideologies vary widely, and their ambitions cannot be readily discerned. Yet political science and gender studies are both dedicated to searching out the patterns that underlie apparently disparate phenomena and actors. And the intellectual resources of presidency and gender studies do reveal commonalities among the modern first ladies. They are singular, but they are not unique.

Among the roles and responsibilities that the first ladies have shared in common are those associated with representation. Encompassing and surpassing the duties of public outreach, representation requires an entrepreneur's skill in communicating and in relationship building. Rather than simply restating or explaining the president's words to the public, the first lady takes on the much more difficult and far riskier task of interpreting one to the other. She is called upon to clarify and calm, or to inspire and motivate, projecting a voicing of confidence, reason, and balance. Lady Bird (Claudia Alta) Taylor Johnson resolutely communicated the success of her husband's domestic programs, for example, and Laura Welch Bush reached out to moderate voters in congressional midterm and presidential reelection campaigns. On other occasions, first ladies have been called upon to remind the people of more intangible ideals with national significance. Rosalynn Smith Carter's decision to wear the gown she wore to her husband's gubernatorial inaugural ball to his presidential inaugural ball was at once sentimental and populist in its frugality. Four years later, Nancy Davis Reagan signaled the glamour and elitism of presidential power with her designer gown, jewelry, and accessories.

Equally telling, when first ladies have not been accepted as representatives, they have had to find a way to reinstate themselves as interpreters and mediators. Eleanor Roosevelt, whose commitment to social justice led her to believe that the war effort would reverse the accomplishments of the New

Deal, nonetheless showcased her patriotism through visits to troops abroad. Pat (Thelma Catherine) Ryan Nixon, castigated for limited travel and press accessibility, conducted public diplomacy in Ghana, Liberia, the Ivory Coast, and Peru. Announcing scholarship programs in the African nations and delivering humanitarian supplies after a devastating earthquake in the Andes, Nixon sought to change public perceptions of the United States internationally. In brief, first ladies have been expected and obliged to facilitate communications and relationships that will bring political success to their husbands' administrations.

Of course, some such contribution is expected of every member of a presidential administration. To compare the president's wife to other members of the White House Office, I draw upon the intellectual insights of presidency research and organizational studies to consider her circumstances as a presidential advisor, a political actor, and the chief executive's wife. Then I turn to gender studies to weigh the resources and the constraints encountered by a woman in a branch of government that some describe as the "most masculine," and by a wife in a society that prizes the autonomous and self-reliant leader. The first lady must negotiate contradictory cultural dictates and competitive political environments, while having her success presumed and her failures publicized. We know much more about what first ladies have not done than about what they have consistently and routinely contributed to the presidency. And this lack of knowledge exists even though outstanding biographies have been written about the individual wives. We know something about the women who have been first ladies, but we have much to learn about the roles and responsibilities that define their post.

This book contributes to that learning, through a study of the work and contributions of the first ladies as representatives in the modern presidency. I reject the notion that the first lady "shares" presidential power, as there is little indication in administration records or first ladies' papers that these women perceived themselves, or were perceived by others, as doing so. There is, however, considerable evidence that first ladies view themselves—and are viewed by others—as exercising influence that is intrinsic to their post within the White House Office. "Presidential partner" is therefore as inappropriate an appellation for the first lady as it would be for the White House chief of staff.

Studying the first lady as a representative reveals this power, situating her within a presidential administration while still acknowledging her distinctive status. Like other representatives within the presidency, she has sometimes presented the president's views to constituents and sometimes presented constituents' views to the president. In mediating president-constituent relationships, she has given a historical and social frame to the presidency that has enhanced its symbolic representation; she has served as a gender role model, enriching descriptive representation in the executive branch; and she has participated in policy initiatives to strengthen an administration's substantive representation. These contributions have been controversial, as might be predicted for a gender outsider, but they attest to the influence that a president's wife may exercise.[1]

During the modern presidency, changes in campaigns, electoral systems, popular participation, interest group mobilization, White House staffing arrangements, executive departments and agencies, and legislative-executive relations fundamentally altered the exercise of power. War and military actions, as well as a volatile domestic and international economy, imposed virtually unprecedented demands upon presidential leadership. An array of civil rights movements, partisan realignments, nativist movements, and a religious reawakening further contributed to reshaping popular expectations of democratic-republican government. Deeply engaged in communications and in building relationships, first ladies were among those mediating these changes for the president and the presidency. The presidents' wives have literally "re-presented" the president, the public, and the presidency to one another.

First Lady Politics as Gender Politics

Any investigation of the first ladies and the first ladies' post must be as rooted in gender studies as it is in presidency research. The origins of the first ladyship are highly informal, reflecting generalized (even essentialist) conceptions of women and of wives.[2] Though there has been a comparative formalization of the office, with statutory and case law explicitly authorizing the first lady's staff and her engagement in policy making, public expectations are still highly influential. Integral to these public expectations, and to first lady priorities, are judgments about gender and gender role modeling.

Surveying the powers of the president, their historic origins and their constitutional expression, gender scholars have concluded that the presidential office is arguably the most intensely masculine post in the United States government. As the commander-in-chief, the president gives modern expression to ideals with ancient and medieval origins, including duty and honor. The sheer multiplicity of powers puts the president in the position of being a

"chief among chiefs," a single leader who literally embodies the nation's interest. The office also gives institutional expression to traits attributed to masculinity in western European traditions. These include self-reliance, autonomy,
competitiveness, and ambition. Forceful (though not abusive) leadership is
expected of those who seek and hold this office, a circumstance that led to
extended debates throughout the 2008 election—was being male a de facto
requirement for being president?[3]

As candidates and as officeholders, presidents have typically conformed
to the mythology of the office, proving their masculinity in traditional terms.
Presidents have stressed their athleticism (and thus their competitive and aggressive spirit), have asserted their intellectual abilities (and thus their incisive
and confrontational thinking), and have showcased their personal strength
(and thus their self-reliance and autonomy). Any suggestion that a president was lacking in these qualities has been hastily reframed, as when presidential illness or injury has been transformed into an expression of courage
and resilience—Ronald Reagan's partisan banter with his surgeons following
the assassination attempt immediately comes to mind. John Kennedy was
particularly emphatic in his self-portrayals, referring to his wartime service
record and to aggressive touch-football games as evidence of his athleticism;
presenting *Profiles in Courage* as evidence of his reflective and analytic talents;
and showcasing his wife as proof of his virility. In these instances and many
others, the president's gender performance was expressive of the gender ideals
of western European, post-Enlightenment, liberal political ideas.

As gender scholars have noted, the result of these beliefs and efforts is an
office that is essentialist and highly exclusive in its masculinity.

> The term *chief* is seldom associated with traditional women's work,
> and women as commanders are even more rare. The "protector" role
> has been almost exclusively a masculine endeavor, beyond the chang-
> ing image of a mother protecting her children. "Voice" is only recently
> something women have been known to have, although surely women
> have always spoken, often in very public ways. As advertising agencies
> and female candidates are well aware, authoritative voices are still ceded
> far more readily to men. This factor also figures centrally into a presi-
> dent's prime power: the power to persuade. The elements that assist per-
> suasion—such as a professional reputation, being seen as a commanding
> presence, and associated elements of public prestige—are also attributed
> more readily to men.[4]

In its turn, the first lady's post has routinely been judged by standards that are exclusively, essentially feminine. The "first lady" title alone, rejected by a number of president's wives, immediately highlights her gender role modeling. The president's wife is a "lady," a term linked to distinctively Anglo-Saxon, white, privileged ideals that confine women to a life of well-mannered civility in the private sphere. As Betty Friedan noted in her searing critique, *The Feminine Mystique* (1963), this is a gender ideology that capitalizes on women's skill (if not their willingness) to tend and facilitate others' ambitions, while denying women the intellectual stimulation and emotional challenge of acting upon their own desires.[5] Today, it is a worldview that surfaces in social conservative thought, which endorses separate spheres and exclusive gender roles.[6] Applied to the first couple, this historical and present-day gender ideology calls for a strong, commanding and authoritative, independent and unequivocal president; and a nurturing, other-directed and thoughtful, reflective moral guardian as first lady. He embodies the best of the public sphere; she embodies the best of the private sphere.

Yet this dichotomizing of the public and private spheres imposes contradictory expectations on the first lady. "Ladies" may be sequestered in the private sphere, but "first ladies" must present themselves in the public sphere as gender role models. Moreover, as the president's wife, a woman finds her role as a political wife expanded, in keeping with her husband's duties and obligations: "A political wife is expected to provide her husband with personal support and encouragement; the president's wife may be the president's protector. A political wife is expected to enhance her husband's image; a president's wife is a public symbol. A political wife is often a campaign surrogate; a first lady may be the president's partner. And while a political wife raises a family, the first lady is elevated to being the nation's hostess."[7] Being an effective first lady therefore means being a controversial first lady, to the extent that the public's demands contradict its expectations.

The modern presidents' wives have responded to this problem in various ways. Some, including Nancy Reagan, Barbara Pierce Bush, and Laura Bush, have framed (and in framing, excused) their public-sphere work as an extension of their private-sphere commitments. These women campaigned as loyal wives and mothers, stressing their familial roles and downplaying their partisanship. In the White House, they similarly presented their policy making as nonpartisan and apolitical, directed more at effecting social change than altering government priorities. Advancing initiatives such as Helping America's Youth, for example, Laura Bush consistently emphasized the need for adult mentors and role models: "Adults should be aware of the challenges that face children, and they should take an active interest in their lives. Adults, and especially parents, should build relationships where they teach their kids healthy behaviors by their own good examples."[8] In these and innumerable other statements, Bush presented herself as a moral guardian, analyzing family relations and calling for change—but not for government intervention. Her words referenced her own values as a parent as much as her professional expertise in child development. Though Bush spoke *in* the public sphere, she was careful to voice her judgments *from* the private sphere, a distinction that finessed concerns about her gender role modeling.

At the other extreme have been first ladies who unapologetically and unequivocally took action in the public sphere, advocating change through formal governmental policy. Eleanor Roosevelt, Rosalynn Carter, and Hillary Rodham Clinton were named to formal positions within their husbands' administrations and testified before Congress. They campaigned independently for their husbands, were clear about their partisan affiliations, and advanced policy initiatives not previously identified with "women's issues." In doing so, these three women contradicted strongly held views of what constituted acceptable behavior for women. Few people were ignorant of their priorities or their actions.

Between these alternatives, however, is a vast middle ground. First ladies "in between" the two extremes include Lou Henry Hoover, Jacqueline Bouvier Kennedy, Lady Bird Johnson, Pat Nixon, Betty (Elizabeth) Bloomer Ford, and Michelle Robinson Obama. Michelle Obama, for example, has repeatedly stressed her role and responsibilities as a mother. Throughout her first year in the White House, she emphasized the importance of seeing her children settled in a new home and a new school, with routines entirely different from their lives in Chicago. When Obama turned to policy, it was with a focus on issues that had historically been associated with the private sphere—food and nutrition, childhood health, gardens and menus. Her communications, with military families and schoolchildren, were congruent with conceptions of the woman as nurturer. Yet Obama added a partisan and autonomous edge to these actions. She claimed the title of "mom-in-chief" and stated explicitly that she was a leader in her family. The kitchen garden initiative unfolded into a public awareness campaign against childhood obesity ("Let's Move!"); an extended set of negotiations with major corporate suppliers in the school lunch program to improve nutritional standards; a presidential task force set an agenda for programmatic reforms throughout the executive branch; and increased budget appropriations to implement the changes. Obama spoke of her work in the public sphere as a reflection of her commitment to the private sphere—"What made me think about nutrition was when I became a mother"—but she was participating and leading in the public sphere.[9]

As different as the first ladies' approaches to gender role modeling and policy making may seem, they are comparatively consistent in responding to public expectations that tie femininity to the private sphere. To suggest that women could or should participate in the public sphere generates immediate controversy. No longer is the president the "public sphere man" to the first lady's "private sphere woman." Consequently, the president may be described as losing power or even as emasculated, charges that were directed at President Bill Clinton in articles, editorials, and political cartoons during his wife's leadership of the Task Force on National Health Care Reform. If the first lady, further, contradicts presidential statements, especially on policy matters, he may be criticized for failing to "control" his wife. Following Betty Ford's controversial *60 Minutes* interview, letters to Gerald Ford expressed just this sentiment.[10] Both political analysts and the general public have viewed first ladies' participation in the public sphere as undermining the presidents' leadership.

It is in the president's interest, therefore, to have the first lady's political and governmental contributions go unrecognized. The wife's substantive expertise is minimized; she is presented as having only personalized understandings of "women's issues." By marginalizing the marriage, there is the hope of preempting charges of presidential manipulation by the first lady. Even so, first ladies have routinely been questioned about their policy conversations and sleeping arrangements with the president.[11] A Clinton cabinet officer, for instance, bluntly attributed the failure of health-care reform initiatives to the first lady's sexual relationship with the president: "The person who's in charge shouldn't sleep with the President, because if you sleep with the President, nobody is going to tell you the truth."[12]

Popular conceptions and expectations of the first lady provide critical insights. They reveal the relevance to the presidency of society's most deeply held conceptions of personal identity and relationship. They teach us about women's status within the society and the political system. And, because gender role modeling affects the first lady's participation in the public sphere, they uncover the connections between identity and power, between gender and representation, in the democratic republic.

THE FIRST LADY AND REPRESENTATION

To identify the first lady as a representative is to conclude that she is performing one of the constitutive tasks of governing in the United States, which
takes great pride in its status as a democratic republic. Representatives in
the U.S. government are entrusted with power to advance the interests of
their constituents or, as described in the *Federalist Papers,* to "refine and ele-
vate" popular demands. They are held accountable through elections, through
nomination and confirmation proceedings, and through the threat of impeachment. It is this equation of empowerment and control that causes such
difficulties for the first lady. As already noted, her claim to and exercise of
power in the executive branch is highly problematic. It seems also that any
possibility of accountability is equally so, as she is not elected, is designated
rather than appointed or nominated, and would have access to the president
through marriage even if she were removed from her post. It appears that the
first lady is more likely to undermine than to strengthen representative government, given these circumstances.

   While such a concern is understandable, it is also mistaken. Powerful
constraints are imposed on, and thereby secure accountability from, the first
lady. Throughout the modern presidency, media coverage of the presidents'
wives has been extensive and carefully monitored by the White House. Precisely because she is married to the president, the first lady's words and actions are considered revelatory of his political and policy priorities. Moreover, because the president is expected to epitomize a masculine ideal of
strength, while the first lady similarly presents a feminine ideal of deference,
their relationship is scrutinized for evidence that he is fit and able to lead.
Although the first lady is not herself elected to office, she is viewed as having
the potential to affect the president's electoral fortunes. As will be shown in
later chapters, this has resulted in stringent checks being imposed on the first
lady. She has, unquestionably, been held accountable as a political actor.

   In addition to media coverage, public opinion, and White House review,
statutes and case law also constrain the first lady. As will be seen, these limit
a first lady's options for holding paid office in the executive branch and for
expanding the range of her voluntary services to the government. Another
statute, however, formally recognizes the role of the president's "spouse" in
providing "assistance to the President in the discharge of the President's duties and responsibilities" with appropriations to support this work. And, acknowledging the longstanding contributions of the first ladies as presidential
advisors, the District of Columbia Circuit Court of Appeals has ruled that

she was a de facto public official for the purposes of the Federal Advisory Committee Act. In brief, the president's wife has been formally authorized and federally financed to serve in the White House Office.

Even if one accepts that a first lady may be held accountable and that she is a member of the government, is she a representative? I argue that this question must be answered in the affirmative because of the tasks that define the first lady's post. She is expected to communicate with diverse publics, explaining and interpreting the president's priorities, policies, and programs. Further, she is expected to explain and interpret the public's response to the president. By performing these roles well, she builds and strengthens relationships with presidential constituents in particular, and with groups, networks, and blocs throughout society more generally. These are the tasks that distinguish representation, and representation requires the exercise of judgment and reason in order to facilitate deliberation about values and interests.

The complexity and power that are such important aspects of this work further distinguish the first lady as providing representation. Outreach to the public is certainly performed by the first lady, but that undertaking is much simpler than representation. Outreach can be unidirectional, need not be interpretive, and may be superficial in its content and its consequences. Representation is far more demanding in the standards it sets for communications and for relationship building. Suzanne Dovi, for example, argues that a "good representative" will manifest three virtues, each contributing to the democratic republic as follows:

- Acting on the virtue of fair mindedness, which will contribute to the realization of civic equality through the protection of individual rights, and perhaps even more importantly, through the recognition and correction of systemic inequalities;
- Acting on the virtue of critical trust building, which will contribute to self-governance by developing the capacity of citizens for deliberation and decision making; and
- Acting on the virtue of good gatekeeping, which will foster inclusion through mutualistic relationships, mobilization, and informed public deliberations.[13]

These are virtues that the first ladies have demonstrated and standards that they have met, assertions that will be supported by the research presented in this book. First, however, the framework used to analyze the first lady's representation needs to be defined and discussed.

Types of Representation

The focus here is on three types of representation, namely, the symbolic, the descriptive, and the substantive. This particular classification schema for representation was chosen because it facilitates study of the first lady's actions and words, as documented through presidential archives, public records, and media accounts. The differences among these three types of representation, in addition to their empirical orientation, reveal the rich diversity of the modern first lady's representation. It is still necessary to give close attention to the historical context in which the first ladies served, but analyzing representation as symbolic, descriptive, and substantive does encompass the extraordinary changes seen in the presidency from the Hoover administration to the first two years of the Obama administration.

Symbolic representation is the use of symbols to evoke emotions and responses, to conceptualize complex ideas, and to give access to their meaning. The White House, for example, is an immediately recognized symbol of the presidency and presidential power. It is also known as a national historic site, a museum, a home, and an office building. And this descriptive, interpretive list could be extended even further, because the rich meaning of symbols can never be "captured" in its entirety. Symbols often represent abstractions that are emotionally as well as intellectually profound in their representations.[14]

In addition to the "re-presentation" provided by the symbol, I argue that symbolic representation also encompasses the interpreting and the making of symbols. These tasks pose significant challenges. The individual who attempts to communicate about symbols is presuming to discuss something that, by definition, cannot be made fully intelligible. The emotional, and perhaps also the intellectual, elements cannot be comprehensively articulated. The individual who is making new symbols must have such strong and well-understood relationships with constituents that the existing emotional resonance aids in the acceptance of the symbol and its meanings.

I do not mean to suggest that the representative manipulates or denigrates the constituents by imposing symbols and meanings.[15] Consider Dovi's three civic virtues and their contributions to realizing democratic ideals—they are relevant to the leadership that is demonstrated in interpreting and making symbols. Fair-mindedness ensures that the symbol's meaning is shared and affirms civic equality. Critical trust building confirms that the symbol is understood and affirmatively valued throughout the polity. And good gatekeeping results in the symbols being used to advance inclusivity in government and society.

Descriptive representation is commonly associated with calls for the legislature or the bureaucracy to mirror the society, in the expectation that these decision makers will then better reflect the values and interests of the people in their deliberations. Though Hanna Pitkin refers to descriptive representation as "standing for" constituents, she notes that this is not merely a passive relaying of information. Descriptive representation is instead an evaluative process that yields accurate information and provides the government with the data needed to formulate effective programs.[16]

Current discussions of descriptive representation, however, exhibit marked contrasts with the theories and recommendations of the proportionalists and of Pitkin. John Stuart Mill, for example, argued for descriptive representation in the legislature, so that this body would have the capacity to debate and to critique the government. The legislature was not to build consensus or to develop policy. In Pitkin's words, "standing for" is an "activity," but it does not involve "agency."[17] Present-day theorists strongly disagree. Identity scholars, especially, observe that when the representative decides which aspects of her or his identity—and thus of her or his constituents—will be represented, and then further determines what information will achieve this goal, the representative is demonstrating agency. Consequently, "standing for" is a form of "acting for," and it is important that representatives be held accountable for the associated decisions and actions.

The dilemmas for a descriptive representative are a product of the multiple and intersecting aspects of people's identities. As Pitkin observed, descriptive representatives are not able to reproduce their constituencies in their entirety, so they (and we) confront the question of setting a standard for their correspondence.[18] Further, priorities need to be assigned to the qualities that are to be descriptively represented. In other words, who counts and how much? Dovi's discussion of fair-mindedness and good gatekeeping is extremely important in this context. Descriptive representation sets the agenda for governing at such an early stage that its consequences may become normative, with great harm if ignored or accepted. Asian American feminists, among others, have referred to this as a problem of "invisible invisibility." Their exclusion from decision- or policy-making processes has passed largely unnoticed, so it was never identified as a problem to be rectified by the democratic republic. Descriptive representation, therefore, allocates power by determining who will be considered in deliberations, negotiations, and decisions.

Substantive representation is "acting for" constituents, whether by advocating policies that the constituents endorse or obtaining resources through government programs. Because substantive representation so obviously provides or denies, is successful or fails, in securing power for citizens, it has been the focus of many theories and studies. Among the more famous debates are those relating to the extent to which representatives should be tied to the preferences of the constituents, serving as their agents (following their directives), their trustees (representatives acting on their more independent judgment), or finding some middle ground. Each has its difficulties, as agents' constituents are seldom unified in their preferences, trustees' constituents often insist upon some accountability and transparency, and any "middle ground" is likely to generate worries about the representative's consistency as a decision maker.[19]

Examining substantive representation with the resources of gender studies reveals the extent to which the government has been involved in defining gender roles, through the norms that it enforces and the power that it allocates. As Gretchen Ritter has detailed in her discussion of civic membership, the state has been intensely involved in the formation and continuation of gender, to the point that it is integral to the nation's "core governing ideologies."[20] As a preeminent mechanism for communication between the society and the government, substantive representation has been a highly gendered enterprise with its power and resources largely reserved to men. Women's widespread participation in and influence over decision making—as legislators, judges, and bureaucratic executives—is a comparatively recent phenomenon. It has also yet to be fully achieved, the United States not having had a woman as majority leader of the U.S. Senate, chief justice of the U.S. Supreme Court, or president. Not surprisingly, feminist theorists have cautioned against an unqualified dependence on government to provide adequate representation for women.[21]

Because women have been underrepresented in the past, even as the government has exerted extraordinary power over their lives, feminist theorists argue that women are needed to represent women. In representing women, they maintain, women representatives will

- provide women with role models, encouraging their political mobilization;
- advance democratic ideals of justice and fairness;
- increase women's trust in government;
- enhance the legitimacy of the democratic republic; and
- improve democratic deliberation at every stage of the policy process.[22]

This is the substantive argument for descriptive representation. The challenge is to achieve these goals without relying on a singular, overly simplified, essentialist conception of women. If a representative falls into this trap, then she or he will give new expression to old practices of exclusion and oppression. All three virtues—fair-mindedness, critical trust building, and good gatekeeping—must be interwoven, and closely reviewed, in the performance of substantive representation.

Modern first ladies have performed symbolic representation, descriptive representation, and substantive representation. Their contributions as symbolic representatives have been particularly evident through their management of White House events, from morning meetings to teas to state dinners to concert series. Jacqueline Kennedy, for example, seized upon these opportunities to place her husband's administration at the center of political, cultural, and artistic networks.[23] She framed the presidency as powerful and as elegant. The modern first ladies have also been widely recognized as gender role models for women, which is to say that they have been acknowledged as descriptive representatives. Mamie Eisenhower's self-presentation as a good housekeeper and homemaker in the White House—checking the pantry, saving and using the leftovers, organizing and presiding over social occasions—aligned with white mainstream expectations of women in her generation. Finally, the modern first ladies have frequently distinguished themselves as substantive representatives. They have held appointive or honorary posts in their husbands' administrations, lobbied state and national legislatures, and mobilized far-flung issue networks. They have addressed a wide range of issues, including economic development, social justice, historic preservation, urban redevelopment and wilderness preservation, mental health care, drug education, literacy, health-care insurance reform, human rights, and childhood nutrition. In each instance, the first ladies have explained the values and interests of the president and the public, each to the other, to win political and electoral support for the chief executive.

Responses to the First Lady as a Representative

First ladies have encountered both criticism and affirmation in serving as representatives. They have typically been evaluated with reference to separate-spheres gender ideology, which reserves the public sphere to men and the private sphere to women. This gender ideology holds that women properly perform their gender roles in devoting themselves to meeting familial and societal needs for civility, collaboration, and consensus. Their voice is corrupted when it advances self-interest and personal ambition. This was the charge directed at Hillary Rodham Clinton, who was portrayed as exemplifying the professional woman committed to equality and individual rights, and disdainful of the private sphere and women's moral obligations as caregivers. When first ladies have attempted to allay these fears, often the outcry has increased. In responding to the public, the first lady only steps further into the public sphere and further away from the private sphere. Betty Ford continually sought to reconcile the separate spheres and women's rights ideologies, articulating a definition of liberation that she believed was suited to all women. She failed in her efforts and mobilized her husband's conservative critics without winning the support of his liberal opponents.

These ideological profiles are admittedly simplified and generalized. Social conservativism recognizes that women may enter the public sphere in order to protect and provide for the private sphere.[24] The agenda of Schlafly's Eagle Forum, for example, is lengthy; it stretches from safety inspections for foreign drug makers to child custody disputes in divorce to video game ratings to international copyright law. In every instance, Schlafly connects her efforts to mobilize people in the public sphere with women's role as moral guardians in the private sphere. Meanwhile, feminists have stressed the values of personal autonomy (as members of the women's rights movement) and complexity (as postmodernists), arguing that women be granted full social, economic, and political opportunities. Pro-choice moderate Democrats, for example, wrote supportive letters to Betty Ford after she incurred criticism for expressing these views (and others) in her *60 Minutes* interview.[25] Notwithstanding the satellite status of some first ladies, therefore, feminists have allied themselves with presidents' wives in order to advance their policy priorities. Still, crosscurrents of support and criticism can shred a first lady's reputation and agenda, leaving her politically and publicly vulnerable.

Understanding the first lady as a representative requires that she be studied as a gender representative *and* as a partisan representative. Neither can be wholly distinguished from the other. Yet this does not make the first lady unique. Gender and presidential power are intertwined throughout presidential administrations, and more generally throughout the executive branch. As a result, there is a wealth of literature, both theoretical and applied, that illuminates the challenges and opportunities confronting the president's wife.

The writings of gender scholars, especially those in applied feminist thought and representation, are unquestionably relevant to the study of first ladyship. These researchers have investigated identity politics, the social construction of femininity and masculinity, the performance of gender roles, and the contributions of representatives to democratic governance. The contrasts among various schools of woman-centered political theory—especially among the mainstream approaches of social conservatives, liberal feminists, and post-modern feminists—outline the conflicts that the presidents' wives have encountered as they became more activist in the public sphere. These ideological confrontations force debate about the social, economic, and political ideals that define the first ladyship specifically and the presidency generally.

No less relevant to analysis of the first lady are White House Office studies, especially those comparing administrations throughout the modern presidency. Many of the influences upon its institutionalization have been systematically weighed and assessed, delineating the impact of the political environment, presidential priorities, and staff ambition. White House units dedicated to public liaison work, for instance, have been among the most affected by changes in the wider political environment.[26] As a representative, the first lady performs public liaison tasks. Accordingly, shifts in the larger political environment could be expected to shape the post and office of the first lady, with implications for her staff and her agenda.

The presidents and the public have expected first ladies to facilitate communication, translating and amplifying the president's message to increase popular support, and to relay public concerns to the chief executive. Yet there has also been popular resistance to first lady activism.[27] A wife's cultivation of political relationships on her husband's behalf may be accepted as evidence of her other-directedness, but there is no such rationale for her serving as his voice. Meanwhile, women's rights and feminist organizations worry about the first lady's accountability.[28] These women's advocates conclude that, as the president's wife, the first lady lacks credibility as a political actor—her marriage is perceived as abolishing her autonomy and thus her effectiveness. What remains to be determined are the strategies, and the associated successes and failures, that first ladies have employed in confronting these contradictions and making their contributions to the modern presidency.

STRATEGIZING REPRESENTATION

Entering the White House today, presidents and their staffs confront virtually empty offices—most files from the previous administration are sent off to be archived, as required by the Presidential Records Act of 1978—and immediate demands from the media, Congress, party leaders, state governments, international leaders and chiefs of state, and more, in an ever-growing list. And however disciplined and tightly scripted a new administration may strive to be, there is always the unexpected event, the missed opportunity, or the surprising proposal that distracts attention from the presidential message, consumes time and other resources, and generally calls into question the coherence and ability of the new administration. A president needs to have a fast and strong start, with a steep and continuous learning curve, in order to exercise leadership.[29]

Circumstances are somewhat different for the first lady, though her position on the White House staff ensures that she shares in these experiences. She, too, encounters immediate questions from journalists and needs considerable staff support to manage the information flow from print, broadcast, and electronic media.[30] She is under considerable pressure to set social outreach priorities and routines.[31] Still, presidents' wives have more time for reflection and planning than do presidents. By the late twentieth century, reporters were routinely asking candidates' wives about the "projects" they expected to pursue as first ladies. The public, however, had not yet begun to presume that those projects would yield formalized policy. That slight lapse in expectation, so at odds with the extraordinary hopes that are directed at a new president, gives the first lady a significant advantage as a representative.

Countering and constraining that leeway are a series of formal and informal checks on the first lady. Among the formal barriers is the limitation imposed by federal anti-nepotism law, which states that a "public official may not appoint, employ, advance, or advocate for appointment, employment, promotion, or advancement, in or to a civilian position in the agency in which he is serving or over which he exercises jurisdiction or control any individual who is a relative of the public official." Familiarly known as the "Bobby Kennedy law" because it was proposed and passed in response to President Kennedy's nomination of his brother as attorney general, this statute is so all-encompassing that it precludes executive branch employment for any member of the president's family. It was on the basis of this statute that the Office of Legal Counsel (OLC) in the Justice Department ruled against Rosalynn Carter's appointment as chair of the President's Commission on Mental Health. She was subsequently appointed the commission's "honorary chairman."[32]

In addition to this and other formal constraints, there are the informal yet powerful limitations that arise from longstanding public expectations that the first lady will uphold a gender ideology that associates women with the private sphere, reserving the public sphere to men. When first ladies challenge this dichotomy, their media coverage becomes far more negative and their approval ratings drop.[33] Formally and informally, it is difficult for a president's wife to sustain herself as a credible, influential decision maker.

Rather than continuing to seesaw between advantages and disadvantages of the first lady's type of representation, we need to consider each in detail and in relation to the other. This approach offers several responses to the basic question of why modern first ladies, who encounter so many disincentives to be representatives, have nonetheless taken on this role. The answers lie in their gender and partisan ideologies, their relationships with their husbands and their husbands' administrations, and their opportunities to exercise influence in the White House Office.

Resources

Changes in policy making during the modern presidency have affected the representation provided by members of the legislative and executive branches, including the first lady. The impact of political organizations on the first lady's representation is great, with more people and more interests making claims and scrutinizing her performance. In the Clinton administration, that group-based engagement led to a series of court cases when the first lady did not accede to demands for greater transparency in the health-care task force deliberations.[34]

Identifying consistent advantages accruing to the first lady as a representative must be done cautiously and with some qualifications. Even so, two advantages are evident, namely, time and staff. First ladies have more time, compared to the president, to set their agenda, and they have acquired larger and more specialized staff to aid them in acting upon that agenda. To be precise, first ladies in the earlier half of the twentieth century had more time to set their priorities, while first ladies in the later twentieth and the twenty-first centuries have had more staff. These changes may be partially attributed to the slow integration of "East Wing" and "West Wing."[35] As stronger relations have been established among the various units in the White House Office, including the first lady's office, it has experienced more of the political pressures felt by the president and the wider administration.

Time is a critical resource for a first lady, as for a president. So long as immediate action or quick responses were not expected of the first lady, she had time to situate herself in the Washington community and society, the administration, and the White House.[36] Having time to assimilate past and present knowledge, and to consult with key actors, gave the first lady an opportunity to make better choices. Moreover, because she was learning while she was the president's wife, her insights were potentially deeper and richer. Each decision built on others, as she saw how people responded to her as a first lady. Her advisors shared in the learning as well. The rush to a conclusion, or the reliance upon tight scripting, which contributes to so many presidential difficulties, does not have to occur in the "East Wing."

At least it did not have to occur so long as the first lady did not make campaign promises that required early actions or quick responses. First ladies who were free of these commitments included Lou Henry Hoover, Bess Wallace Truman, Mamie Doud Eisenhower, Jacqueline Kennedy, Lady Bird Johnson, Pat Nixon, Nancy Reagan, and Michelle Obama. Barbara Bush and Laura Bush made general references to literacy and reading, respectively. Rosalynn Carter promised mental health-care reform, and Bill Clinton repeatedly stated that his wife would be an active participant in presidential policy making.

First ladies who had committed themselves to representation found themselves the focus of intense public scrutiny. The difficulties that first lady policy entrepreneurs, in particular, encounter are exemplified by Hillary Rodham Clinton's experiences. On January 25, 1993, President Clinton appointed the first lady to chair the Task Force on National Health Care Reform. There was wide consultation within the administration, but public interest and advocacy organizations were excluded. Congress members subsequently confronted an intricate program to which they had made few contributions. Negotiations were conducted late, with a push to meet overly ambitious deadlines, and there was little opportunity for reflection. Ultimately, the proposals were rejected. This failure, together with a series of scandals and investigations, so damaged the first lady's reputation that she stepped back and away from the policy process. She no longer publicly commanded others in presidentially centered decision-making processes; she did not attend "West Wing" briefings.[37]

What is striking about Rodham Clinton's actions is the extent to which they mirror those of presidents. Many difficulties in a presidential administration come early or late, when time constraints and close scrutiny exacerbate the tensions already being generated by ignorance, weariness, and political and partisan conflict.[38] Failure follows more often than not. These were the results for Rodham Clinton, with further gender consequences because she was a woman failing in a presidential (masculine) policy arena (medical finance and insurance).[39] Whether, and to what extent, a first lady sacrifices her time advantage depends on factors such as her campaign promises, her contributions to her husband's policy agenda, and her self-presentation as a representative.

While presidents' wives in the late twentieth century have more often faced pressures to act quickly and to achieve great things, they have had far more staff resources with which to satisfy their constituents. In the Johnson administration, press and communications work was removed from the social secretary's list of responsibilities, and a separate "East Wing" office was established with specialists in print and broadcast media. Johnson's successors continued this specialization and departmentalization. As always, some innovations resulted from careful planning while others were unexpected.

Among the more carefully planned innovations was the staffing structure instituted by Rosalynn Carter in 1977. A detailed assessment of Betty Ford's office, conducted by the Carter transition team in 1976–77, made recommendations, but Rosalynn Carter surpassed them.[40] Expecting to be a policy entrepreneur, she recruited a staff to support her activism. Like her predecessors, she had staff specialists in press relations, advance, and scheduling; she added a chief of staff (titled "staff director") and a policy director ("director of projects"). Carter was also an adaptive manager. The work on mental health-care reform, which stretched through the entire term, had a comparatively formal, somewhat hierarchical staffing arrangement. Her response to the Cambodian refugee crisis in 1979 was more organic and team-oriented. Mental health policy required close coordination of staff in a presidential commission, the White House, and executive departments. Outreach was conducted to the public, relevant professions, the media, both congressional chambers and their leaders, the Office of Management and Budget, and policy councils—it was a very long list, for a very complex policy. A single individual, Peter Bourne, was charged with continuing responsibility for policy development. The refugee crisis, in marked contrast, was centered in the first lady's staff, with support and outreach to the State Department, the National Institutes of Health, the Center for Disease Control, the United Nations, and a series of national and transnational interest groups. A great deal of effort was expended in a comparatively short space of time, and a more participatory management style facilitated its achievement.[41] Staff was critical to Carter's effectiveness as a representative.

As first ladies lost the time to reflect and orient themselves to their post, they gained a more extensive and specialized staff. As they became more involved in policy and decision making, there was more coordination of the first lady's staff with other units in the White House Office. These are correlations, not causal relationships, but they are events that make the first ladies' representation even more interesting. In order to achieve their goals while managing the risks and pressures of the political environment, the women have acted strategically. Even so, as first ladies have become more closely associated with presidential politics and policy, and as their politics and parti-

sanship have become more evident, the women have become more controversial—and staff have not been able to wholly deflect public criticism.

Constraints

In addition to presidential power, and in addition to the judgments of the
Washington community and society, the media, and the general public, there
are statutory laws, case law, and OLC opinions that delineate the first lady's
policy-making roles.

The Anti-Deficiency Act of 1884 sanctioned virtually all voluntary service in the government. There were few exceptions, the most notable of
which allowed people to take action to save lives (as during war or natural
disasters) or to perform roles that had not previously been salaried (such
as the first ladyship). Even so, the prohibitions were stringent. Given these
strictures, the Office of Legal Counsel ruled that if a president's wife took on
new responsibilities (as when President Carter intended to appoint the first
lady to chair a presidential commission), she would violate this law and be
susceptible to legal challenge. If the first lady sought to avoid this problem by
accepting a salary, she would violate the federal anti-nepotism law. Together,
the two laws caught the first lady in a seemingly inescapable catch-22.[42]

A third law—the White House Personnel Act of 1978—was a product
of President Carter's efforts to bring transparency and order to the White
House Office following the Watergate scandals. For first ladies, Section
105(e) is key: "Assistance and services authorized pursuant to this section to
the President are authorized to be provided to the spouse of the President in
connection with assistance provided by such spouse to the President in the
discharge of the President's duties and responsibilities. If the President does
not have a spouse, such assistance and services may be provided for such
purposes to a member of the President's family whom the President desig-
nates."[43] These words formally authorized the first ladyship in gender-neutral
language. The president's spouse was explicitly acknowledged as contributing
to the presidency, and more generally, to the government. Budgetary alloca-
tions were to be made for staff and resources to support her performance of
this work. This was more formal recognition than had been given to other
posts or units within the White House. The wording, however, set the president's spouse apart from other executive branch personnel. She or he was
not hired, appointed, or nominated to her White House post; she or he was
"designated."

The choice of the word "designated" to describe the first lady's recruitment has proven of critical importance and resulted in a fourth law—this time, case law—defining the first lady's post. Previously, the first lady was described in negative terms. She was not a member of the civil service, not a public official (by accepted legal definitions), not a presidential appointee or nominee. Following extended litigation, however, the District of Columbia Circuit Court provided an affirmative definition, ruling on appeal that the first lady was a de facto public official for the purposes of the Federal Advisory Committee Act (FACA). Even this narrow ruling was accompanied by a tightly reasoned dissenting opinion, which maintained that the federal anti-nepotism law precluded the first lady holding office in the executive branch. Though Section 105(e) acknowledged her existence, the dissenting opinion concluded, authorizations to support her political or policy work could be contested.[44]

Reinforcing these legal constraints are informal gender norms, which become more imposing as the first lady steps further into the public sphere. As noted previously, the executive branch is rooted in a historical context of war and military leadership. Its theories and practices of leadership are presumptively hierarchical, valuing traditionally masculine traits such as competitiveness and strength. Though the White House staff and various other administration officials might seem to compromise the image of a self-reliant chief executive, comity actually conflates masculinity and executive branch service. A president's closest advisors evidence extraordinary loyalty and dedication to the chief executive, a modern echo of medieval "fealty" and "archetypical camaraderie." As Georgia Duerst-Lahti has stated, "[T]he palace is not guarded by women."[45] When the president's wife has been present at meetings of the inner circle, she has often been silent—Lou Henry Hoover and Lady Bird Johnson were very clear about this, and it is unlikely that they are unique. Mere attendance at high-level meetings does not constitute membership in the inner circle and does not facilitate the first lady's success as a representative.

Also constraining the first lady's opportunities for effective representation is her status as the president's wife. The closeness of their relationship, and the fact that it is a sexual relationship, complicate all judgments about her competence and credibility. While many may be willing to grant that a woman can be a thoughtful decision maker, fewer are comfortable with accepting the first lady as a proactive representative. How can a president's wife be held accountable? The presumption is made that she cannot be fired or removed from the White House, that she cannot be distanced from the president. Of course, none of these assertions is necessarily accurate. Many presidential couples lead compartmentalized lives before and during their White House years, including the Eisenhowers, Kennedys, and Nixons. And as the Roosevelts and Trumans found, the presidency does not always bring husband and wife closer together.

For those who embrace separate-spheres ideals, the concern is slightly different, with observers fearing that a first lady active in the public sphere will be ineffective or, if effective, will impose heavy costs on the private sphere. Whether this fear is allayed depends upon the first lady's framing. If she presents a conservative agenda and herself as a moral guardian, then separate-spheres advocates may accept her efforts as an extension of women's roles in the private sphere. The fact that the first lady has identified herself as a moral guardian for generations also shifts the legal calculations—historical practice is one of the exceptions to the anti-deficiency law's prohibitions.

"Designated" for their post and given few legal protections, typically unable to expand their portfolio through paid or voluntary government service, their accountability and their credibility questioned, the odds are against the first lady succeeding as a representative.

OVERVIEW

This book examines the modern first ladies, investigating the contributions these women have made to their husbands' administrations and to the presidency through their service as representatives. The focus is on the modern presidency, beginning with the Hoover administration in which the president was staffed by multiple professional aides, each formally appointed and paid, and each charged with formal governmental responsibilities.[46] The first lady also was assisted by multiple staff members—similarly appointed, paid, and charged—making this administration highly appropriate as a starting point for this study. Notably, first lady historians also tend to associate Lou Henry Hoover with the modern presidency. Though she did not present herself as a strong policy advocate, as did Eleanor Roosevelt, Hoover's initiatives evidence a number of continuities with those of her successors. During the modern presidency, there were dramatic changes in gender roles. These are also the administrations in which the White House Office emerged as a complex bureaucratic organization. As a result, the challenges confronting the first lady multiplied, even as she acquired more staff and resources to facilitate her participation in the public sphere. How did first ladies respond to these contradictory forces, in order to contribute to the modern presidency through the performance of representation?

Each woman has had to interpret the first lady's post for herself, albeit within a context set by her predecessors, by her husband's administration, and by society. The next chapter, "Before They Were First Ladies," delineates the resources that these women have called upon in developing their strategies as representatives.

"The Nation's Hostess: The First Lady and Symbolic Representation" then investigates the first lady role that is generally accepted, though little understood. Social outreach to international leaders and domestic elites has provided the presidents' wives with opportunities to shape the deeper symbols and rituals of power. More pragmatically, the first lady and the social secretary allocate the scarcest of all White House resources—the president's time—in determining the format and seating for all events. Quite simply, White House occasions frame, and sometimes even structure, the exercise of power.

"Voice and Message: The First Lady and Descriptive Representation" examines the first ladies' gender role modeling and use of mass communications. Reaching beyond the direct contact of White House–centered events, the first ladies have delivered the president's message, fine-tuned their own priorities, and discerned constituent preferences through their use of mass communications. Modeling a definition of femininity that empowers a wife to speak for her husband, and to pursue her own interests politically, places the first lady firmly in the public sphere. Separate-spheres advocates then worry that the private sphere will be neglected and the public sphere undermined, while women's rights advocates often question the first lady's accountability as a decision maker. The associated gender-role controversies have been deep and strong, forcing the first ladies (especially in the later twentieth and early twenty-first centuries) to addresses charges that they were fostering a harmful, essentialist conception of women's gender roles.

The final chapter, "Gender and Policy: The First Lady and Substantive Representation," investigates modern first ladies' strategies for participating in the policy-making process. Their use of rhetoric, their societal activism, and their political entrepreneurship are closely linked to their gender and partisan ideologies. Revealing their policy priorities and concerns, substantive representation requires first ladies to defend their ideological judgments in both gender and partisan terms. Not surprisingly, first ladies and presidents have sometimes coordinated their agendas, the first lady acting on behalf of presidential interests. And yet, first ladies have never merely echoed their husbands. Instead, the presidents' wives have advanced their agendas from their own distinctively gendered perspective. The interplay of gender, credibility, and power that characterizes every aspect of representation may be most easily perceived in the first ladies' substantive representation, with profound implications for their contributions to the theory and practice of representative, democratic governance.

Thus, this book explores how and why modern first ladies have served as representatives in their husbands' administrations. Recognizing that the political environment, as mediated by the president, impacts every White House office, careful assessments are made of the constraints imposed upon first ladies by popular expectations, their strategies for establishing credibility, and their consequent effectiveness. Before reaching conclusions about the first ladies' contributions and legacies, however, the experiences and expertise they brought into the White House must be delineated. This is the subject of the next chapter.

BEFORE THEY WERE FIRST LADIES

The successful presidential campaign is an ending and a beginning for the woman who becomes first lady. Immersed in public outreach—traveling independently or with the presidential candidate, confronting the scrutiny of the media and the electorate, responding to diverse gender and partisan ideologies—future first ladies refine their skills and talents throughout the campaign. The key word, however, is "refine." These women, like their husbands, have had rich lives before entering the White House. Their actions during the presidential term rest on wisdom acquired in their pre-presidential years. It is in this sense that the successful presidential campaign is both an ending and a beginning: the first lady and the president bring experience and knowledge to the White House, which they rely upon in responding to the expectations, requirements, and demands of the presidency.

This chapter, accordingly, investigates the modern first ladies' pre-presidential careers. Though not always sharing their husbands' White House ambitions, these women have been highly political. More often than not, they have been strategic entrepreneurs within their families, the private sector, the not-for-profit sector, the public sector, or some combination of the four. Their associated successes and failures foreshadow the representation they provide once they become first ladies.

THE EXPERTISE THAT THE PRESIDENCY REQUIRES

Like every other member of a presidential administration, first ladies bring considerable and diverse expertise to the White House. Their pre-presidential careers typically encompass work outside the home, before and sometimes during their marriages; marital and family responsibilities; and partisan political experience, including but not limited to campaigning and policy making. Their marriages sometimes evidence profound power inequities, but at other times are partnerships. As several first ladies acknowledge in their autobiographies, marriage and politics set the context for their lives. Like others in the White House Office, personal, partisan, political, and professional relationships decisively shaped the modern first ladies' careers.

To inventory the first ladies' pre-presidential lives in terms of employment, family, and politics, however, is to echo the biographical approaches of the past. What is needed instead is an analytic framework that draws connections between the expertise that the women acquired before they became first ladies *and* the learning and expertise that they demonstrated throughout their husbands' presidential terms. Just such a framework can be drawn from White House Office studies.

After interviewing senior staff members in presidential administrations of the later twentieth century, political scientist Martha Joynt Kumar concluded that an effective White House Office required the following four kinds of expertise:[1]

Knowledge of the future president, so that the chief executive's thought processes and values are recognized, understood, and anticipated. This expertise facilitates communication, especially the negotiations associated with agenda setting, legislative bargaining, and programmatic implementation. However, this knowledge may also lead to groupthink, with alternative perspectives and possibilities disregarded.

Knowledge of campaigning and governing, so that the staff appreciates the strategic impact of campaign promises on the administration, and in turn, the effect of the administration's actions on a reelection campaign. The constant campaign makes these effects infinitely more complex, especially given the heightened scrutiny of the 24/7 news cycle.

Knowledge of policy, so that partisan bargaining does not ignore or discount the substantive consequences of political decision making. Party polarization has made this empirical knowledge even more important, as a counter to misinterpretations or misstatements, and as a source of credibility in the midst of acrimonious debates.

Knowledge of the Washington community, its rituals and symbols, so that the expectations of the powerful are anticipated. The formal practices and informal expectations that govern relationships in the capital are critically important to any administration. Trust and credibility facilitate all forms of representation and decision making. Conversely, betrayal—whether real or imagined—inhibits dialogue well into the future.[2]

As the executive of a unit within the White House Office, the first lady needs access to each type of expertise. As a member of the White House Office herself, the president's wife must possess and demonstrate at least some of these different kinds of knowledge. The first lady's expertise, at its most expressive and expansive, will bridge the masculine gender role constructions and politics ascribed to the president's senior staff, and the feminine gender role constructions and politics ascribed to her staff, so that the first lady communicates and builds relationships within the administration and throughout the wider society.

Knowledge of the Man Who Is President

This expertise is arguably foundational for the first lady. Knowledge of the chief executive's political priorities and willingness to compromise, his professional interests and judgments, and his character and ambition are necessary resources for any senior staff member who wants to facilitate constructive relationships between the president and the public. As the president's wife, however, the first lady is expected to contribute a distinctive set of insights, with consequences for her descriptive representation in particular. Her marriage and her self are publicly analyzed as evidence of the president's attitudes toward women in the private and public spheres. To the extent that a first lady is ignorant of her husband, or is unwilling to recognize how her self and her marriage will be objectified, she will be surprised by these judgments and demands. Rather than taking the lead as a representative, she will find herself scrambling to compensate for her lack of insight.

Hillary Rodham Clinton found herself in this situation in 1998. Having defended her husband against all accusations, insisting that he was the victim of a conservative conspiracy, she was (or claimed to be) blindsided by his admission of an extramarital affair with Monica Lewinsky. Both of their autobiographies stressed this point, with Rodham Clinton explicitly stating that she had previously told a member of the White House staff, "My husband may have his faults, but he has never lied to me."[3] Clinton, in his memoir, paraphrased his speech to the nation, except for his reference to the first lady: "At ten o'clock I told the American people about my testimony, said I was solely and completely responsible for my personal failure, and admitted misleading everyone, 'even my wife.'"[4] By excusing the first lady's contributions to the cover-up as unwitting, however, the president reinforced conclusions that she lacked judgment about her husband's character and politics.

Rodham Clinton sought to counteract this effect by presenting herself

as a betrayed wife, and as a model of faith and forgiveness. In an early statement, a member of the first lady's staff stressed, "It's at times like this when
she relies on her strong religious faith. She is committed to her marriage and
loves her husband and daughter very much."[5] Five years later, in her autobiography, Rodham Clinton wrote, "I have found my way through a lifetime
of uncharted territory with good fortune and abiding faith to keep me on
course." And then, having paraphrased a famous sermon by theologian Paul
Tillich, she concluded the chapter titled "August 1998" with the statement,
"Grace happens. Until it did, my main job was to put one foot in front of the
other and get through another day."[6] Her public approval ratings throughout
the month were the highest in her tenure as first lady, 64 percent.[7]

Even so, many challenged the first lady, believing that she had been well
aware of the affair. At the least, these individuals charged, she had known her
husband to be unfaithful and sexually promiscuous, a "wild-child President."
Articles, editorials, op-eds, and letters to the editor referred to her codepen-
dency and to her desire for power; she was variously described as a "steely
Lady Macbeth" and as "nourish[ing] a moral decline in our society." For still
others, Rodham Clinton was too loyal and too deferential to her husband.
Rather than a strong and independent participant in a marriage of equals,
she was now being perceived as a satellite who accepted and enabled her husband's duplicity and infidelity. Her high favorability rating was attributed to
her marital steadfastness, not to her political acumen.[8] Accordingly, her status as a representative for the administration was questioned, with observers
and decision makers deeply divided in their assessments of her effectiveness
within the administration.

Rodham Clinton endured events among the more extreme to have confronted a president's wife, but her experiences reveal the difficulties that arise
when first ladies are publicly mistaken in their assessments of their husbands. It is therefore imperative to ask whether these women have had pre-
presidential opportunities to become well informed about the future presidents' judgment and politics. Do these wives know their husbands well
enough to anticipate their actions as chief executives? Have they known their
husbands as decision makers and policy makers? Are they able to make use
of that knowledge as representatives?

Knowledge of Campaigning and Governing
For first ladies with policy agendas, a strategic expertise in campaigning and
governing is critical to their success. Yet even when first ladies have limited

their participation in policy making, they have needed this knowledge to advance the priorities of their husbands' administrations. Each meeting that she conducts with current or prospective presidential constituents, domestic and international decision makers, opinion leaders, and journalists provides an opportunity to advance the president's interests. Doing so, however, requires the first lady to consider how her ascribed identity frames the president's message, and then to think about how that frame may be utilized to best advantage for her and for the administration. This strategic awareness is critical if the president's wife is to sidestep failure and realize the full potential of her representation.

Lady Bird (Claudia Alta) Taylor Johnson was among the modern first ladies most dedicated to public communication and relationship building. During the five years of the Johnson administration, working closely with the social office and her own press office, and with senior White House aides and cabinet officers, she implemented a multifaceted communications strategy designed to focus public attention on successful federal programs. Notably, she inaugurated this work immediately after her husband's first State of the Union address, in which the president declared, "Poverty is a national problem, requiring improved national organization and support. But this attack, to be effective, must also be organized at the State and the local level and must be supported and directed by State and local efforts."[9] Just three days later, Lady Bird Johnson's one-day visit to Scranton and Wilkes-Barre, Pennsylvania, both hit hard by industrial failure, showcased these collaborations as well as private-public partnerships. Receiving extensive print and broadcast coverage, the trip testified to the first lady's ability to show the connection between the administration's policy goals and ordinary citizens' lives.

Lady Bird Johnson's knowledge of campaigning and governing was even more clearly on display during her 1964 whistle-stop campaign trip through eight southeastern states. The whistle-stop was intended to facilitate party outreach and advocate civil rights. Lyndon Johnson's support for civil rights legislation had alienated a great many white voters in the South, who were as strongly supportive of segregation as they were strongly opposed to federal involvement. As the election approached, Democratic Party operatives, members, and leaders became increasingly worried about their ability to sustain electoral majorities. Commenting on the campaign strategies of 1964, Scooter (Virginia) Miller, who had campaigned with Lady Bird Johnson in 1960, argued, "You can't stay out of the South when you're the first southern president. You can't write it off."[10] But Miller also believed that the campaign would only be effective if it was persuasive rather than confrontational. In

Miller's words, "[T]his campaign needed to go into the South, and it needed to go in as gracious a way as it could. And Mrs. Johnson is a real southern person. . . . Mrs. Johnson was a person who carried some political power herself."[11] Marshaling and directing that power was accomplished by designing a route that, as several governors' wives recommended and other advisors seconded, took the first lady into several white segregationist strongholds.[12] The whistle-stop did not secure the South for the president, but it testified to the first lady's deep engagement in representation, her commitment to mediating between the president and the public.

Whether the opportunities are made for or by the first lady, the expectations and the scrutiny directed at the presidents' wives requires them to be sophisticated strategic actors. And so, how have the first ladies participated in politics during the pre-presidential years? How can their talents be applied to communicating and relationship building once they assume their responsibilities as representatives?

Knowledge of Policy

Mastery of the substance of domestic and foreign policy has brought numerous benefits to the modern first ladies. Their command of data and access to information has added content to their communications and momentum to their relationship building. It has also contributed to their gender role modeling, their expertise being publicly interpreted as a statement about those issues that should concern all women. Presidents' wives with policy knowledge have therefore understood the importance of limiting their agenda and clarifying their goals.[13] In brief, policy knowledge has made the president's wife a more credible and more effective substantive representative.

Rosalynn Smith Carter's White House experiences show the wider benefits that presidents' wives have derived from their policy knowledge. In the 1976 presidential campaign, Rosalynn Carter claimed to make only one promise that was wholly her own, namely, to reform the nation's mental health-care system. It was a commitment rooted in earlier promises made during her husband's gubernatorial campaigns, which she had fulfilled as Georgia's first lady. As the president's wife, she served as the honorary chair of the President's Commission on Mental Health, attending all of the hearings and meetings. After its recommendations were made public, she conducted a nationwide media campaign to build grassroots support for their adoption. She became known as a relentless lobbyist within the legislative and the executive branches, testifying before the Subcommittee on Health and Scientific Research of the Senate Committee on Labor and Human Resources, and pushing the Office of Management and Budget for increased appropriations.[14] At every juncture, Rosalynn Carter was obliged to prove her strategic and substantive skills as a policy entrepreneur.

Mental health-care reform was not the only initiative that Rosalynn Carter advanced as a first lady, but it was the issue that brought coherence and consistency to her substantive representation. Most of her other policy initiatives—especially those relating to elder care, education, and neighborhoods—were similar to mental health-care reform in that they emphasized decentralized, community-based programming.[15] Such consistency facilitated the first lady's communications and her relationship building. It could also be expected to mute criticism of her involvement in the public sphere: her practice of an ethic of care would appeal to those who embraced the separate-spheres ideal, while her political entrepreneurship would win support from those who favored activism.

In her husband's single term, Carter presided over a policy reform that advanced from commission recommendations to statutory law to appropriations in a time of budget cutbacks. It was a remarkable achievement and it indicates that a first lady's policy expertise can serve as a basis for representation. It is therefore important to determine whether other first ladies have brought policy expertise to the White House that may redound to the administration's credit. Has the first lady's established herself as a policy maker in the years before she entered the White House Office? Do opinion leaders and issue networks view her as a credible activist? Why? Has she cultivated the skills that will bring her success in policy making among elites in the legislative and executive branches of the national government?

Knowledge of the Washington Community and Society

This final category of expertise may be the most difficult to assess. Discerning the informal pathways of power in the Washington community is always problematic, and the intricacies of Washington society add additional layers of uncertainty. Women established in and accepted by Washington (such as Lou Henry Hoover, Lady Bird Johnson, and Barbara Pierce Bush), start the presidential term with allies—and with the experience to capitalize on their resources. But women who are new to Washington (such as Nancy Davis Reagan) or who resist participating in these rituals (such as Bess [Elizabeth] Wallace Truman, Rosalynn Carter, and Hillary Rodham Clinton), may make mistakes as representatives, with high costs for their husbands' administrations.

Lou Henry Hoover reveals the power to be exercised by a president's wife who is well known to the Washington community and Washington society. With an extended record of international and domestic accomplishments, and an extraordinary reputation as a hostess while her husband was in the Harding and Coolidge cabinets, Lou Henry Hoover had the credibility to effect changes that altered public perceptions of the presidency. The Coolidges had limited their hospitality in the White House to offering cold water at receptions held on especially hot days. Lou Henry Hoover, however, provided a sandwich buffet at receptions and a full tea for other afternoon events. Dinners and lunches were similarly generous, and invitations were routinely extended to members of the staff and the administration, as well as others present for meetings in the mansion. The president and first lady rarely ate alone, and were typically joined by twenty or more guests. The associated costs were paid by the Hoovers, who were determined that visitors be received in comfort. Ultimately, Herbert Hoover estimated that he paid for 140,000 meals each year. This included meals for guests (except the major diplomatic receptions, which were paid for by the federal government), family, servants and staff, and all meals at Rapidan.[16] There was less stiffness and a warmer welcome in the Hoover White House.

In addition to changing the tone of the occasions, the first lady included women and children in her guest lists. Though Lou Henry Hoover had resigned her leadership positions in the Girl Scouts when she became first lady, she invited a number of individuals and groups from the organization to teas and receptions. Though the focus of White House entertainment was still the Washington community, this inclusion of women and children nuanced its exclusivity.[17] It was a quiet but notable change, continued and magnified by Eleanor Roosevelt.

Yet Hoover sustained as many practices as she altered. After trying to abolish receiving lines, Hoover reinstated them to ensure each guest was welcomed and security concerns were allayed. Hoover also continued the social season and the New Year's Day reception, the former welcoming Washington elites to the White House and the latter opening the mansion to the public.[18] The balance of monarchical and democratic elements in Hoover's symbolic representation was correspondingly familiar to many observers.

As the "nation's hostess," the first lady frames and interprets the presidency in the White House, a setting that is intimately connected to the exercise of presidential power. It is therefore important to ask about the first lady's pre-presidential experience in and with Washington. Is she familiar and at ease with its networks? Does she understand that power may be wielded informally as well as formally? Is she aware that ritual and symbol are integral to the achievement of substantive political goals?

These forms of expertise only become more important as the first lady's participation in the public sphere increases. Her words and actions receive closer scrutiny; she must prove herself in an environment that is suspicious of her motives and abilities. Have first ladies entered the White House with the kinds of expertise known to be useful to the presidency? to their own performance of representation?

Knowledge of the Future President as a Decision Maker and a Policy Maker

Modern first ladies observed and worked with their husbands for many years before entering the White House. With just four exceptions—Jacqueline Bouvier Kennedy (married eight years at the time of her husband's presidential inauguration), Hillary Rodham Clinton (married eighteen years), Laura Welch Bush (married twenty-three years), and Michelle Robinson Obama (married seventeen years)—modern first ladies celebrated their twenty-fifth wedding anniversary well before their husbands were elected to the Oval Office. During these decades of married life, the women fulfilled significant familial responsibilities *and* contributed to their husbands' success through public and political outreach. A number of first ladies gained considerable knowledge of their husbands' professional strengths and weaknesses. That insight was critical to their ability to represent the chief executive to diverse constituencies, and in turn, to represent those constituencies to the president.

Marriage and Family

Modern first ladies married between the ages of eighteen (Rosalynn Carter) and thirty-four (Bess Truman). The timing of their marriages reflected both historical and personal circumstances, though the personal often dominated. History intervened in the Truman and G. H. W. Bush marriages, which did not occur until after the men had completed wartime military service. The Ford and Reagan marriages were reflective of personal circumstances: Betty Bloomer Ford had to wait until her divorce was finalized and Ronald Reagan was reluctant to marry after his divorce. The personal and the professional overlapped for the Hoovers and Clintons, who waited until the women

Table 2.1 Biographical Data for the Modern First Ladies

First lady	Birth and death dates	Postsecondary education	Marriage date	Children
Louise (Lou) Henry Hoover	b. March 29, 1874 d. January 7, 1944	Teaching certificate, 1893, San Jose Normal School BA, 1898, Stanford University, Geology	February 10, 1899	Herbert Clark Jr., 1903–1969 Allan Henry, 1907–1993
Anna Eleanor Roosevelt Roosevelt	b. October 11, 1884 d. November 7, 1962		March 17, 1905	Anna Eleanor, 1906–1975 James, 1907–1991 Elliott, 1910–1990 Franklin Delano Jr., 1914–1988 John Aspinall, 1916–1981
Elizabeth Virginia Wallace Truman	b. February 13, 1885 d. October 18, 1982		June 28, 1919	Mary Margaret, 1924–2008 (also, at least 2 miscarriages)
Mamie Geneva Doud Eisenhower	b. November 14, 1896 d. November 1, 1979		July 1, 1916	Doud Dwight, 1918–1921 John Sheldon Doud, b. 1922
Jacqueline Lee Bouvier Kennedy Onassis	b. July 28, 1929 d. May 19, 1994	BA, 1951, Vassar College, George Washington University, Journalism	September 12, 1953	Caroline Bouvier, b. 1957 John Fitzgerald Jr., 1960–1999 Patrick Bouvier, 1963 (also 1 miscarriage, 1 stillborn)
Claudia Alta (Lady Bird) Taylor Johnson	b. December 22, 1922 d. July 11, 2007	BA, 1933 and 1934, University of Texas–Austin, History and Journalism	November 17, 1934	Lynda Bird, b. 1944 Lucy Baines, b. 1947 (also at least 3 miscarriages)
Thelma Catherine (Pat) Ryan Nixon	b. March 16, 1912 d. June 22, 1993	Fullerton Junior College Radiology course, Columbia University BA cum laude, 1937, University of Southern California, School of Education	June 21, 1940	Patricia, b. 1946 Julie, b. 1948

Name	Born	Education	Married	Children
Elizabeth Ann (Betty) Bloomer Ford	b. April 8, 1918		October 15, 1948	Michael Gerald, b. 1950 John Gardner, b. 1952 Steven Meigs, b. 1956 Susan Elizabeth, b. 1957
Eleanor Rosalynn Smith Carter	b. August 18, 1927	1946, Georgia Southwestern Junior College, two-year program	July 7, 1946	John William, b. 1947 James Earl III, b. 1950 Donnel Jeffrey, b. 1952 Amy Lynn, b. 1967
Anne Frances (Nancy) Robbins Davis Reagan	b. July 6, 1923	AB, 1943, Smith College, Theater	March 4, 1952	Patricia Ann, b. 1952 Ronald Prescott, b. 1958 (also two stepchildren)
Barbara Pierce Bush	b. June 8, 1925	Smith College (attended)	January 6, 1945	George Walker, b. 1946 Pauline Robinson, 1949–1953 John Ellis, b. 1953 Neil Mellon, b. 1954 Marvin Pierce, b. 1956 Dorothy Walker, b. 1959
Hillary Diane Rodham Clinton	b. October 26, 1947	BA, 1969, Wellesley College, Political Science JD, 1973, Yale Law School	October 11, 1975	Chelsea Victoria, b. 1980
Laura Lane Welch Bush	b. November 4, 1954	BS, 1968, Southern Methodist University, Elementary Education MS, 1972, University of Texas–Austin, Library Science	November 5, 1977	Barbara, b. 1981 Jenna, b. 1981
Michelle LaVaughn Robinson Obama	b. January 17, 1964	BA, 1985, Princeton University, Sociology JD, 1988, Harvard Law School	October 3, 1992	Malia Ann, b. 1998 Natasha, b. 2001

had completed their educations and, in the Clintons' case, until both of the marriage partners had begun their professional careers. The marriages thus reflected the couples' diverse values and priorities from their earliest days.

These differences notwithstanding, there were commonalties in the challenges that the couples encountered, especially in their early years. Mamie Doud Eisenhower, Lady Bird Johnson, Pat (Thelma Catherine) Ryan Nixon, Betty Ford, and Michelle Obama were each surprised (or perhaps appalled) by the demands imposed upon them by their husbands' careers. Others, most notably Eleanor Roosevelt and Bess Truman, encountered profound tensions within their families. Additional external pressures came from living in a war zone (the Hoovers) or living within tight financial budgets (the Trumans, Carters, and Reagans). More often than not, wives and husbands grew to know one another under adverse conditions.

Many of the couples suffered tragedies while seeking to have and raise their children. Bess Truman, Jacqueline Kennedy, and Lady Bird Johnson were among those enduring miscarriages and stillbirths. Bess Truman, Lady Bird Johnson, Pat Nixon, Betty Ford, Rosalynn Carter, Nancy Reagan, and Laura Bush all had high-risk pregnancies accompanied by various health problems. The Eisenhowers, Kennedys, and George H. W. Bushes each lost a child in infancy or at a very young age. With few exceptions, the wives were the primary caregivers, the husbands typically absent in furtherance of their careers.

Even as they were coming to know their husbands and learning to be mothers, therefore, the women found themselves isolated by their husbands' ambitions and their children's needs. Whether they married early or late, few of the future first ladies sustained their premarital networks. Relocations severed many ties for the wives of servicemen and Washington-based elected officials. Especially for the women who married young and began families, independence came after the children were older.

Just four modern first ladies—Lou Henry Hoover, Eleanor Roosevelt, Hillary Rodham Clinton, and Michelle Obama—had well-established professional lives after their marriages. All four women were highly entrepreneurial, though that can be said of many other presidents' wives. Lou Henry Hoover and Eleanor Roosevelt, however, had the additional resources of wealth, which meant that they could afford staff to share their familial responsibilities and to soften the impact of continuing relocations. Hillary Rodham Clinton and Michelle Obama had the profound advantage of geographic stability, to which they added elite educational and professional credentials. Rodham Clinton sustained her premarital networks and established a further set of professional associations following her marriage, incorporating the latter into the former. (Though a number of wives had lifetime friendships and alliances, Rodham Clinton appears unique in having such long-running professional associations.) Obama began her professional career in an elite law firm, then entered city government before transitioning to the not-for-profit sector. In each instance, she established herself as a creative and formidable leader, earning promotions and increased responsibilities. The four women were located in cities that were centers of power—London (Hoover), New York (Roosevelt), Chicago (Obama), and Washington, DC (Hoover, Roosevelt, and Rodham Clinton). In brief, though the lives of Lou Henry Hoover, Eleanor Roosevelt, Hillary Rodham Clinton, and Michelle Obama were shaped by their husbands' choices, they did sustain comparatively autonomous professional networks and careers.

Even so, the husbands' careers did compromise the independence of all the modern first ladies. At times, it forcefully constrained the women's choices by prioritizing the men's interests. The following edict, attributed to Dwight Eisenhower, was imposed in more presidential families than his: "Mamie, there's one thing you must understand. My country comes first and always will. You come second."[19] For men engaged in public service, "country" and personal ambition were seldom distinguishable. The demands of the husbands' careers shaped even the most mundane aspects of daily life. As Betty Ford wrote of her husband's years as House minority leader, "I lost a husband. There followed a long stretch of time when Jerry was away from home 258 days a year. I had to bring up four kids by myself. I couldn't say, 'Wait till your father comes home'; their father wasn't going to come home for maybe a week."[20]

The Hoover, Roosevelt, Clinton, and Obama marriages notwithstanding, the pre-presidential gender roles of the first ladies and their husbands were generally congruent with separate-spheres ideals. Husbands were routinely the primary source of the family's income, and the men's careers determined the family fortunes. Wives provided support for their husbands and guidance for their children. The emotional strength required for these undertakings was formidable, especially when husbands were not yet well known, and childbearing and -rearing included failed pregnancies and childhood fatalities. Further, while men sometimes encountered destructive competition in the public sphere, women consistently had to accept a loss of independence and meet familial demands for selfless nurturing.[21]

The appeal of the separate-spheres domestic ideal is often attributed to its clarity and efficiency, as men's ambitions and women's care are rendered

neatly complementary. Conversely, the ideal is criticized for the hierarchy
that it imposes upon men and women, which leads to alienation and hardship for all involved. And yet, as we will see, few of the modern first ladies
accepted secondary status to the point that they entirely sacrificed their creativity or their influence.

Marriage as Profession

Virtually every modern first lady had an extended professional association
with her husband during their pre-presidential careers. The notable exceptions were Mamie Eisenhower and, by some accounts, Jacqueline Kennedy.
Every other couple, to a greater or lesser extent, has claimed and could often
give evidence of regular conversations about politics and policy. Wives reviewed and analyzed media coverage, lobbied on behalf of particular issues
and programs, reviewed schedules, and edited speeches.[22] These were all
public-sphere tasks, though the consultations were not always conducted
publicly, and prepared the women for communications and relationship
building, the tasks of representation.

    Couples who conducted their professional relationships in the public
sphere and in the public eye included the Roosevelts, Johnsons, Carters, and
Clintons. Eleanor Roosevelt was credited with sustaining her husband's political reputation while he endured and then convalesced from infantile pa-
ralysis. Though their marriage was periodically strained, and their political
partnership was far from easy, Eleanor Roosevelt's contributions to her husband's decision making, particularly regarding domestic policy, were widely
recognized. Lady Bird Johnson and Rosalynn Carter were in business with
their husbands: Lady Bird Johnson financed and managed their media hold-
ings, and Rosalynn Carter became the chief accountant for the family business. Similarly, as first ladies of Georgia, Arkansas, and Texas, Carter, Rodham Clinton, and Laura Bush each advanced social policy initiatives that
strengthened the political reputations of their husbands' administrations.

    Further consideration of these marriages as professional associations
continues in the following sections, which assess the wives' pre-presidential
knowledge of political strategizing, public policy, and Washington networks.
The analysis consistently reveals that while the public sphere was ostensibly
reserved to the husbands, the wives actually facilitated the husbands' achievements by shuttling between the private and public spheres. This contrast
between appearance and reality grew as the men entered successively higher
offices. With few exceptions, public-sphere man and private-sphere woman

became the dominant presentation of the future presidential couples, allowing the husband to claim as "his" the career to which the wife was an important and continuing contributor. Thus, Lady Bird Johnson's work as an effective legislative staff member, personal assistant, and business manager were seldom publicly admitted, notwithstanding her skill in facilitating constituent relationships, in easing her husband's personal and political transitions between Washington and Texas, and in building the family fortune.[23]

Belief in the self-reliant and autonomous male leader is deeply rooted in the history of Western political thought and practice. No one can win presidential office alone, but time and again men claim to have done so. And when acknowledgments are made, they seldom extend to the wife's professional and political contributions. Though few modern presidential marriages are apolitical and nonpartisan, they are repeatedly presented as such because doing so protects and advances the husbands' ambitions. Yet there are real costs to this practice. The man may be reelected, but the creativity of the couple and the expertise of the wife go unrecognized.

Did the wives know their husbands well enough as decision makers and policy makers to anticipate their behaviors as presidents? Setting aside the issues of whether a wife would want to make such assessments of her husband, answering this question is certain to generate debate. Those who see life as compartmentalized into private- and public-sphere relationships will likely judge the pre-presidential insights of the future first ladies as being of questionable or limited relevance. In contrast, those who see the private and public spheres as mutually influential will expect many wives to have unparalleled opportunities for evaluating their husbands. The truth of the matter undoubtedly lies somewhere between the two extremes, at a different point for each couple.

The argument that actions in the private and public spheres reflect different priorities and values is a logical extrapolation of separate-spheres gender ideology. Commenting upon this perspective in reference to the sexual probity of the modern presidents, political scientist James P. Pfiffner notes, "For some, the private sexual behavior of presidents should not be a public issue since it usually does not have to do with the performance of official duties or public policy. . . . This view holds that regardless of the personal morality of the behavior, it is not the public's business to be concerned with the sexual conduct of presidents."[24] Arguably, the personal intimacy of the private sphere is on a scale very different from that of the public sphere. The character of marital and family relationships, accordingly, may be viewed as having little to do with success in professional life. A man may be a caring husband and father but fail to achieve his career goals. Conversely, competitive (even abusive) husbands and fathers may succeed publicly. Wives, to this way of thinking, do not observe their husbands in a context relevant to politics. Strong separate-spheres adherents would argue, moreover, that wives lack the judgment to evaluate their husbands' potential for achievement in the public sphere. Immersed in the private sphere, the women have inadequate knowledge of the public sphere, its requirements, and its expectations.

The modern presidential couples whose pre-presidential lives are most congruent with the separate-spheres ideology are the Eisenhowers and the Fords, followed by the Kennedys and the Nixons. There is little evidence that Mamie Eisenhower or Betty Ford had many opportunities to observe their husbands at work. During Dwight Eisenhower's military career, the couple was often separated. When they were together, military protocol set stringent gender boundaries, and available evidence suggests that these were also in place while Dwight Eisenhower served as the president of Columbia University.[25] Eisenhower's first elective office was the presidency, so Mamie Eisenhower did not have any earlier campaign experience. Similar circumstances, though varying in degree, held for the Kennedys, Nixons, and Fords. Jacqueline Kennedy's participation in her husband's political career was sporadic and limited, given their brief marriage and the timing of her pregnancies. Pat Nixon's involvement was significantly greater—she was second lady in the Eisenhower administration and a participant in her husband's congressional, Senate, gubernatorial, and presidential campaigns—but existent records indicate few opportunities for her to evaluate her husband as a partisan decision maker. Betty Ford's autobiographies make few references to her husband's twenty-four-year congressional career, though she does describe the effect of his absences on her health and their family. For these couples, limited professional associations may well have constrained the wives' knowledge of their husbands as decision and policy makers.

Analysts and observers who instead see the private and the public spheres as interactive expect political wives to provide important and useful insights on their husbands. To this way of thinking, personal and familial relations are a microcosm of the larger society. While accepting that a man's public success cannot be predicted from his care or abuse of family members, they argue that these relationships do reveal deeply held values and critical character traits. A husband who would not be faithful to the vows made to his wife or promises made to his children could not be expected to keep his word

in political or business dealings. If a man cannot be trusted when the consequences of his actions are intimately evident, why trust him when the stakes
are more abstract in terms of legislation or budgets? The exercise of power
in the private sphere, then, becomes indicative of the exercise of power in
the public sphere; the actions of the individual are expected to be consistent
and even somewhat predictable.[26] Having had the longest and most intimate
experience of those behaviors, the wife would presumably have the greatest
knowledge of the future president. Even if she was not willing to verbalize
her judgments, she could still act upon them. Like all aides, her influence
would be (should be) determined by her ability to anticipate and respond to
the needs of the president, her husband.

Award-winning biographer Robert Caro embraced this approach, describing Lyndon Johnson's treatment of his wife, staff, and political colleagues as similar. Behavior in one context was revealing of behavior in all
others.[27] In each instance, the "Johnson treatment" was an exercise in domi-
nation that sometimes crossed into emotional abuse. The lack of respect that
Lyndon Johnson demonstrated toward his wife—the public reminders of
the chores he assigned her to perform, the orders she was to obey, the weight
he expected her to lose, the clothes he insisted she wear—had a parallel
in the "psychological dependence" he required of the men who worked for
him. Caro found layers of truth in one congressman's statement that Lyndon
Johnson "treated [Lady Bird Johnson] like the hired help."[28] Though Lady
Bird Johnson herself publicly rejected these negative judgments, she did endorse the underlying assessment that public and private could not be distinguished in their marriage: "His life became my life. I respected it. I wanted
to learn from it, to excel in it." In the words of biographer Jan Jarboe Russell,
"She viewed her marriage as a career as much as a relationship."[29]

I take a middle road, as indicated by the position of "knowledge of the
president" as first among the types of knowledge, I believe the future first
lady's understanding of her husband is extraordinarily important to her performance as a representative in the presidential administration. Further, I
argue that the historical and documentary record shows that modern first
ladies have derived this knowledge in part from their marriage and family
lives, in part from their professional and political lives. This approach makes
the best possible use of all information and reaches the most comprehensive conclusions possible. Gender roles in the United States throughout the
twentieth century also recommend this approach. If the private and public
spheres were actually exclusive, the electorate would not expect to meet the

spouses and children of elected officials. In this book, then, all aspects of the wife-husband relationship—familial, professional, and political—are viewed as sources of knowledge for women and for men.

Future first ladies may gain considerable insight on their husbands during the pre-presidential years. At a very powerful minimum, they would have a clear sense of their husbands' ambitions and what they would be willing to sacrifice on behalf of those ambitions. Because most of the presidential couples had experienced some hardship and tragedy, the wives could also know how their husbands responded to failure and loss. To the extent that there was some shared decision making within the family (Hoovers and Trumans), or in building a business (Johnsons and Carters), or constructing a political reputation (Roosevelts, Reagans, George H. W. Bushes, and Clintons), wives would also know how their husbands negotiated and compromised. Presumably, these women could anticipate their husbands' performances as chief executives, fine-tuning their own performance as representatives to bolster and to compensate for the president's strengths and weaknesses.

KNOWLEDGE OF CAMPAIGNING AND GOVERNING

Of the fourteen modern first ladies, just two—Lou Henry Hoover and Mamie Eisenhower—were introduced to campaigning when their husbands ran for the presidency. The other women had previously participated as candidates' wives in races for the U.S. House of Representatives (five), the U.S. Senate (six), governors' offices (six), the vice presidency (five), and the presidency (four). Of the twelve women with election experience, six had campaigned for a range of offices, including one or more national campaigns before the one that put their husband in the Oval Office (see Table 2.2). During these electoral apprenticeships, the future first ladies learned about winning and losing political contests, with all the associated partisan and policy lessons.

Among the most unremitting of those lessons were the expectations confronting the candidate's wife. She was to attend all events, presenting herself as feminine and photogenic, showcasing her husband's strength, virility, and masculinity.[30] This was particularly important in the 1960 presidential campaign, when Jacqueline Kennedy's presence was an implicit refutation of concerns about John Kennedy's health.[31] The husband's identity subsumed the wife's. She became another piece of evidence, testifying to his fitness for office.

Table 2.2. Campaign Experience, Gubernatorial and Federal, of the First Ladies prior to Their Husbands' Successful Presidential Campaign

Governor's Office

    Eleanor Roosevelt (1928, 1930)
    Pat Nixon (1962 unsuccessful)
    Rosalynn Carter (1970, 1966 unsuccessful)
    Nancy Reagan (1966, 1970)
    Hillary Rodham Clinton (1978, 1982, 1984, 1986, 1990, 1980 unsuccessful)
    Laura Bush (1994, 1998)

U.S. House of Representatives

    Lady Bird Johnson (1936, 1938, 1940, 1942, 1944, 1946)
    Pat Nixon (1946, 1948)
    Betty Ford (1948, 1950, 1952, 1954, 1956, 1958, 1960, 1962, 1964, 1966, 1968, 1970, 1972)
    Barbara Bush (1966, 1968)
    Hillary Rodham Clinton (1974 unsuccessful)
    Laura Bush (1978 unsuccessful)
    Michelle Obama (2000 unsuccessful)

U.S. Senate

    Bess Truman (1934, 1940)
    Jacqueline Kennedy (1958)
    Lady Bird Johnson (1941, 1948, 1954)
    Pat Nixon (1950)
    Barbara Bush (1964 unsuccessful)
    Michelle Obama (2004)

Vice Presidency

    Eleanor Roosevelt (1920 unsuccessful)
    Bess Truman (1944)
    Lady Bird Johnson (1960)
    Pat Nixon (1952, 1956)
    Barbara Bush (1980, 1984)

Presidency

    Eleanor Roosevelt (1928 [Smith campaign])
    Jacqueline Kennedy (1956 preconvention only)
    Lady Bird Johnson (1960 preconvention only)
    Pat Nixon (1960 unsuccessful)
    Nancy Reagan (1968 preconvention only, 1976 primary season only)
    Barbara Bush (1980 primary season only)

The wives' awareness of this role was evidenced in their blunt recommendations for surviving campaigns. Bess Truman viewed the experience as a more specific instance of the public expectations confronting all wives in the public sphere. She concluded, "A woman's place in public is to sit beside her husband and be silent and be sure her hat is on straight."[32] Michelle Obama agreed but observed that political husbands were also sometimes objectified, saying of her appearances with her husband, "We accessorize one another well."

Conforming to these standards demanded a great deal. Bess Truman suffered in crowds, finding them overwhelming and even frightening, especially when people stretched across barriers to touch or pull at her.[33] In a rare complaint, Lady Bird Johnson said she had only elections to anticipate for years, having neither a home nor children.[34] Pat Nixon saw the money she had earned and saved for a home spent by her husband on his first congressional campaign.[35] Hillary Rodham took her husband's name, after keeping her birth name throughout their married life, following widespread criticism during her husband's early gubernatorial campaigns.[36] Women who resisted changing their identity typically did so by absenting themselves from campaigning. Bess Truman, Jacqueline Kennedy, and Betty Ford all minimized their electoral participation. Truman detested campaigning, and her husband later commented, "I did my best to keep the Boss and Margaret out of it as much as I could, but that didn't always happen."[37] In 1958 Jacqueline Kennedy limited her participation in her husband's Senate reelection campaign, claiming her responsibilities as a mother; in the 1960 presidential campaign, her pregnancy constrained her travel.[38] Betty Ford's autobiography refers to just two elections, her husband's first in 1948 and his last in 1976. His other twelve congressional campaigns are mentioned only briefly, with the note that they routinely caused Gerald Ford to miss celebrating his wedding anniversary.[39]

Governing, like campaigning, required a political wife to undergo close scrutiny in a highly competitive environment. In governing, however, the competition was more open-ended and more enduring. For the wives of governors, serving as a state's first lady was a test of their political style and policy priorities. Eleanor Roosevelt, Rosalynn Carter, Nancy Reagan, Hillary Rodham Clinton, and Laura Bush rehearsed their communications, their performance as representatives, and their policy agendas as first ladies in their home states.

During her husband's gubernatorial inaugural, Laura Bush, for example, announced that her "interests" would reflect her professional and personal commitment to "reading and writing and children." Bush earned her undergraduate degree in elementary education and then her master's degree in library science, focusing on child development and reading. Before her marriage, she worked as a public school teacher and librarian, and as a public librarian. As the first lady of Texas, Bush accented her strategic expertise. This was most evident in her founding of the Texas Book Festival, arguably her greatest contribution. Begun in 1995, the two-day gathering featured Texas literature and authors, fostered literacy, and raised money for Texas public libraries. Fifteen years later, as this book is being written, over forty-six thousand attend the annual festival, which has awarded over $2 million to hundreds of public libraries throughout the state. The public-private partnerships that Bush inaugurated are strong and enduring, dedicated to sustaining the festival and its commitment to public libraries. In fact, two of the festival's grant programs are supported by corporate and foundation funds.[40]

Wives whose political experience was centered in Washington also manifested strategic expertise, though the extent of their participation in politics varied. At one extreme was Bess Truman, Jacqueline Kennedy, and Betty Ford, whose political involvement was minimal. Even so, all three women observed first ladies closely and were well socialized to Washington networks.[41] Truman and Ford are credited, by their husbands, with serving as their political confidantes.[42] Among those at the other extreme were Lou Henry Hoover and Lady Bird Johnson, who participated extensively in politics throughout the pre-presidential years.

Lou Henry Hoover did not hold a post comparable to those of Rosalynn Carter and Hillary Rodham Clinton, but she did undertake initiatives similar to Laura Bush's. Hoover's organizational affiliations and contributions closely paralleled those of her husband. When hundreds of thousands of Americans were stranded throughout Europe at the start of the war in 1914, Herbert Hoover led the organization that financed their return home, while Lou Henry Hoover led the Women's Committee that provided "unaccompanied women and children" with economic and emotional support. When Herbert Hoover became chair of the Commission for Relief in Belgium, Lou Henry Hoover traveled to occupied Belgium and "visited every sort of relief activity." She also acted independently. She led the American Women's Committee for Economic Relief, which founded a knitting factory for unemployed women (the products were distributed to sailors and soldiers), provided rehabilitation services for injured servicemen, and established relief programs for soldiers' wives. She focused her efforts, however, on the American Women's Hospital in Paignton, England, a two-hundred-bed surgical hospital for wounded soldiers, which was financed and staffed by Americans throughout the war.[43]

When Herbert Hoover was subsequently appointed U.S. food adminis-
trator, Lou Henry Hoover once again led related organizations. At the Food
Administration, she established the Food Administration Girls' Club to provide housing and assistance to women working in the agency. She also lobbied for and helped to run a large cafeteria, which provided, in the words
of Herbert Hoover, "good and cheap food." It served "thousands of meals
daily—and made a profit. They devoted the profit to their other activities on
behalf of the women employees with a grim determination that the men employees must thereby contribute to their resources." During the influenza epidemic of 1917–18, the organization provided support to the sick and dying,
and to the families of the dead. Hoover also joined the Girl Scouts at this time
and soon held local, council, and national leadership positions. She founded,
led, and fundraised for the Women's Division of the National Amateur Athletic Federation and established enduring networks among women's political
organizations such as the League of Women Voters and the General Federation of Women's Clubs. She was adept in mobilizing the public across gender
and class boundaries, and would later utilize these same skills and connections to publicize the president's agenda.[44] Lou Henry Hoover's leadership was
often linked to Herbert Hoover's, but her successes were her own.

As the wife of the Senate majority leader and then of the vice president,
Lady Bird Johnson was well socialized to Washington. Her apprenticeship
as second lady was particularly intense, as she routinely served as Jacqueline
Kennedy's surrogate. In 1961 alone, she hosted over fifty official functions
at the White House, with all associated networking and political responsibilities.[45] Though Bess Truman, Pat Nixon, and Betty Ford also served an
apprenticeship as second ladies, Johnson's was the more intensive. In part,
this reflects Jacqueline Kennedy's own willingness to make use of Johnson's
talents. In both the campaign and the White House, Johnson was among the
administration's primary emissaries to women leaders and women's organizations. The strategic expertise she acquired in this role was put to greater use
in her husband's administration, when her outreach and representation signaled that this president recognized women as his constituents.

A strategically knowledgeable staff member understands the needs and
incentives that leads to campaign promises, and is capable of balancing those
forces with the stresses of a system of separated powers and checks and balances. The power of the presidential office and the limits of its authority are
especially important when the individual is one of the few able to say "no"
to the chief executive. This is a great deal to expect, but further demands are
made of the first lady as a representative. The president's wife is also expected

to aid her husband in capitalizing on the constructive effects of gender, identity, political symbolism, tradition, and presidential character. Mistakes cannot be easily corrected.

Several of the first ladies entered the White House with strategic expertise. The wives routinely expected to serve as their husbands' political
confidantes and consultants, feeling a sense of loss and alienation when circumstances dictated otherwise. Barbara Bush, for example, acknowledged
that she was "depressed, lonely, and unhappy" when conversations with her
husband, newly named as the Central Intelligence Agency director, were
constrained by security clearances.[46] When her husband campaigned for the
presidency, however, Barbara Bush's networking skills placed her at the center
of the action—her index of friends, acquaintances, and associates generated
the earliest lists of supporters and donors.[47]

Responses to questions about the first ladies' strategic expertise would
therefore be generally affirmative. The women had, with few exceptions, been
politically active in their pre-presidential years. Several came to expect that
they would participate in campaigning and governing, as the husband's career
became an expression of their marital relationship. Even those more removed
from campaigning and governing could not be considered amateurs. Mamie
Eisenhower, for example, had married an army lieutenant who became a five-
star general and then president of an Ivy League university. She had acquired
a comprehensive understanding of military and academic life, in all their
formal and informal aspects. The future first ladies had demonstrated their
understanding of the power exercised through gender ideologies during campaigns and while their husbands held office. Time and again, these women
renegotiated their relationships with their husbands and the public, sometimes accepting and sometimes manipulating expectations that they would
be their husbands' satellites. Though few of the women could fully anticipate
the pressures they would encounter as first ladies, virtually all had a well-
honed ability to meet the kinds of challenges they would encounter as representatives in the White House.

KNOWLEDGE OF POLICY

Six of the modern first ladies were engaged in policy making during their
pre-presidential careers, though not all of the six would describe themselves
as doing so. Lou Henry Hoover and Michelle Obama were both active in an
arena distinct from government, for example, though it had significant soci-

etal consequences. Hoover devoted herself to the development of leadership skills in girls and young women, seeking to engender rich self-confidence. Through the Girl Scouts and the National Women's Athletic Association, she fostered self-expression, self-reliance, and self-esteem. She therefore brought a significant background in leadership training and child development into the White House, in addition to her strategic expertise in management and development. Michelle Obama was also deeply engaged in the not-for-profit sector, first administering community service programs and then facilitating community relations for the University of Chicago hospital system. She acquired a corresponding expertise in the workings of health and education programs, at the grassroots and in larger organizations.

Four others had substantive policy expertise, as that term is more routinely defined. Eleanor Roosevelt and Hillary Rodham Clinton each engaged in extensive government-centered policy work in their pre-presidential careers. Throughout the 1920s, Eleanor Roosevelt first developed and then put to use her substantive (and strategic) policy expertise through leadership roles in the Women's City Club, the League of Women Voters, and the Women's Division of the New York Democratic State Committee. In each instance, she advocated for reform by highlighting the relevance of the issues and the policies to the lives of ordinary people. Human suffering, she argued, compelled change. Her agenda included the provision of good, affordable housing; the passage of protective labor legislation (especially the forty-eight-hour work week) for women and children; and initiatives that advanced women within the Democratic Party. She collaborated across gender boundaries even as she established a formidable network of women political activists. This was the strategic manifestation of her firm belief that change was best effected from within the political system, an explicitly incremental approach to wielding power. When she became the first lady of New York, she sustained her influence even after she stepped down from formal leadership positions. Her fact-finding tours for the governor provided her with important information, allowed her to continue her political relationships, and enabled her to advertise her programmatic priorities.[48]

Rodham Clinton's analytic training and political development were primarily fostered through professional and governmental associations. A graduate of Yale Law School, she was a staff attorney and then board member of the Children's Defense Fund, a staff member on the House Judiciary Committee when it prepared the articles of impeachment against President Nixon, and a Carter appointee to the U.S. Legal Services Corporation. She became a partner in the Rose Law Firm and served on several corporate boards. As

Arkansas's first lady, she chaired the Arkansas Education Standards Committee (which set public school accreditation guidelines), was the governor's designee to the Southern Regional Task Force on Infant Mortality, and chaired the state's rural health committee.[49]

Rosalynn Carter and Laura Bush became involved in public policy making while serving as first ladies of Georgia and of Texas, respectively. Carter's commitment to mental health-care reform was initiated in her husband's 1970 gubernatorial campaign, when prospective supporters spoke out about their concerns for mentally ill family members. Carter subsequently served her policy apprenticeship as one of four members of the Governor's Commission to Improve Services to the Mentally and Emotionally Handicapped. Finding that Georgia was "five to seven years behind the national trend in developing comprehensive community centers," the commission recommended a wide-ranging set of reforms despite the state's limited eligibility for federal funding. Community-based mental health services, education of the public, humane treatment of the mentally ill and mentally handicapped, coalition building with community organizations and health-care volunteers, and public health (especially family planning and prenatal, postnatal, and children's health) were among the commission's highest priorities. A decentralization of the mental health-care system was subsequently effected, with 111 community mental health centers and twenty-three group homes opened while Jimmy Carter was governor. The number of individuals receiving services was increased by 56 percent, while the number of resident hospital patients dropped by approximately 30 percent.[50]

Laura Bush became more involved in the policy process after her husband declared his presidential candidacy. In 1999 she hosted a conference on child development, laying the groundwork for efforts to secure passage of a bill to provide state funding for reading readiness programs and Head Start educational programs. This initiative made Bush the first of Texas first ladies to lobby the state legislature; she was careful, in the words of an *Austin American-Statesman* reporter, to keep "a low profile during the session." Yet her activism was interpreted as a public statement of her ambition to move "onto the national political stage" as a first lady with an issue agenda.[51] She was presenting herself—and was being presented—as a strong and effective successor to Hillary Rodham Clinton. And she was doing so in her area of professional expertise, child development and literacy. All of this augmented her work in establishing the Texas Book Festival to raise funds for public libraries throughout the state.

Self-evidently, each of the policy activists among the modern first ladies was determined to effect change. They were not interested in abstractions or ideologies, though they were highly analytic thinkers. Their commitment was less to ideas than to applications, to doing politics rather than to theorizing. Their substantive and strategic expertise, therefore, was always closely intertwined. In her tours of hospitals and clinics as New York's first lady, Eleanor Roosevelt gathered the data and established the relationships that made her a more persuasive, influential advocate for public health reforms, for example. And, in keeping with the reality that these marriages were also professional alliances, the women's policy work neatly complemented their husbands' priorities. Lou Henry Hoover led women's organizations that were the female counterpart to the predominantly male organizations led by her husband. Michelle Obama's career in the not-for-profit sector paralleled her husband's early career as a community organizer. The governors formally endorsed their wives' issue priorities and recommendations, as evidenced by Eleanor Roosevelt being requested to conduct fact-finding tours, Rosalynn Carter being appointed to a gubernatorial commission, and Hillary Rodham Clinton being named to task forces and committees. Similarly, Laura Bush found her legislative lobbying timed to coincide with her husband's presidential campaign.

A further, substantive commonality among the women is found in their connection with "women's issues" throughout the pre-presidential years. Children, women, and leadership development (Lou Henry Hoover), social policy and social justice (Eleanor Roosevelt), mental health and public health (Rosalynn Carter), children, education, and health (Hillary Rodham Clinton), reading (Laura Bush), and mentoring and childhood health (Michelle Obama) are widely viewed as falling within women's ascribed roles as homemakers and caregivers. They are issues that have led to the foundation of philanthropic organizations, research foundations, interest groups, and professional associations—many of them with a preponderance of women among their members and officers, and many of them with agendas that prioritize the needs and concerns of women. As policy activists, the women who became first ladies knew and mobilized these issue networks. Lou Henry Hoover, Eleanor Roosevelt, and Hillary Rodham Clinton held leadership positions in women-centered organizations; Lou Henry Hoover and Laura Bush established new organizations to realize their goals; and Eleanor Roosevelt and Rosalynn Carter facilitated strong relationships between policy networks and government offices. Michelle Obama served on the boards of community organizations and schools. All of this work in the public sphere could be accepted and endorsed because it could be seen as an extension of a woman's tra-

ditional responsibilities in the private sphere. Even as these women fully engaged themselves in the public sphere, they could be presented as supporting
a separate-spheres gender ideology. A commitment to the interests of women
and children, as separate-spheres advocates have argued, is an expression of
morality and guardianship, a judgment that women are distinctively able to
provide.

Yet another similarity among these policy activists is the breadth of their
networking. Though their issue agendas relate to women and to "women's
issues," none hesitated to reach across gender boundaries or to appeal to diverse publics. Lou Henry Hoover was one of the first women to earn an undergraduate degree in geology from Stanford University and subsequently
published in that male-dominated discipline with her husband. As a founding officer of the National Amateur Athletic Federation of America, and of
its Women's Division, Hoover built coalitions with national men's athletic
organizations.[52] Eleanor Roosevelt established an early and strong association
with the Democratic Party and did not hesitate to use partisan organizations
to gain support for policy reforms. Rosalynn Carter's mental health initiatives affected professions that were predominantly male as well as predominantly female. Hillary Rodham Clinton worked with party organizations
and government agencies that were predominantly male. As a fundraiser and
legislative lobbyist, Laura Bush was well aware that a broad (but focused)
appeal was essential to achieving success. She took care to present children's
reading as a priority for men and women of all ages, backgrounds, and in-
comes. Michelle Obama worked in settings that had varying gender ratios,
and was mentored by men and by women. She herself was her husband's
mentor during his law school summer internship. For all of these women,
the consistent concern was to build a strong coalition of supporters, which
meant that the future first ladies were intertwining their substantive and strategic expertise.

The ideological content and outcomes of this activism are even more revealing of the close connection drawn by these women between policy substance and political strategy. The two Republicans—Lou Henry Hoover and
Laura Bush—were skilled organizers and fundraisers.[53] Their activism was
conducted mostly in the not-for-profit sector, with occasional government
partnerships. At times, they relied upon market mechanisms to achieve their
policy goals. Thus, Lou Henry Hoover established first a knitting factory in
London to provide employment for women dislocated by war, and then a
cafeteria at the Food Administration building in Washington to provide affordable meals for the office workers and to generate funds for social services

for women and for victims of the 1917–18 influenza epidemics. Laura Bush focused her efforts on the Texas Book Festival, turning to legislation much later in her tenure as the state's first lady. These women acted on their belief that society's needs should be met through a creative marshaling of society's own resources. If individuals could not be wholly self-reliant, neither was there reason to create a dependence upon government and government programs. Enduring Republican ideals of small government and minimal intervention in the market were very much a part of the pre-presidential coalition building performed by these women, which reinforced their credibility as loyal wives of strong Republicans.

The Democratic activists were similarly consistent in the ideological underpinnings of their policy making. Each woman believed that the suffering that permeated society was sometimes exacerbated by the market and too often ignored (or inadequately addressed) by the government. They saw government-centered programs as the desired corrective and advocated on behalf of far-reaching reforms. Eleanor Roosevelt's commitment to protective labor legislation, Rosalynn Carter's advocacy on behalf of community mental health centers, and Hillary Rodham Clinton's contributions to setting public school accreditation standards are just a few of the instances in which the Democratic women pushed for a more responsive government. Michelle Obama's work was centered in the not-for-profit sector, but her stress on community service resonated with this theme. The shared ideal of democracy and responsive government positioned the women in the liberal mainstream of their party.

Significantly, the wives who were pre-presidential policy activists were Republicans and Democrats. Each was rewarded for her efforts with national offices (Hoover and Clinton), media coverage (Hoover, Roosevelt, Carter, and Bush), and promotions (Clinton and Obama). Though the five women would express and perform very different gender ideologies as first ladies, their policy activism was a powerful similarity in their earlier careers.

While prior participation in issue networks was not a requirement for undertaking policy making as a first lady, it did provide experiences and knowledge that advantaged these five women. Policy negotiations with legislatures and executive agencies, in gubernatorial commissions and not-for-profit organizations, tested the women's gender and partisan commitments. Their communication and relationship-building skills were refined while they developed substantive and strategic expertise. Policy knowledge, in brief, brought an understanding of the dilemmas that would characterize their representation as first ladies.

KNOWLEDGE OF THE WASHINGTON COMMUNITY
AND OF WASHINGTON SOCIETY

For the modern first ladies, knowledge of Washington has had two facets. One is an extension of their strategic knowledge of campaigning and governing, focused upon partisan processes and personalities. Knowing the role each U.S. representative and U.S. senator plays in policy networks, party caucuses, committees, and chambers, for example, is essential for the political wife. No less important is her skill in anticipating public responses to her husband's speeches and actions. The other facet of a first lady's Washington expertise relates to Washington society. Washington opinion leaders control many networks and hierarchies that infuse and reach beyond the purely governmental.

Strategic expertise and sensitivity to the Washington community is a difficult blending of talents, often more easily recognized when it is absent than when it is present. It requires a president and a president's wife to acknowledge and respect a wider array of actors than is usually associated with the permanent campaign or the policy-making process. As Clinton's social secretary Ann Stock explained, social outreach to Washington society could "neutralize your yip-yappers" and "create a buzz to go around town about the good, wonderful things that you do." In other words, it could preempt criticism, replacing it with a strong and positive momentum that favored the administration. Doing so requires a first lady to use and honor "the grandeur and cachet" of the presidency, especially its most visible symbol, the White House.[54] In Washington and throughout the country, the president's status as chief executive is augmented by the widespread recognition that he is also a chief of state, the leader of a nation as well as the highest officeholder in one branch of its government. But this requires a first lady to see the connections between policy and protocol.[55]

Five of the women who became first ladies had comparatively little knowledge of the Washington community and its society. Mamie Eisenhower, Rosalynn Carter, Nancy Reagan, Laura Bush, and Michelle Obama had their first extended contact with the Washington community as a president's wife. Mamie Eisenhower's prior status as the wife of a five-star general, however, meant that she was familiar with many of its social networks. Rosalynn Carter had not prioritized social outreach as Georgia's first lady, though Reagan had done so while she was California's first lady. As the daughter-in-law of a former president, Laura Bush was well acquainted with both Washington and White House folkways. Obama had been the wife of a

U.S. senator, though she did not relocate to Washington until shortly before she moved into the White House.

Five other women had a working familiarity with the Washington community and society. Eleanor Roosevelt, Bess Truman, Jacqueline Kennedy, Betty Ford, and Hillary Rodham Clinton interacted with Washington networks on their own terms throughout their pre-presidential years. As the wife of the assistant secretary of the navy, Eleanor Roosevelt's interaction with Washington society had been highly ritualized. She spent the majority of her afternoons calling, spending a few moments with each of ten to thirty other political wives, and she hosted formal dinners of ten to forty guests at least one weekday each week and two Sundays each month. She also attended diplomatic dinners, where her gift for foreign languages was well known and respected. During World War I, she worked at canteens and visited sick and wounded soldiers. This was expected of a subcabinet wife; Roosevelt performed the tasks dutifully, without finding them fulfilling or rewarding.[56] Bess Truman also met social expectations, but more minimally. Roosevelt had ten or more servants and a family fortune to draw upon, while Truman had little help and only her husband's Senate salary, which they augmented by hiring Bess Truman as a full-time staff member in Harry Truman's Senate office. In addition to these familial and financial constraints, neither of the Trumans viewed entertainment as a priority, or even as appropriate, during the depression and war years. Bess Truman attended the expected events, such as the Senate ladies' luncheons, but was not herself a recognized hostess.[57]

Other political wives, similarly, balanced the expectations of Washington society, their personal inclinations, and their family resources. Jacqueline Kennedy attended Senate ladies' luncheons and did the Red Cross service expected of Senate wives, but generally avoided diplomatic dinners and larger receptions. Instead, she hosted smaller and more intimate dinners in her Georgetown home.[58] Betty Ford stressed that raising four children limited her attendance at White House social occasions. When she did talk about these events, it was in terms of her personal enjoyment, not their political character.[59] And Hillary Rodham Clinton, who would stress policy and political networking throughout her years as first lady, spent far more time with those power brokers in the Washington community than with arbiters in Washington society.[60] Each of these political wives revealed their priorities through their social outreach. Jacqueline Kennedy's selective entertaining, Betty Ford's self-distancing from partisan politics, and Hillary Rodham Clinton's dedication to the policy process foreshadowed the representation they would perform as first ladies.

The remaining four women—Lou Henry Hoover, Lady Bird Johnson, Pat Nixon, and Barbara Bush—were well known in Washington society and were familiar with the Washington community of decision makers. Hoover was an eminent hostess. As a cabinet wife, she deftly facilitated changes in protocol. She also reached out more widely to the Washington community through her work with the U.S. Food Administration and her leadership of the Girl Scouts. Her knowledge of legislative and executive networks, though, went largely undocumented; there are only brief references to her as an attentive listener in her husband's political conversations. The documentary record is similarly limited for Lady Bird Johnson, though her memoir offers evidence of her political acumen, particularly in regard to legislative-executive relations. As a congressional and Senate wife, Johnson had entertained extensively and often on short notice, as her husband frequently brought home colleagues and staff members. As second lady, Johnson continued to cope with these spontaneous demands when Jacqueline Kennedy excused herself from events.[61]

Pat Nixon and Barbara Bush, like Lady Bird Johnson, were well socialized to the Washington community and society. They had been political wives for decades, with a corresponding expertise in Washington's formal and informal relationships. Each had been a second lady, with an opportunity to closely observe a president's wife and her communications with Washington networks. Although Hoover and Johnson had greater expertise, neither Nixon nor Bush were amateurs.

Governmental organizations are only a few of the arenas in which policy is made. Also important are Washington social and cultural networks, which set a context for so many perceptions of a presidential administration, shaping its reputation and its prestige. Knowledge of both the formal and the informal networks of political and governmental decision makers is an invaluable resource for an administration.

CONCLUSION

Presidents' wives have routinely been valued as their husbands' satellites, or as evidence of their husbands' masculinity and virility. Their political contributions as representatives have seldom been systematically assessed. To lay the foundation for doing so, this chapter has examined the kinds of expertise that the modern first ladies have brought into the White House, revealing their likely strengths and weaknesses. In other words, it suggests when the first ladies may act as comparatively independent representatives, expressing

well-founded judgments and insights, and when they will be silent or dependent upon the guidance of others.

Unquestionably, the women are diverse. However, if this study is to
move beyond a biographical analysis, it is the larger, more constant similarities and contrasts that merit investigation (see Table 2.3).

First, the modern presidents' wives had considerable expertise when they
entered the White House. Their pre-presidential careers were varied, making it difficult to compare the extent and content of one woman's knowledge
with that of another. Still, with the exception of Mamie Eisenhower, every
modern first lady could reasonably claim two of the four kinds of expertise.
Those with relatively weaker claims—Bess Truman, Mamie Eisenhower, and
Betty Ford—had distanced themselves from politics and yet were well socialized to the Washington community. If not well prepared, they were at least
well braced for life in the White House. Truman, Johnson, and Ford had
even served as second lady immediately prior to becoming first lady.

Second, the knowledge shared by the greatest number of modern first
ladies was strategic, meaning that the women were knowledgeable about the
processes of campaigning and governing. Experientially, wives participated
in their husbands' campaigns, often traveling independently as surrogates.
Wives routinely served as their husbands' confidantes and advisors, providing
insights that ranged from the political to the psychological. Not all the wives
enjoyed politics, but there were those who proactively sought opportunities
to participate in campaigning and governing. Eleanor Roosevelt, Rosalynn
Carter, and Hillary Rodham Clinton are the most obvious examples, earning
reputations as formidable political entrepreneurs.

Third, substantive policy expertise was perhaps the least common form of
knowledge possessed by the future first ladies. Just six could be considered to
have such a background, and Lou Henry Hoover and Michelle Obama might
dispute such a characterization. In part, this scarcity of knowledge reflects
some wives' decision to distance themselves from politics, because policy-
related expertise requires a considerable investment of time and other resources. Lack of policy expertise also can be attributed to the wives' family
responsibilities and to the husbands' failure to facilitate their participation in
the policy process.

Gender studies, however, offer further and deeper insight on this apparent lack of expertise. Precisely because policy making involves the allocation
of resources and reveals the distribution of power, it is a highly competitive undertaking that resists substantive and procedural change. Newcom-
ers and new ideas, therefore, must surmount significant barriers. As women,

Table 2.3 Pre-presidential Political Expertise of the Modern First Ladies

	Knowledge of the future president as a decision and policy maker	Knowledge of campaigning and governing	Knowledge of policy	Knowledge of the Washington community and society
Lou Henry Hoover	x		x	x
Eleanor Roosevelt	x	x	x	x (less)
Bess Truman	x	x (less)		x (less)
Mamie Eisenhower	x (less)			x (less)
Jacqueline Kennedy	x	x (less)		x (less)
Lady Bird Johnson	x	x		x
Pat Nixon	x	x		x
Betty Ford	x (less)	x (less)		x (less)
Rosalynn Carter	x	x	x	
Nancy Reagan	x	x		
Barbara Bush	x	x		x
Hillary Rodham Clinton	x	x	x	x (less)
Laura Bush	x	x	x	x (less)
Michelle Obama	x	x (less)	x	

the future first ladies were gender outsiders in the policy process. Moreover, the self-reliance, power, and autonomy required of a hard-bargaining policy advocate are almost exactly the reverse of what is praised in a political wife. Overcoming, circumventing, or reconciling these contrasts requires extraordinary resources, which were available to few of the wives. It also requires acceptance, if not affirmative support, from husbands immersed in campaigning and governing, determined to succeed and correspondingly less likely to question prevailing presumptions. Certainly the husbands often demonstrated their willingness to sacrifice their family and personal relationships to their political ambitions.

Studying the constraints upon the first ladies' political learning, and their responses, quickly reveals the ways in which the first ladyship affects a woman's choices and actions. For modern first ladies in the earlier administrations, who confronted a society resistant to women in the public sphere and who had few staff resources, the first lady's post would seem to offer few opportunities for political engagement. Eleanor Roosevelt ultimately set a high standard for first ladies committed to electoral, policy, and governance work, but she entered the White House with an acute awareness of what she would be expected to sacrifice as a president's wife.

> [F]or myself I was deeply troubled. As I saw it, this meant the end of any personal life of my own. I knew what traditionally should lie before me; I had watched Mrs. Theodore Roosevelt and had seen what it meant to be the wife of a president, and I cannot say I was pleased at the prospect. By earning my own money, I had recently enjoyed a certain amount of financial independence and had been able to do things in which I was personally interested. The turmoil in my heart and mind was rather great.[62]

From the Johnson administration onward, multiple staff members aided the first lady. Gradually, the first lady gained a press secretary, speechwriter, scheduling and advance team, and chief of staff, among others. Also gradually, women began to fill decision-making positions throughout the legislative, executive, and judicial branches. With her own staff, contacts extending into issue networks, and a continuing awareness of the influence wielded by other women, first ladies in the latter twentieth century were less isolated and potentially more empowered.

And yet there remains the matter of the first lady's own interests, priorities, and expertise. The next chapter examines the links between the first lady's knowledge of the Washington community and the symbolic representation provided by the president's wife. As might be expected, the first ladies' pre–White House careers are a useful but not wholly accurate predictor of their performance. Like their husbands, the presidents' wives change as they learn and fulfill their responsibilities as representatives.

3

THE NATION'S HOSTESS:
The First Lady and Symbolic Representation

Symbols are numerous and diverse in the presidency, but the White House may be the most conspicuous and the most meaningful. Well into the twentieth century, those attending White House receptions and dinners wore "court dress," conforming to standards set in western European royal courts. Women, for example, were expected to wear gowns with six-foot trains. And yet in this same period there was a public White House reception on New Year's Day. People stood for hours in the cold, waiting to be welcomed into the White House by the president and first lady, who shook hands with every individual in line. Time and again, the White House has symbolized both the monarchical qualities of the presidency and its close ties to democratic-republican ideals. Dwight Eisenhower reinforced these perceptions, writing in his memoirs that "the White House is not just a well-run home for the Chief Executive; it is a living story of past pioneering, struggles, wars, innovations, and a growing America. I like to think of it as a symbol of freedom and of the homes and future accomplishments of her people."[1]

To recognize the White House as a symbol of great importance to the presidency is to acknowledge its power in framing both an enduring office and an effervescent administration. There is an immediacy to the social outreach that is conducted in this setting. The rituals associated with ceremonies, receptions, teas, luncheons, and state dinners are subtly shaped by each administration to reflect its principles and priorities. Along the way, the administration hopes, these rituals will encourage observers to draw constructive connections between a widely valued political symbol (the White House) and a sometimes controversial organization (the administration). Even when communications and relationship building are less personal and are mediated by mass communication, attention to the symbolic value of the White House continues. The decision to broadcast from the Oval Office or the East Room, as one example, is carefully considered.

Given these circumstances, the individuals who manage the White House wield considerable influence. Serving as the nation's hostess is arguably the oldest of the roles informally assigned to the president's wife; it remains central to the first lady's performance as a representative. As the nation's hostess, the first lady in consultation with others in the White House Office decides who will be invited to the White House. Not merely a gatekeeper or a chatelaine, the first lady is among those deciding who will be recognized by the presidency.

Identifying the first lady as the nation's hostess may seem to magnify the private-sphere roles that have historically been ascribed to women. These duties appear marginal to the public-sphere responsibilities of political decision making, which are traditionally reserved to men. And yet, because symbols have such great meaning, and because the role of nation's hostess empowers the first lady to frame and interpret such formidable political symbols as the White House, these duties have led to increased presidential interest in the work of the social office. This in turn has drawn the first lady and her staff into closer contact with the president and other units in the White House Office. These changes have led to a renegotiation of the political and gender boundaries within the White House Office. In more recent administrations, there has been greater coordination between the social office and other units in the White House Office, though ties to the first lady have not necessarily lessened.

This chapter investigates and assesses the first ladies' performance of symbolic representation and their social outreach, the latter referring to the audiences targeted for their symbolic representation. The kinds of events hosted at the White House and in other settings, and their design, execution, and guest lists, give form to the first lady's and the president's perceptions of presidential power. More important, the extent to which longstanding practices are continued, changed, or rejected reveals the willingness of the first lady and president to confront history and exercise power, claiming their own authority. Study of the first lady's symbolic representation provides insight on an administration's understanding of such fundamental symbols as the White House and such elemental abstractions as presidential power.

STRATEGIZING SYMBOLIC REPRESENTATION: FIRST LADIES AND SOCIAL SECRETARIES

The symbolic representation provided by the first lady has undergone many changes, which have been uneven, inconsistent, and somewhat unpredictable. And yet, in true contradictory fashion, they have also been cumulative.

Lou Henry Hoover opened the White House to white women's organizations, initiating a gender desegregation that Eleanor Roosevelt accelerated. Roosevelt also abolished many traditional events, citing the need for economies during the Depression and the war. Bess Wallace Truman also limited her social outreach to Washington society; White House reconstruction and her mother's illness were the public reasons for her restraint. Mamie Doud Eisenhower briefly reinstated some past traditions, before Jacqueline Bouvier Kennedy and Lady Bird Taylor Johnson effected enduring changes. From Pat Ryan Nixon onward, each first lady has worked to establish a distinctive social, political, and cultural frame for the chief executive. And presidents became increasingly involved in this endeavor. The following analysis is based upon the records of the social secretaries and the social office, which are available through the G. H. W. Bush administration; analysis of the more recent administrations awaits the release of documents currently in the presidential archives or held at the White House.

Lou Henry Hoover: Tradition, Updated?

As the wife of the commerce secretary in the Harding and Coolidge administrations, and as an organizational activist in her own right, Hoover had entertained extensively before entering the White House. A well-established member of Washington society, she accepted most of its rules and conformed to most of its practices. Most, but not all. She was judged inappropriate and even dangerous by her first social secretary, Mary Randolph, whose 1936 memoir extensively critiqued the first lady. She objected to the social priorities and preferences of the Hoovers, advocating a more formal and self-conscious display of presidential power.[2]

By June 1930, Randolph had left the Hoover administration. Her post was vacant for almost sixteen months, until Doris Goss was hired in October 1931. Even then, the first lady continued to act, in large part, as her own social secretary.[3] And while Hoover did come to adopt some practices of past administrations, this first lady's social outreach was known for its spontaneity. Guest lists were constantly augmented, except for the most formal events. The hospitality was generous: Hoover receptions always included a buffet.[4] Randolph considered this overwhelming and ostentatious, and judged the first lady contrary and undisciplined.[5]

Table 3.2 summarizes social outreach during the Hoover administration, though it records only the occasions for which formal invitations were sent. As such, it dramatically understates the extent of this administration's social outreach.[6] Still, the numbers do indicate which social outreach events

Table 3.1. White House Social Secretaries, 1929–2011

First lady	Social secretary	Years in office
Lou Henry Hoover	Mary Randolph	1929–1930
	Doris Goss	1931–1933
Eleanor Roosevelt	Edith Benham Helm	1933–1945
Bess Wallace Truman	Edith Benham Helm[a]	1945–1953
	Reathel M. Odum[a]	1945–1953
Mamie Doud Eisenhower	Mary Jane McCaffree	1955–1961
Jacqueline Bouvier Kennedy	Letitia Baldrige	1961–1963
	Nancy L. Tuckerman	1963
Lady Bird Taylor Johnson	Elizabeth Clements Abell	1963–1969
Pat Ryan Nixon	Lucy Alexander Winchester	1969–1974
Betty Bloomer Ford	Lucy Alexander Winchester	1974
	Nancy Lammerding Ruwe	1974–1975
	Maria Anthony Downs	1975–1977
Rosalynn Smith Carter	Gretchen Poston	1977–1981
Nancy Davis Reagan	Mabel Brandon	1981–1983
	Gahl Hodges [Burt][b]	1983–1985
	Linda Faulkner	1985–1989
Barbara Pierce Bush	Laurie Green Firestone	1989–1993
Hillary Rodham Clinton	Ann Stock	1993–1997
	Capricia Penavic Marshall	1997–2001
Laura Welch Bush	Catherine S. Fenton	2001–2005
	Janet Lea Berman	2005–2009
Michelle Robinson Obama	Desirée Rogers	2009–2010
	Julianna Smoot	2010–2011
	Jeremy Bernard	2011

[a]Edith Benham Helm and Reathel M. Odum were both identified as the Truman social secretary in internal memoranda and in several editions of the *U.S. Government Manuals*. Though they shared certain duties, Helm seems to have had responsibility for organizing social events while Odum focused on family-related tasks. For example, Odum was Margaret Truman's chaperone when she traveled.

[b]Gahl Hodges Burt married and took her husband's name after leaving the social secretary post.

consumed the most resources and also indicate that formal dining occasions were relatively infrequent. Cumulatively, breakfasts, luncheons, and dinners, of which there were seventy, account for just 10.2 percent of the events. Larger events—receptions, "receiving" afternoons, and teas, of which there were 593—account for 86.5 percent of the total. While a limited budget

Table 3.2. Symbolic Representation: Events during the Hoover Administration, 1929–1933

Events	Percentage	Frequency
Breakfasts	0.3%	$n = 2$
Luncheons	2.3	16
Dinners	7.6	52
Receive/At home	50.0	343
Receptions	9.5	65
Teas	27.0	185
Parties	2.0	14
Music/Play[a]	0.4	3
Other	0.9	6
TOTAL	100.0	686

[a]Events in this category were entirely independent of all others. When musical entertainment accompanied or followed a dinner, it was not included in this count.

Sources: Social Functions [Scrapbooks], [Vol. 1] March 4, 1929, to November 18, 1930, and [Vol. 2] December 2, 1930, to March 4, 1933, Herbert Hoover Library; "Groups Received by Mrs. Hoover" and "Teas Given by Mrs. Hoover," compiled by Archivist Mildred Mather, Herbert Hoover Library.

may have played a part in the number of events, it is notable that the more frequent events had slightly fewer social strictures. Racial barriers endured in most instances, but some boundaries were being blurred.

Of the events organized by the social office, eighty-five, or 12.4 percent, were for white women and eighty-eight, or 12.8 percent, were for children. There were no stag events. Unquestionably, there were occasions when only men were invited, given that women held few significant positions in the public or private sector during these years. However, those privileges were not reinforced through purposely exclusive social outreach by the Hoover administration, as they would be in later administrations. Instead, the social outreach to white women and children made the White House more accessible, especially when the first lady's commitment to the Girl Scouts led her to go beyond established Washington social circles.[7] A final example of the priorities of this first lady was her insistence upon continuing the New Year's Day public receptions, the president's opposition notwithstanding. Lou Henry Hoover believed that a powerful message was sent in having one day—the first of the year, especially—when any citizen could come to the

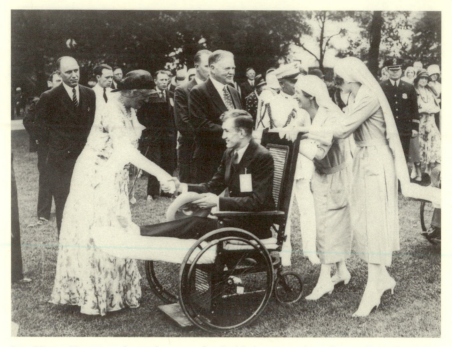

Lou Henry Hoover at the garden party for disabled veterans, hosted annually at the White House, June 10, 1931. Lou Henry and Herbert Hoover are pictured in a receiving line, with veterans greeted first by the president and then by the president's wife. This was a celebratory event, not an occasion for awarding military honors. It was racially integrated with African American and white soldiers among the guests. Photo provided by Herbert Hoover Library, West Branch, Ia.

White House and be personally welcomed by the president and first lady. She believed that denying people this welcome would be taken as proof that the president was, at the least, uncaring. This, she maintained, would be an unmistakable and injurious statement.[8]

Lou Henry Hoover also made a significant structural innovation as a symbolic representative. The Hoovers built a presidential retreat, Rapidan, in Virginia's Blue Ridge Mountains. Constructed at the Hoovers' own expense to the first lady's detailed specifications and subsequently gifted to the nation, Rapidan expressively symbolized many aspects of the Hoovers' political philosophy. Believing that nature and recreation were integral to human wellness, they were confident that time spent at Rapidan could only facilitate wise decision making.[9] As property owners, the Hoovers also considered themselves members of the local community. Recognizing the limited resources of families in the surrounding area, they built a school and paid the teacher's salary to provide local children with an education.[10]

Rapidan also pointed to the Hoovers' willingness to augment the venues in which presidential power was displayed and exercised. In 1930 and 1931, the Hoovers spent the majority of weekends from April through October in whole or in part at Rapidan. In 1932, an election year, they spent just the majority of weekends there from April to early July. Many of the guests were government officials, military officers, or journalists.[11] All of these individuals, many of whom visited Rapidan repeatedly, mixed work with recreation. The time was spent so profitably that Franklin Roosevelt quickly decided in favor of building his own presidential retreat, Camp David.

Lou Henry Hoover, then, reformed, upheld, and invigorated traditions. She also established some new practices that would last long enough to become traditions. She invited a more diverse array of white women and children to the White House. She was the primary force in building and then welcoming government officials, military personnel, and journalists to Camp Rapidan, facilitating the exercise of presidential power in a new setting. Along the way, Lou Henry Hoover confronted the tension that would define first ladies' performance of symbolic representation throughout the modern presidency, namely, balancing the hierarchical traditions of the past and the more democratic pressures of the present.

Eleanor Roosevelt, Bess Truman, Mamie Eisenhower: Fractured Symbolism

Social outreach showed considerable variation throughout the Roosevelt, Truman, and Eisenhower administrations. In part, the differences could be attributed to changing historical and political contexts. The Depression and World War II, the tensions of the Cold War, the reconstruction and refurbishing of the White House, and partisan change and the so-called doldrums of the 1950s all affected the presidency and thus the first lady. The changes in social outreach also reflected the first ladies' and social secretaries' priorities. Each had her own approach to symbolic representation. To an extent greater than would be seen in later administrations, these first ladies chose which traditions they would continue and which symbols they would interpret.

Eleanor Roosevelt would strongly disagree with the assertion that she exercised discretion in performing symbolic representation. In her autobiography, Roosevelt claimed that she would have preferred to abdicate the role of nation's hostess and that she challenged her social secretary, Edith Helm, to defend the utility of social occasions. She only reluctantly came to view them as meaningful.

Eleanor Roosevelt with her personal assistant, Malvina Thompson, and her social secretary, Edith Benham Helm, April 1, 1941. Though Helm disagreed with the characterization, Roosevelt presented herself as impatient with social outreach, being far more interested in policy making, and correspondingly in need of Helm's guidance. That self-portrayal is visually conveyed in this portrait. Photo provided by the Franklin D. Roosevelt Library, Hyde Park, N.Y.

Certain duties, however, which I thought at first were useless burdens I later grew to realize had real meaning and value. For instance, the teas. It seemed to me utterly futile to receive anywhere from five hundred to a thousand people of an afternoon, shake hands with them, and then have them pass into the dining room to be given a cup of tea or coffee by Mrs. Helm and Miss Thompson.

I soon discovered that, particularly to people from out of town, the White House has a deep significance. It is a place where the people's hospitality is dispensed to the representatives of other countries; in a way, it is with a sense of ownership that citizens of the United States walk through the simple but dignified and beautiful rooms. To many people the White House symbolizes the government, and though standing and shaking hands for an hour or so, two or three times a week, is not an inspiring occupation, still I think it well worth while.[12]

Margaret Truman believed that her mother also found it difficult to come to terms with a first lady's obligations and responsibilities as a symbolic representative. Though Bess Truman did reconcile herself to the demands of the presidency, her social outreach did not resemble Eleanor Roosevelt's. As much could have been predicted from their earlier actions and choices as political wives. As the wife of an assistant secretary of the navy, with the resources that accompany wealth, Roosevelt had dutifully acquiesced to elaborate calling and dining rituals. In subsequent years, she had augmented these social networks with wide-ranging relationships in reform and policy organizations, many of them women-centered. Roosevelt, therefore, brought financial and relational resources with her into the White House to support and shape her performance of symbolic representation. Bess Truman, a U.S. senator's wife, had not participated extensively in Washington society for reasons of personal preference and limited financial resources. Truman found Washington society to be indulgent and extravagant, and she had little desire to endorse or encourage those qualities. Though Harry Truman enjoyed the rituals that celebrated presidential power, he and Bess Truman suspended the social season for several years, giving international crises, family obligations, and the White House reconstruction as their reasons for doing so.[13]

Such contrasting approaches to symbolic representation did not, however, result in a change in social secretaries. Edith Benham Helm served through both the Roosevelt and Truman administrations. Like Mary Randolph, Helm was well connected socially; her family tree included numerous high-ranking military officers. Before her White House appointment, Helm had been the social secretary for several leaders in Washington society, for the Russian ambassador to the United States, and for the U.S. ambassador to Great Britain. A widow, she came out of retirement for the Roosevelt administration; reappointed by President Truman, she ultimately served for twenty consecutive years as the White House social secretary, in addition to six years as social secretary in the Wilson administration. Unlike Mary Randolph, Helm could adapt to changing expectations, though she was never at ease in serving as Bess Truman's de facto press secretary, as I will discuss in the next chapter.

Helm self-evidently appreciated the value of symbolic representation to the presidency. Her memoir repeatedly emphasized that symbolic representation could strengthen the reputation of a president and first lady, contributing to their effectiveness and to the influence wielded by the administration as a whole. As social secretary, she sought to capitalize on every opportunity to present the president as a chief of state. Helm proposed White House ceremonies to award military honors, as a means of drawing greater attention to the president's status as commander-in-chief. Previously, these events had been held in relative obscurity in the cabinet departments.[14]

Mamie Eisenhower had no Washington experience, but as the wife of a military officer and university president, she was well accustomed to the intricacies of social outreach in an unforgiving environment. When she entered the White House, she continued the division of labor that had for decades characterized her marriage. As first lady, she assumed responsibility for the private sphere and its extensions, including symbolic representation.

Yet Mamie Eisenhower's symbolic representation defies categorizing. On one hand, she instituted (or reinstituted) practices that had been discontinued for several decades. Like Lou Henry Hoover, Eisenhower served as her own social secretary; no one was listed in that post until the 1955–56 *U.S. Government Manual.* Eisenhower also returned to a pre-Hoover practice of receiving visitors, an undertaking that had been abandoned as tedious and inefficient. (Better a large reception or tea, with more people in and out, and more opportunity for mingling and assessing.) On the other hand, Eisenhower was decidedly independent and even progressive in her social outreach. Biographer Marilyn Irvin Holt lists a series of occasions at which the first lady showed her support for African American civil rights, including the integration of the Easter egg hunt, the invitation to Mahalia Jackson to perform for the first lady's birthday, her provision of tours for African American groups, and her own honorary membership in the National Council of Negro Women. She also invited Lucille Ball and Desi Arnaz to the president's birthday celebration, seating them with her husband, even though Ball had been called before, and only grudgingly cleared by, the House Committee on Un-American Activities.[15] Mamie Eisenhower understood the power that could be expressed through symbolic representation, and she exercised that influence in ways that blended conservative and liberal ideals.

Table 3.3 reveals three significant changes in the social outreach of Eleanor Roosevelt, Bess Truman, and Mamie Eisenhower. First, there were

Table 3.3. Symbolic Representation: Events during the Roosevelt, Truman, and Eisenhower Administrations, 1933–1961

	E. Roosevelt 1933–37	E. Roosevelt 1937–41	E. Roosevelt 1941–45	E. Roosevelt 1945	B. Truman 1945–49	B. Truman 1949–53	M. Eisenhower 1953–57	M. Eisenhower 1957–61
Events:								
Breakfasts	0% (n = 0)	0% (n = 0)	0.3% (n = 1)	0% (n = 0)	0% (n = 0)	0% (n = 0)	2.8% (n = 15)	7.2% (n = 16)
Luncheons	19.3 (57)	20.7 (80)	26.8 (101)	34.5 (10)	16.6 (52)	27.4 (74)	26.0 (139)	25.1 (56)
Dinners	20.3 (60)	18.1 (70)	15.9 (60)	13.8 (4)	6.7 (21)	8.1 (22)	18.0 (96)	26.9 (60)
State dinners	1.7 (5)	0.8 (3)	3.7 (14)	0 (0)	3.2 (10)	4.1 (11)	1.9 (10)	9.4 (21)
Receptions	9.5 (28)	9.3 (36)	16.2 (61)	10.3 (3)	24.8 (78)	24.1 (65)	4.3 (23)	2.7 (6)
Receive/At home	1.7 (5)	12.4 (48)	2.7 (10)	0 (0)	0 (0)	0 (0)	36.9 (197)	15.2 (34)
Teas	28.5 (84)	24.3 (94)	17.8 (67)	17.2 (5)	33.8 (106)	34.4 (93)	7.5 (40)	10.3 (23)
Music/Play	3.4 (10)	2.8 (11)	0.3 (1)	0 (0)	1.9 (6)	0 (0)	0 (0)	0.4 (1)
Parties	8.1 (24)	8.3 (32)	6.1 (23)	0 (0)	2.9 (9)	0.4 (1)	1.7 (9)	2.7 (6)
Other	7.5 (22)	3.4 (13)	10.3 (39)	24.1 (7)	10.2 (32)	1.5 (4)	0.9 (5)	0 (0)
TOTAL	100.0 (295)	100.1 (387)	100.1 (377)	99.9 (29)	100.1 (314)	100.0 (270)	100.0 (534)	99.9 (223)
Tours	0	0	0	0	20	6	537	381

Note: Numbers may not add to 100.0% due to rounding.

Sources: Records of the Office of the Chief of Social Entertainments, 1933–1945, Franklin D. Roosevelt Library; Social Functions File, Harry S. Truman Library; Social Office (A.B. Tolley) Records, 1952–1961, White House Office, Dwight D. Eisenhower Library.

real and meaningful differences among the first ladies that reflected their political priorities, not merely their historical circumstances. Eleanor Roosevelt, in addition to the expected array of White House occasions, hosted meetings and conferences at the mansion. (These are recorded as "other" in the table.) Roosevelt's social secretary, therefore, provided this first lady with logistical support to advance her policy agenda. Symbolic representation was closely intertwined with the first lady's substantive representation.

Bess Truman conducted most of her symbolic representation through teas and receptions, events that were less formal than luncheons and dinners, and that allowed for more conversation among invited guests. The number of organizations and professional associations invited to the White House during this administration was remarkable; the White House was registering the effects of an expansion in the number of interest groups and their increasing attentiveness to the presidency and the executive branch. Though Roosevelt and Truman responded very differently to political networks, they were both willing to use their social outreach to establish relationships with organizational activists. Roosevelt often proceeded to mobilize these groups. Truman generally monitored them. She was perhaps more passive than Roosevelt, but she also kept the White House and the presidency connected to the interest-group community.

Mamie Eisenhower placed the White House itself on exhibit. The White House was gutted and rebuilt during the Truman administration; Eisenhower put the improvements and innovations on display. Describing it as her "home"[16]—a reference that immediately conflated her self and the historical significance of the building, her husband and the power of the presidential office—she self-evidently saw White House tours as a form of social outreach. More than nine hundred groups, almost two hundred of which were school or other children's groups, were escorted through the mansion. She also returned to or surpassed prewar numbers for formal White House dining. The constraints that Eleanor Roosevelt and Bess Truman claimed—economic deprivation, war, world hunger, postwar tensions—were not identified by Mamie Eisenhower. Only the president's health (his 1955 heart attack, 1956 ileitis-related surgery, and 1957 cerebral hemorrhage) limited social outreach, as presidential and family illness had in the past.[17] Even then, over the two terms of her husband's administration, Eisenhower hosted more state dinners than did the first ladies who came before her in the modern presidency. Social outreach accelerated during this administration, which meant that the first lady was communicating more widely, and building more and more diverse relationships through her symbolic representation.

The second change relates to the gender dynamics of social outreach, which showed similarities for women and marked contrasts for men across the three administrations. As seen in Table 3.4, gender-exclusive events for women increased across the three administrations. Gender-exclusive events for men also increased, though at a very different rate. There were 140 events formally designated as stag in the Eisenhower administration, four in the Truman administration, and none in the Roosevelt administration.

Of course, the numbers of gender-exclusive events do not indicate the full extent of gender disparities and gender segregation within the administration. The count for stag events, for instance, does not include those that were all male because all the invited officeholders were male. Moreover, women often came to the White House for events that were more ceremonial than consultative. Dwight Eisenhower emphasized this contrast in explaining why he valued his stag dinners.

> "[S]tag dinners . . . were usually small, rarely involving more than sixteen guests. . . . My guests were drawn from government, business, publishing, the professions, agriculture, the arts, labor, and education. . . . The after-dinner period was devoted to extended informal conversation, with the group seated in a circle in the Red Room. . . . I used these dinners to try to draw from leaders in various sections of American life their views on many domestic and international questions. Thus the stag dinners were, for me, a means of gaining information and intelligent opinion as well as of enjoying good company. . . .
>
> I remember one evening when, after walking a friend to the door, I looked at him and saw that tears were running down his face. He was a strong man, a hardheaded businessman, and I exclaimed, "What's the matter?"
>
> "Mr. President," he said, "I just wanted to tell you what it has meant to me, a farm boy from the Midwest, to spend an evening and dine in the White House. . . ."
>
> He did not have to explain any further. The White House seen quickly in a photograph or in passing, is one thing; but if a man pauses long enough to contemplate what it has meant to so many Americans, it is something else again. The castles of Europe are splendid, but they were built by monarchs and rulers of all sorts, including despots; they have

Table 3.4. Symbolic Representation: Constituent-Specific Events during the Roosevelt, Truman, and Eisenhower Administrations, 1933–1961

	E. Roosevelt 1933–37	E. Roosevelt 1937–41	E. Roosevelt 1941–45	E. Roosevelt 1945	B. Truman 1945–49	B. Truman 1949–53	M. Eisenhower 1953–57	M. Eisenhower 1957–61
Attending:								
Children only	3.1% (n = 9)	5.9% (n = 23)	11.7% (n = 44)	0% (n = 0)	3.8% (n = 12)	4.4% (n = 12)	(n = 198)[a]	(n = 100)
Stag	0 (0)	0 (0)	0 (0)	0 (0)	1.0 (3)	0.4 (1)	15.9% (85)	24.7% (55)
Women only	14.6 (43)	19.1 (74)	10.9 (41)	13.8 (4)	28.0 (88)	28.1 (76)	(215)[a]	(118)[a]

[a]Many of these individuals participated only in White House tours, so percentages were not calculated.

Note: All percentages are calculated for the total number of all social outreach events, not merely those that are child- or sex-specific.

Sources: Records of the Office of the Chief of Social Entertainments, 1933–1945, Franklin D. Roosevelt Library; Social Functions File, Harry S. Truman Library; Social Office (A.B. Tolley) Records, 1952–1961, White House Office, Dwight D. Eisenhower Library.

meant pomp and splendor. This house, from the beginning, has meant freedom.[18]

What is striking about this assessment is the unequivocal tone of the president's judgments. In essence, the stag dinners functioned as focus groups of elites. At the same time, they reminded the powerful of the greater power of the president, who controls access to the political symbols of the polity. Though Dwight Eisenhower speaks of the White House as a symbol of freedom, he describes an evening in which power and privilege are intertwined. Further, it is a place of kings rather than queens. Men, not women, are invited to share their wisdom with the president; loyalty and leadership are thereby reserved to men. Masculinity is elevated and honored.

The president hosted the stag dinners, but the first lady and social secretary organized them. And while these events may seem to reflect the president's military experience, which was acquired in a masculine enclave, it is important to note that this social outreach also reflected Mamie Eisenhower's symbolic representation. She embraced the separate-spheres gender ideology, seeing the private sphere as the source of women's authority. A woman made significant contributions as a homemaker. And making a home was an extraordinarily difficult task, encompassing every aspect of the family's relationships and resources. As Mamie Eisenhower explained, "[W]ith *our* Army career, a wife played a very big part. And if she doesn't measure up, or if she was a trouble maker, a gossiper, or if she doesn't know the proper things to do, these things all play a great part."[19] For her, not inviting women to discuss affairs of state with the president would have been as important as the affirmative act of inviting men.

Third, and finally, the role of political and policy groups in facilitating public-presidential communication became more evident in these years. Jill Abraham Hummer has examined the ways in which first ladies' social outreach has advanced the interests of successive women's movements. First ladies have provided access to the White House not only to organizations associated with what have been historically identified as women's interests, but also to reform movements and interest groups, professional and charitable associations, and political and policy organizations.[20] An extension of social outreach, very much related to symbolic representation, was the various honorary affiliations and memberships accepted by these first ladies.

Having the first lady as a patron adds to the status of the group, and it reveals—or is perceived to reveal—something about the priorities and interests of the president's wife and, by extension, the president's administration.

Mamie Doud Eisenhower with President Dwight D. Eisenhower, leaving Washington, DC, on a reelection campaign trip, November 1, 1956. Eisenhower models the supportive satellite wife: her attention is wholly focused on the president, while he projects his personality outward toward the crowds. The physicality of the couple reinforces this gender message, with the first lady positioned to the side and gazing upward, and the president confronting the viewer and raising his arm in a victory salute. Photo provided by the Dwight D. Eisenhower Library, Abilene, Kansas.

When the Daughters of the American Revolution (DAR) refused to allow Marian Anderson to perform in Constitution Hall because she was African American, Eleanor Roosevelt resigned and published her reasons for doing so in her syndicated column.

The question is, if you belong to an organization and disapprove of an action which is typical of a policy, should you resign or is it better to work for a changed point of view within the organization? In the past, when I was able to work actively in any organization to which I belonged, I have usually stayed until I had at least made a fight and had been defeated.

Even then, I have, as a rule, accepted my defeat and decided I was wrong or, perhaps, a little too far ahead of the thinking for the majority at that time. I have often found that the thing in which I was interested was done some years later. But in this case, I belong to an organization in which I can do no active work. They have taken an action which has been widely talked of in the press. To remain as a member implies approval of that action, and therefore I am resigning.[21]

A reader has to be struck by Roosevelt's detailing of her choices in responding to the DAR—though she does not actually name the organization—and by her consideration of past lessons learned from similar experiences. Roosevelt stresses her credentials as an activist, highlighting her strategic expertise. The presentation changes abruptly when she states her decision to resign, however. The final sentences are abrupt. The first lady writes in absolutes, stating the values she upholds through her symbolic representation. She stands for civil rights. She insists upon the opportunity to "work actively" in any organization with which she is affiliated. She demands that she be publicly recognized as doing that work, so that there is no mistake about her agenda or her beliefs. These conditions identify the first lady as an actor in the public sphere, affiliated with and yet independent of political organizations. Roosevelt's resignation from the DAR was endorsed by 67 percent of the American public, according to Gallup polls. When Interior Secretary Harold Ickes arranged for Anderson to perform on the steps of the Lincoln Memorial, seventy-five thousand attended in person and many more tuned in on the radio.[22] The obvious connections between civil rights and the Lincoln Memorial, and the clarity of Eleanor Roosevelt's position, delivered a strong message about the administration's values.[23] Policy and substantive representation would lag, as we will see in a later chapter, but the symbolic representation was assertive.

The symbolic representation provided by Eleanor Roosevelt, Bess Truman, and Mamie Eisenhower cannot be easily summarized. The similarities and differences associated with their social outreach—the selection and frequency of events, the weakening or reinforcement of tradition, the gender segregation of guests, the organizational agendas endorsed or critiqued—are complex and shifting. Public expectations of the modern first lady were not so established that the administrations and first ladies had no leeway. Though

Eleanor Roosevelt is credited with being a revolutionary force, each first lady made her own innovations in symbolic representation. And that distinctiveness, in its turn, facilitated even greater changes during the Kennedy and Johnson years.

Jacqueline Kennedy and Lady Bird Johnson: Symbols as Power

During the Kennedy administration, and continuing throughout subsequent administrations, the first lady's symbolic representation was explicitly recognized as political and partisan. In previous administrations, the social office had been presented as an extension of a woman's private-sphere role as a hostess. From the Kennedy administration onward, however, the responsibilities associated with symbolic representation drew the first lady and her staff into the public sphere of presidential politics.

Jacqueline Kennedy's first social secretary was Letitia Baldrige, whom she contacted even before the election. Then Tiffany's director of public relations, Baldrige had spent the greater part of her professional career in diplomatic circles, like Mary Randolph and Edith Helm. Drawing upon her family's political connections, Baldrige secured social secretary posts with the U.S. ambassadors to Paris and to Italy, and had a brief stint in the Washington offices (the East European Division) of the Central Intelligence Agency. She negotiated aggressively for the White House appointment, however, and secured both a higher salary and more staff support than had been initially offered. During her two-and-a-half years at the White House, Baldrige continued to take a confrontational approach to her work. She implemented and enhanced the first lady's ideas, fiercely protesting any "West Wing" intrusions except those of the president. In compiling guest lists, for example, she saw no reason to substitute political supporters or campaign donors for patrons of the first lady's initiatives. Baldrige reported that the president once told her that she "fought like a Kennedy," a comment that she chose to take as a compliment, though she acknowledged that her drive and assertiveness eventually led to the acceptance of her resignation.[24]

Nancy Tuckerman was named social secretary when Baldrige left the White House in mid-1963. Tuckerman's principal credential was her strong relationship with the first lady, whom she had known since they roomed together at Miss Porter's School. Yet Tuckerman was Baldrige's equal in planning and hosting events, and she was credited with lessening tensions between the social office and the first lady, and perhaps also between the social office and other units in the White House Office. Like many other midterm presidential appointees, Tuckerman sustained the commitments and expectations established earlier in the presidential term, while contributing the creativity and the initiative to keep political relationships fresh and constructive.

When Lady Bird Johnson became first lady, some thought that she might ask Baldrige to return to the White House. Instead, she selected her own assistant, Bess (Elizabeth) Clements Abell, for the post. It was a calculated risk. Abell had no experience organizing large-scale events. Her White House service had been limited to working for the then–vice president's wife, which involved her in tasks more personal than managerial: "Everything from cutting flowers in the backyard and arranging them on the table to getting the clothes from the cleaners, to paying the bills, to writing the letters, keeping track of the appointments."[25] Leveraged against this lack of formal credentials, however, were Abell's political affiliations and networks. She had known the Johnsons for years—her father, Earle C. Clements (D-KY), had been Democratic whip and then director of the Senate Democratic Campaign Committee when Lyndon Johnson was majority leader. Abell was at ease with local, state, and national political networks, again as a result of her father's career, which had included service as a county sheriff, governor, U.S. representative, and U.S. senator, before he retired as president of the Tobacco Institute. Abell's marriage to Tyler Abell, columnist Drew Pearson's stepson, had augmented these political-social connections. She had proven her loyalty to the Johnsons as a volunteer in the 1960 campaign and in the presidential transition, as well as her term-time position as the second lady's assistant. And Abell badly wanted the social secretary post.[26] Though her professional expertise was limited, her longstanding association with the Johnsons, her familiarity with political networks and Washington society, and her demonstrated allegiance to the president and first lady gained her the appointment.

The three social secretaries—Letitia Baldrige, Nancy Tuckerman, and Bess Abell—are interesting for what they suggest about the first ladies' staffing priorities. Baldrige alone had experience as a social secretary prior to her White House appointment, and she was charged with implementing significant changes in symbolic representation, lifting presidential occasions to a continental style and standard. She was reportedly the first social secretary charged with a programmatic level of responsibility, and she did not hesitate to act on her own judgment, even to the point of arguing with the president or the first lady.[27] Tuckerman continued Baldrige's innovations but with minimal confrontation or consultation with the first lady. Lady Bird Johnson placed tremendous confidence in Bess Abell, giving her even more responsibility than had been granted the Kennedy social secretaries. Comparing the administrations, Chief Usher J. B. West concluded that Bess Abell "did for Mrs. Johnson what Mamie Eisenhower and Jacqueline Kennedy had done for themselves. . . . It wasn't just that Bess *assumed* more authority than previous social secretaries, she'd been *granted* that authority by Mrs. Johnson. The 'Chairman of the Board' approved or disapproved all Bess' written plans and scenarios."[28] Symbolic representation and social outreach were critically important during these administrations, and only a closely coordinated staff could carry the workload. A first lady would never again serve as her own social secretary, though varying degrees of trust and discretion would be invested in those individuals.

During the Kennedy administration, that endorsement was given so that the social secretary could help to fulfill a campaign promise to bring freshness and "vigor" to the White House. As one Kennedy campaign speech concluded, "We will need . . . what the Constitution envisioned: a Chief Executive who is the vital center of action in our whole scheme of government."[29] This commitment, with the value it placed on such historically masculine traits as forcefulness, autonomy, and aggressiveness, reinforced the separate-spheres ideals that reserved the public sphere to men. Yet the first lady and the social office played an important role in keeping this campaign promise. Jacqueline Kennedy, Letitia Baldrige, and Nancy Tuckerman borrowed liberally from western European traditions, identifying the White House with European standards of elegance and power. J. B. West saw stark contrasts between the Kennedy and Eisenhower administrations.

> The tone of the Kennedy entertaining was lighter, gayer, more fun: Black tie rather than white tie; for the first time, cocktails before dinner; and smoking was allowed. . . . They had a formal receiving line only at state dinners. At the few large receptions they held, President and Mrs. Kennedy mingled among the guests and "received" as they walked through the room. . . . The Kennedys cut down on the number of courses at meals and changed the tone of after-dinner entertainment (Eisenhowers: 6 courses, with 21 items, followed by Fred Waring and the Pennsylvanians. Kennedys: 4 courses, with 8 items, followed by the Metropolitan Opera Studio). Gone was the formal E-shaped banquet table. Instead, Mrs. Kennedy selected fifteen round tables seating ten each for the State Dining Room. . . . Delicate, multi-colored flower arrangements, yellow organdy tablecloths, and candlelight highlighted the formal entertaining. . . .

In 1961, Jacqueline Kennedy dispensed entirely with the traditional
social season. . . . The next year, she reshaped the "season," combining
dinners. . . . Instead of concentrating on the Washington social season,
which had been primarily a series of political evenings, the cosmopolitan
First Lady turned to her own strong suit, entertaining foreign visitors.[30]

Jacqueline Kennedy had preferred to host small dinners when she was the
wife of a U.S. senator, and she did as much as possible to continue that more
personal, more intimate social outreach in the White House. The Eisenhower
receiving lines, banquet tables, and traditional service had focused the guests'
attention on the president, but these were acts of symbolic representation
that simply placed the president at the top of easily identifiable hierarchies—
the central figure in the receiving line, the head chair at the banquet table, the
first to be served at dinner. Jacqueline Kennedy's symbolic representation instead created an ambiance that made everyone aware of the presidency. With
this shift in emphasis, the first lady succeeded in placing the president at the
"vital center." These practices were continued and enhanced during the Johnson administration, when the diversity, scale, and extent of the first lady's
symbolic representation took a quantum leap upward.

The magnitude of the change in symbolic representation is indicated by
the jump in the number of events from the Kennedy to the Johnson years,
presented in Table 3.5. Receptions, dinners, parties, and state dinners were all
more frequent. The number of state dinners—arguably the most intricate of
all White House events—in 1964 (thirteen) was almost equal to the number
hosted throughout the entire Kennedy administration (fourteen). The numbers are also significant because this event was most strongly associated with
Jacqueline Kennedy's symbolic representation. The Johnson administration
also hosted more receptions, especially during the 1964 election year (fifty-
one). Groups, professional associations, and even conference gatherings were
invited to the White House and courted for their political support.

As the first lady's symbolic representation increased in extent, it also became more focused and precise. Broadcast correspondent Nancy Dickerson
observed, "[T]he keynote to the Johnsons' hospitality was that it had a purpose. Just as LBJ capitalized on news events to get action on legislation and
to achieve his goals, both of them used entertainment to further their pet
projects."[31] While Lady Bird Johnson and Bess Abell lacked Jacqueline Kennedy's talent for staging powerful visual images, they had a gift for presenting
the most appealing characteristics of the nation's identity. It was a talent that
the press recognized and even celebrated. Syndicated columnist Betty Beale,

Table 3.5. Symbolic Representation: Events during the Kennedy and Johnson Administrations, 1961–1969

	J. Kennedy 1961–63	C. T. Johnson 1963–65[a]	C. T. Johnson 1965–68
Event:			
Breakfasts	0.8% (n = 2)	0% (n = 0)	0% (n = 0)
Luncheons	49.6 (122)	24.8 (39)	19.7 (100)
Receptions	12.6 (31)	32.5 (51)	32.5 (165)
Dinners	20.7 (51)	12.7 (20)	16.0 (81)
State dinners	5.7 (14)	8.3 (13)	7.9 (40)
Receive/At home	0 (0)	0 (0)	2.4 (12)
Teas	4.5(11)	3.8 (6)	1.6 (8)
Music/Play	2.8 (7)	6.4 (10)	0.2 (1)
Parties	0.4 (1)	8.3 (13)	12.8 (65)
Tours	1.2 (3)	—	—
Other	1.6 (4)	3.2 (5)	6.9 (35)
TOTAL	99.9 (246)	100.0 (157)	100.0 (507)

[a]Virtually all social outreach was canceled from the assassination of John F. Kennedy in November 1963 through December 1963. Lady Bird Johnson is identified as C. T. Johnson, or Claudia Taylor Johnson, to avoid confusion with her husband. This is also how the first lady signed her personal checks.

Note: Numbers may not add to 100.0% due to rounding.

Sources: White House Staff Files of Sanford Fox, John F. Kennedy Library; Indexes, Social Secretary Scrapbooks, Bess Abell Files, Lyndon Johnson Library.

for example, highlighted the cultural message of the Johnsons' first state dinner, drawing readers' attention to the Kennedy continuities and the Johnson innovations in terms that favored the Johnson administration: "The Johnsons wanted to present to the Segnis [the Italian prime minister and his wife] not just operatic selections by an Italian composer but something as authentically American as folk music, which, explained noted composer and producer Richard Adler, the musicale's emcee, 'is as indigenous to our country as opera is to yours.'"[32] The phrasing is as judgmental as it is supportive: "*not just* operatic selections by an Italian composer but something as *authentically American* as folk music." The Continental emphasis of the Kennedy years was lightened. During the Johnson years, the first lady presented the artistic, intellectual, and philanthropic character of the United States to national and

Table 3.6. Symbolic Representation: Constituent-Specific Events during the Kennedy and Johnson Administrations, 1961–1969

	J. Kennedy 1961–63	C. T. Johnson 1963–65	C. T. Johnson 1965–68
Attending:			
Children only	2.8% (n = 7)	7.0% (n = 11)	3.6% (n = 18)
Stag	31.3 (77)	15.9 (25)	0.8 (4)
Women only	4.9 (12)	8.3 (13)	13.4 (68)

Note: All percentages are calculated for the total number of all social outreach events, not just those that are child- or sex-specific.

Sources: White House Staff Files of Sanford Fox, John F. Kennedy Library; Indexes, Social Secretary Scrapbooks, Bess Abell Files, Lyndon Johnson Library.

international audiences. In other words, Lady Bird Johnson interpreted the identity of the nation, an action that presented the presidency as "the vital center" at home and abroad.

There was also a shift in the audiences targeted by the social secretary and first lady (see Table 3.6). The core constituents—domestic and international decision makers—remained constant across the Kennedy and Johnson administrations, but gender segregation practices changed. The number of stag events dropped precipitously in the full Johnson term. Though the limited number of women in high governmental offices meant that many White House gatherings were all male, the first lady's social office was less engaged in facilitating the exclusion of women from the White House. In fact, the first lady and her staff reached out to women and women's organizations. Johnson slightly exceeded the number of Kennedy's women-centered events (most of which Johnson had actually hosted) in her first twelve months and then more than quintupled that number during the full presidential term. In addition to the long-established luncheons and teas for political wives, there were also gatherings to recognize women as leaders and activists. Eminent women from the arts, sciences, politics, public health, education, and other fields were honored at the White House. Often these occasions were coordinated with presidential policy initiatives to gain greater media coverage. For instance, Betty Furness, special assistant to the president for consumer affairs, was a featured guest at the all-women Doers Luncheon on consumer concerns, held just days after the president had submitted his special message to Congress on consumer issues.

Lady Bird Johnson and Bess Abell also initiated changes in the setting of the first lady's symbolic representation. The White House had always been a rich and powerful symbol of the presidency. Rapidan and Camp David had also become settings associated with presidential deliberation and decision making. During the Johnson administration, however, a president's private home became a symbol of the presidency, an innovation whose significance was immediately recognized by the national media.

> White House sources said today that the ranch-style entertainment that captivated [West German Chancellor Ludwig] Erhard may be in store for many foreign visitors during this administration. There are three reasons:
> First, the guests will be able to see the land west of the Mississippi, get out of the big cities of the United States and away from stiff, stuffy rituals like the state banquets at the Waldorf-Astoria in New York and the White House here.
> Second, foreigners are usually fascinated with this country's frontier traditions. . . .
> Third, overseas visitors will be able to do business with the President in an intimate atmosphere, over the deer meat sausage at breakfast or in the Johnson family's cozy ranch living room.[33]

Internal White House memoranda indicate that these "three reasons" were the subject of intense negotiation. The president was the leader of the nation, and as a chief of state, needed to be seen as the first among a guest list of executives from across the country. To be seen only in the company of Texans would have merely reiterated a single facet of Lyndon Johnson's personal identity; it would not have added to his stature as a chief executive. If, however, the event balanced Johnson's claim to power as president and his personal identity as a Texan, then the office and the individual might be conflated in the minds of observers, to Johnson's advantage. The powers of the office would be Johnson's powers, an association that could only be helpful to a man who had entered the Oval Office when his predecessor was assassinated and who had only just been elected to the office in his own right.

The effect of these innovations was to reinforce the authority of the president. More social outreach, to a more diverse audience and in an additional venue, extended the reach and influence of the president. When anti-war protests limited social outreach, they profoundly constrained the administration. In fact, the protests were considered so limiting that the staff members committed themselves to sustaining social outreach to the greatest extent possible. The social secretary, with other members of the first lady's staff, devoted extraordinary resources to reviewing guest lists and prospective performers to ensure that the president's message, not that of his critics, would be presented at the White House.

The Kennedy and Johnson administrations dramatically altered the meaning and significance of the first lady's role as the nation's hostess. Presidents—though not always first ladies—had viewed these responsibilities as an extension of women's traditional responsibilities in the private sphere. Yet Jacqueline Kennedy and Lady Bird Johnson made the role of hostess emphatically, unequivocally public. They set a new standard for a first lady's symbolic representation, which would now be judged by how she presented the White House, designed and staged events that wove a president's priorities into the nation's identity, and delivered the president's message to the targeted audience. And all of these responsibilities drew the first ladies further into the public sphere.

From Pat Nixon to Barbara Bush: Constancy and Change

With the potential influence of symbolic representation acknowledged, and its rituals well established, it might seem that there was little likelihood of variability or innovation. Even as the White House became "an indispensable social entity with a unique way of doing business and a life of its own,"[34] first ladies and social secretaries found new ways to capitalize more fully on the potential of symbolic representation to facilitate relationship building with influential publics.

The social office was drawn into closer association with the president. In the Nixon administration, the commanding power of the chief of staff and president led to tensions with the social secretary and the first lady. Pointed memoranda regarding guest lists and events, addressing issues from serving order to staff decorum, were sent to the "East Wing" and subsequently leaked to the press.[35] In the Ford administration, as recounted in Social Secretary Maria Downs's unpublished memoir, these practices led to a direct confrontation between the first lady and the president's aides.

> I landed in the midst of an all out war when I became Social Secretary. Mrs. Ford had caught the West Side boys with their fingers in the cookie jar! The cookies being the guest lists for all social events. Especially the state dinner guest lists! She raised uncharacteristic hell! . . .
>
> Some [presidential aides] argued that, at that time, the guest lists were not doing the job they were intended to do, were not being used to

their fullest potential in furthering the aims of the President. And many sought to use them as a vehicle for personal gains.

The problem of the guest lists was thoroughly discussed. The First Lady issued an ultimatum to the effect that names would continue to be contributed from various sources, but all input would be channeled through the Social Office.

"Control of the guest lists would stay with the Social Office and not be taken over by the West Side."[36]

As Maria Downs was a former member of the "West Wing" staff, her own loyalty was raised as an issue in her earliest interview with the first lady. Downs believed that she enjoyed a close working relationship with the first lady, though her memoir indicates that she conducted symbolic representation in order to advance the presidential agenda. There were no crosscutting loyalties to the first lady, as there had been in the Kennedy administration.[37] This connection between presidential staff and the social secretary would strengthen in subsequent administrations. Always recognized as an assistant to the nation's hostess, the social secretary's work would be more closely integrated with that of the president. Evidence of these developments is presented in Table 3.7.

As in the past, there are shifts among the different administrations, with some placing greater reliance upon luncheons, and others upon receptions or dinners. These differences are important. They impact communications and relationship building, decisively altering the symbolic representation performed by the first lady and the president. The lengthier and more etiquette-bound exchanges of a dinner (favored in the Nixon administration) contrast sharply with the casual elegance of White House luncheons (more numerous in the Carter, Reagan, and G. H. W. Bush administrations).

These alterations in the first ladies' symbolic representation reflected developments occurring in the wider political and governmental systems. As interest groups, professional associations, and political groups of all kinds entered more fully into policy dialogues and election campaigns, White House social outreach expanded to recognize, accommodate, and advance the priorities of their leaders and members. A privileged set of organizations—among them, the Daughters of the American Revolution, the National Council of Negro Women, and the White House Historical Association—received annual invitations to the White House. By the time of the Carter, Reagan, and G. H. W. Bush administrations, the list of groups welcomed to the White House had lengthened and diversified. The number of receptions increased,

Table 3.7. Symbolic Representation: Events during the Nixon, Ford, Carter, Reagan, and G. H. W. Bush Administrations, 1969–1993

	P. Nixon 1969–73	P. Nixon 1973–74	B. Ford 1975–77	R. Carter 1977–81	N. Reagan 1981–85	N. Reagan 1985–89	B. Bush 1989–93
Events							
Breakfasts	4.1% (n = 14)	4.5% (n = 3)	4.3% (n = 12)	1.5% (n = 6)	2.8% (n = 21)	3.1% (n = 21)	1.0% (n = 9)
Luncheons	8.8 (30)	6.1 (4)	10.1 (28)	18.5 (74)	21.9 (165)	17.6 (119)	12.0 (108)
Receptions	16.1 (55)	13.6 (9)	56.0 (155)	30.8 (123)	20.3 (153)	12.3 (83)	22.6 (203)
Dinners	31.0 (106)	25.8 (17)	10.5 (29)	11.3 (45)	5.1 (38)	5.6 (38)	3.7 (33)
State dinners	7.9 (27)	21.2 (14)	14.1 (39)	8.8 (35)	4.9 (37)	3.8 (26)	3.6 (32)
Teas	5.6 (19)	6.1 (4)	0.4 (1)	2.8 (11)	4.4 (33)	3.0 (20)	10.3 (92)
Music/Play	0.6 (2)	3.0 (2)	0 (0)	2.8 (11)	0.1 (1)	0.4 (3)	0 (0)
Parties	9.6 (33)	10.6 (7)	4.3 (12)	6.5 (26)	2.8 (21)	5.6 (38)	6.7 (60)
Tours	0 (0)	0 (0)	0 (0)	1.8 (7)	2.5 (19)	2.8 (19)	0.1 (1)
Other	16.4 (56)	9.1 (6)	0.4 (1)	15.5 (62)	35.1 (264)	45.7 (309)	40.0 (359)
TOTAL	100.1 (342)	100.0 (66)	100.1 (277)	100.0 (400)	99.9 (752)	99.9 (676)	100.0 (897)

Note: Numbers may not add to 100.0% due to rounding.

Sources: "Official Calendars, Activities, and Honorary Affiliations, 1969–1974" Folder, Box 19, Susan Porter Files, White House Central Files, Richard M. Nixon Presidential Materials; Maria Downs Files, 1974–1977, and Maria Downs Papers, 1975–1977, Gerald R. Ford Library; Gretchen Poston Social Office Files, Jimmy Carter Library; Mabel (Muffie) Brandon Files, 1981–1984; Gahl Hodges Files, 1983–1984, and Linda Faulkner Files, 1981–1989, Ronald Reagan Library; Laurie Firestone Files, White House Social Office, George H. W. Bush Presidential Records, 1989–1993, George H. W. Bush Library.

predictably, from thirty-five in the first term of the Nixon administration to 203 in the G. H. W. Bush administration. But this was only part of the social outreach directed at organized publics.

Receptions, ceremonies, and awards testified to an administration's responsiveness to a mobilizing, diversifying, and fragmenting society. The Carter administration hosted events for Polish Americans, Jewish leaders, Armenian Americans, Asian Americans, Italian Americans, Lithuanian Americans, and various other demographic blocks. The G. H. W. Bush administration hosted ceremonies for Reading Is Fundamental, the National Endowment for the Humanities Teacher-Scholar Program, the Institute for Museum Studies, the National Arboretum Project, and the Ebony Excellence Awards.

Rather than merely acknowledging changes in political structures and routines, the first ladies became decidedly proactive. These women sought to directly influence relationships among the groups, thereby reworking political and societal agendas, in order to change the salience of various issues and identities. In the Johnson and Carter administrations, especially, White House conferences drew public attention to administration initiatives. During the Johnson years, gatherings such as the White House Conference on Natural Beauty spotlighted policy areas of interest to the president and first lady. In the Carter administration, conferences centering on the first lady's agenda—aging, employment, mental illness—linked these issues to the president's domestic priorities. In these instances, the first lady and social secretary were interweaving symbolic and substantive representation, drawing upon the historical authority of the White House to present and advance legislative and programmatic change.

A second change was the decline in gender-segregated events (see Table 3.8). Stag events were relatively common in the Nixon administration: close to one in five events in the first term, and one in eight in the second term, were formally limited to men. Subsequent administrations virtually abandoned this practice. Gender patterns in presidential appointments and nominations continued to ensure that there were a number of occasions on which the guest list was all male, as women were only gradually named to senior executive posts. Still, by hosting fewer stag events, presidents lowered one of the more formalized barriers to women's participation in the conversations and relationships fostered through symbolic representation and social outreach.

At the same time, women were losing their longtime access to the president through the first lady's social outreach. Even Rosalynn Smith Carter, who demonstrated some responsiveness to women as presidential constituents, hosted only fourteen all-women events, just 3.5 percent of the total organized

Table 3.8. Symbolic Representation: Constituent-Specific Events during the Nixon, Ford, Carter, Reagan, and G. H. W. Bush Administrations, 1969–1993

	P. Nixon 1969–73	P. Nixon 1973–74	B. Ford 1975–77	R. Carter 1977–81	N. Reagan 1981–85	N. Reagan 1985–89	B. Bush 1989–93
Attending:							
Children only	1.8% (n = 6)	1.5% (n = 1)	1.1% (n = 3)	1.0% (n = 4)	0.5% (n = 4)	0.6% (n = 4)	0.3% (n = 3)
Stag	18.1 (62)	12.1 (8)	0 (0)	0 (0)	0 (0)	0 (0)	0.1 (1)
Women only	7.9 (27)	7.6 (5)	6.1 (17)	3.5 (14)	4.7 (35)	2.1 (14)	2.1 (19)

Note: All percentages are calculated for the total number of all social outreach events, not only those that are child- or sex-specific.

Sources: "Official Calendars, Activities, and Honorary Affiliations, 1969–1974" Folder, Box 19, Susan Porter Files, White House Central Files, Richard M. Nixon Presidential Materials; Maria Downs Files, 1974–1977, and Maria Downs Papers, 1975–1977, Gerald R. Ford Library; Gretchen Poston Social Office Files, Jimmy Carter Library; Mabel (Muffie) Brandon Files, 1981–1984, Gahl Hodges Files, 1983–1984, and Linda Faulkner Files, 1981–1989, Ronald Reagan Library; Laurie Firestone Files, White House Social Office, George H. W. Bush Presidential Records, 1989–1993, George H. W. Bush Library.

by the social office. Nancy Davis Reagan met with very few women's or "women's issue" groups, reserving all-women and women-centered events to those few for political wives. Reagan's social outreach reflected the strategic priorities of the Reagan administration's communications and campaign teams, which sought to appeal to women along dimensions other than those of gender.

A third innovation in these administrations is suggested by the growth in "other" events—the social secretary was assuming responsibility for a more diverse array of events. In addition to the expected breakfasts, luncheons, teas, receptions, dinners, and state dinners, there were now coffees, brunches, cocktails, picnics, barbecues, and tennis and horseshoe tournaments (in the Reagan and G. H. W. Bush administrations, respectively). This change in the social secretary's workload reflected the increased demands made on and by the president. Expectations that the chief executive would provide leadership extending from the social to the political to the artistic dictated that more time and attention be devoted to symbolic representation.

Meeting those expectations drew the social office into closer association with other White House offices and with the chief executive. The social secretary contributed to presidential communications by staging photo opportunities; supported the rhetorical presidency by framing presidential addresses, speeches, and proclamations; and facilitated legislative-executive relations by coordinating signing and swearing-in ceremonies. The office that had once been gender segregated and located at the core of the first lady's staff was now being integrated into the wider White House Office. Once associated with feminine hostessing routines, it was now participating in the masculine competitions of presidential politics. These organization and gender shifts were significant. When President Carter delegated campaign travel to the first lady throughout 1979 and 1980, the social secretary "became very accustomed to working for the president and the West Wing."[38] The first lady took the lead in a role previously reserved to the president, and the president became more involved in a role previously reserved to the first lady. Masculinity and femininity were becoming somewhat less dichotomous, less exclusive.

No single office owns any White House event. Each occasion has many architects, though it does not take much imagination to understand why rhetorical events might be viewed with special attentiveness by those in communications, why public liaison and policy initiatives would be of particular concern to the associated offices and councils, and so on. Among the first contributors, however, are the president's wife and the social secretary, who present and frame the administration's priorities through their interpretation of such meaningful symbols as the White House.

CONCLUSION

Examining the symbolic representation provided by the first lady, with the social secretary, leads us to assess which symbols are being interpreted and to what ends. Like all studies of representation, this analysis requires close attention to the representative's constituents and to the individuals whom she considers politically relevant and with whom she communicates. Finally, there is also the reflective element of representation. Interpreting symbols, identifying constituents, and communicating all reveal the perceptions and priorities of the first lady and the White House Office in which she works. Each of these points has been examined in this chapter.

Like the president, the first lady has provided symbolic representation by interpreting important symbols. Of the symbols interpreted—and wielded—by the first lady, the White House has been most important to her performance of symbolic representation. From a reception open to the public on New Year's Day in the Hoover administration to the continental elegance of state dinners in the Kennedy administration to award ceremonies in the George H. W. Bush administration, the White House has given meaning and significance to presidential power. Gradually, with the support of the social secretary, the first lady has realized, utilized, and increased the influence and power inherent to her role as the nation's hostess. In event after event, the modern first ladies and their social secretaries have validated the president's exercise of power by associating him with enduring (even mythic) values and priorities, as President Eisenhower noted in regard to the stag dinners he hosted at the White House. At its most effective, the first ladies' skillful use of the White House has elevated partisanship into leadership and transmuted power into authority.

No less significant has been the role of the first lady and social secretary in determining *who* would be invited *when* to the White House. Guest lists have typically originated with the social secretaries, appointed for their knowledge of Washington political networks. "West Wing" and presidential reviews follow, with sometimes protracted negotiations. Which individuals, groups, and organizations are welcomed to the White House, and for which events and occasions, reveal the increasing pluralism—in terms of diversification and fragmentation—of national politics across the administrations. Guest lists indicate which actors a presidential administration chooses to publicly recognize as politically relevant.

This process of inclusion and exclusion was particularly evident in regard to gender. In the Eisenhower, Kennedy, and Nixon administrations, women's inclusion in politics and government was symbolically and substantively constrained by a presidential preference for stag events. These formally all-male events supplemented occasions when the guest list was all male because the officeholders were all male. Women often came to the White House as political wives, their status and influence tied to their husbands.' Greater pluralism in the issue networks, and the mobilizing force of the second women's movement, did lead to women-centered social outreach in the Johnson and Ford administrations. This lessened in the Carter administration. Gender segregation in social outreach decreased further in the Reagan and G. H. W. Bush administrations, which virtually eliminated stag events and hosted few women-centered events. It remained to be seen whether this change would facilitate gender integration in symbolic representation, with women recognized as autonomous decision makers, and thus, as presidential constituents.

The role of hostess is one of the most enduring of those assigned to the first lady. It is congruent with historically mainstream, white, and middle-class conceptions of femininity as centered in the private sphere. Guests come to the home, where they are welcomed and served by the woman, who displays her talents to a select audience in a controlled and confined environment. When the woman is the nation's hostess, the scale and the consequence of the hostess role increases dramatically. Now the guests are decision makers and policy makers. The home is the White House, a historic site revered by the nation and the location of the presidential office. The first lady's expertise must correspond to these public-sphere characterizations: she is a representative, her symbolic representation expressing the ideals and advancing the interests of her husband's administration. Because she is at once hostess and representative, her contributions may go unnoticed—hostesses are often dismissed as servants and facilitators. Yet modern first ladies have made lasting contributions, some controversial and some accepted, through their performance as symbolic representatives. First ladies have exercised influence through—not in spite of—their role as the nation's hostess.

The high stakes associated with symbolic representation have become more evident throughout the modern presidency. The first lady, perhaps more than any other member of the White House staff, has confronted increasing public and media scrutiny. Not surprisingly, a press secretary was the second full-time, federally funded post on the first lady's staff. These developments are the subject of the next chapter, which examines modern first ladies as descriptive representatives.

VOICE AND MESSAGE:
The First Lady and Descriptive Representation

Technology has dramatically affected presidential responsibilities and opportunities for rhetorical leadership. Broadcast and electronic media outlets, from radio to television to the Internet, have multiplied and diversified, driving a twenty-four-hour news cycle. Print media, meanwhile, has found its circulation numbers fluctuating and often falling. Papers have dropped editions, changed formats, consolidated, gone online, and closed. Coverage has become even more adversarial, with investigative efforts spurred by covert operations that expanded wars, presidential cover-ups of criminal actions and personal failures, and policy decisions that changed the balance of power among the branches. In an effort to turn these journalistic practices to their own advantage, presidents have recruited aides specializing in communications, media relations, and public relations.[1] First ladies have similarly diversified and departmentalized their staff.

The changes in media coverage throughout the modern presidency were arguably even greater for the first ladies than for the presidents. The chief executive has long been of interest to journalists—presidency scholar Martha Kumar concluded that the presidency emerged as "the national news center" in the 1880s. Media coverage created a public record of presidential politics, a "first draft of history," as one aphorism put it. Yet decades and generations passed before there was any widespread expectation that first ladies would appear in the media as other than presidential appendages.[2] The president's wife was present in campaign photos, as evidence of the candidate's virility and familial credentials, and examined in the society pages, as an arbiter of proper behavior. As another old dogma went, a lady appeared in the newspapers only at her birth and her death, perhaps also on the occasion of her marriage.[3] There was no need of a public record, many felt, because she properly centered her life in the private sphere. Earlier in the twentieth century, media coverage of the first lady outside the society pages routinely focused on novel or inappropriate behavior, as when Lou Henry Hoover drove her car in DC or out to Rapidan. Even later in the twentieth century, first ladies found it difficult to secure substantive coverage. Rosalynn Smith Carter, for example, was frustrated and even angered by the effort required to draw media attention to her policy work.[4] Yet coverage of the first ladies did change. While still attentive to their symbolic representation, journalists gradually gave greater consideration to the first ladies' substantive representation. In fact, within a few decades, first ladies became a subject of intense and continuing interest to reporters and the public. Why? What happened? And how did the first ladies respond?

Media Coverage and the Modern First Ladyship

Changes in media coverage of the first ladies, as of the presidents, reflected trends in the wider society. The popular appeal of Theodore White's Pulitzer Prize–winning volume, *The Making of the President, 1960,* at once tapped into and generated tremendous interest in campaign processes, practices, and personalities. It contributed to changes in media coverage—including the so-called goldfish bowl journalism—and to an increasing focus on the candidates. With such attention given presidential aspirants, it was only to be expected that spouses would also be scrutinized. As in the past, wives were studied for what they revealed about their husbands, the femininity of the woman presumed to complement the masculinity of the man. But as the women's rights movement gathered force through the 1960s, there was also interest in women as decision makers and actors in their own right.

The suffrage movement of the nineteenth and early twentieth centuries gave a lasting push to social reform, specifically to advances for white and professional women. As historian Susan Ware has demonstrated, the New Deal women's networks then transmuted this movement into a social feminism that evidenced gender consciousness and pride, but saw itself as transcending gender through a commitment to all of humanity.[5] Historian Cynthia Harrison has shown that these efforts continued into the 1950s, refuting those who described these years as the "doldrums" for women and women activists.[6] When the women's rights movement began to gather momentum, it drew upon the expertise acquired and the momentum generated through these decades of political entrepreneurship. The women who led the government initiatives of the women's rights movement knew how, why, and to what ends they wanted the government to act.

The women's rights movement was distinct from the suffrage movement in important ways. Rather than arguing, as had a number of the suffragists, that women should have rights because they would then be able to contribute more to the nation, those in the women's movement of the 1960s and 1970s maintained that women should have rights in order to realize their creative potential as individuals. Self-expression, with all its associated joys and sufferings, was intrinsic to being human and ought to be as much a part of a woman's life as it was a man's. This was the argument of Betty Friedan's *The Feminine Mystique* (1963), published just a few years after *The Making of the President, 1960,* and unquestionably one of the great forces in the women's rights movement. Not incidentally, *The Feminine Mystique* included a lengthy and detailed critique of the mass media, delineating how the industry had broken women's spirits, leaving them intellectually stunted and emotionally barren.[7] The book, like the movement, called upon women to take action, to claim responsibility, and to insist upon being recognized. Those expectations were also directed at the first ladies, just as these women were becoming somewhat more individualized as surrogates in electoral politics and as representatives in government, and just as media interest in first ladies (both prospective and current) was on the increase.

All of these developments came together to create new expectations for the first ladies. Media interest was on the rise, with journalists studying the wives of candidates and presidents for what they revealed about their husbands, and what they were in and of themselves. Women looked to these political wives as gender role models and policy activists.

This interest in the first ladies as participants in the public sphere was a significant development. Presidents' wives had always been the focus of some public interest, and as already noted, of highly gendered expectations. Studying a wife for what she revealed about her husband expressed a gender ideology in which femininity and masculinity were both mutualistic and exclusive, premised upon heterosexuality and the predominance of the masculine. The first lady was expected to uphold a standard of behavior that typified the aspirations of white, Anglo-Saxon, middle-class, conservative, nuclear-family Americans—the comfortable, mythic mainstream. This standard placed the woman firmly in the private sphere as caregiver and homemaker, occasionally allowing her to express herself beyond the family as a gracious hostess or moral guardian. But her role was one of inspiration, not direction. The first lady could appropriately speak of values and ideals, but she was not to command their adoption through policies and programs.[8]

With the rise of the women's rights movement, this restraint became a matter for discussion, then debate, and finally for confrontation. If women had the ability to see what changes would improve the society, why shouldn't they also use their voice and exercise power to effect them? When the post-modern women's movement gathered force in the late 1980s, it added new indictments and brought more energy to this dialogue. With its attentiveness to identity politics, and to the intersectionality of identities in the life and judgment of every woman, postmodern feminists argued that the president's wife should prioritize diversity rather than conformity to an essentialist ideal. When an African American woman became first lady, this question became even more significant. How would Michelle Robinson Obama negotiate gender-race expectations, providing descriptive representation that earned voters' support? This would be especially difficult given the diversity of views regarding the role of race in gender ideologies and practices.

Jill Abraham Hummer has written that the American public has, for generations, expected the first lady to be a "cultural everywoman" who embodies and thereby validates a singular ideal of womanhood in the United States.[9] So long as there was one dominant ideal, this expectation might be fulfilled—if the first lady could express in words and actions such an intangible and slippery conception without encountering conflict or scandal. Often, she also had to set aside her own interests and ideologies. Lou Henry Hoover routinely undertook to meet the cultural everywoman standard of her time. During her husband's presidential term, Hoover withdrew from the public life she had created for herself. Adopting the gender ideology of the separate spheres, she confined herself to the private sphere, or to those public-sphere roles that could be defended as extensions of private-sphere responsibilities.[10] She did not speak on the record to journalists, declined virtually every public-speaking invitation, resigned from her leadership positions in national organizations, and even answered virtually all of her White House mail in the third person. And, with some event-specific exceptions (including what may have been the first White House tea to include an African American congressional wife among the guests), Hoover was generally considered a noncontroversial first lady. Bess Wallace Truman, who seemingly also limited her public-sphere participation, was complimented on doing so by the editors of the *Los Angeles Times*:

> She has—and we say this sincerely—been a model First Lady and a loyal and dignified partner to the President during every difficulty that has beset him and the nation.
> This is not to say that every First Lady must elect the retiring role that Mrs. Truman chose, but to express the feeling most Americans share

that she always has been simply herself, a genuine and gracious lady, without any desire to capitalize on her husband's office or to mirror its importance.[11]

Though the editorialist claims to accept politically active first ladies, the criticism that would be directed at such individuals—and that had been directed at Eleanor Roosevelt—is clear. Bess Truman was her husband's confidante and advisor.[12] But because she did not publicize her contributions in and to the public sphere, she was praised as a "model First Lady" and honored as a cultural everywoman.

Once there was widespread debate about what constituted women's gender role, first ladies could not hope to win such endorsements, even if they were willing to follow Hoover and Truman's lead. No single gender ideal or ideology drew such widespread support that it silenced those with opposing or contrasting philosophies. As a highly identifiable public figure, who was widely viewed and judged as a gender role model, the first lady became a lightning rod in the culture wars about women's status in politics, society, the market, and the family. Close media scrutiny fueled the ensuing controversies.

First ladies have had most of their representation mediated by print, broadcast, and electronic outlets. To state the obvious, the mass media prioritizes communication. Feminists, moreover, have focused upon "voice," with all that it suggests about an individual's uniqueness and personal autonomy. The first lady's use of her voice, in the mass media, as a descriptive representative, generates pointed questions about the influence, power, and contributions of the president's wife. Should she exercise her voice? Should she express or constrain it? Every statement made by the first lady, as a descriptive representative, has wider societal implications.[13]

As a symbolic representative, the first lady interpreted national political symbols such as the White House, enhancing her husband's authority by demonstrating the congruence between his priorities and the accepted mythologies and ideologies of presidential power. The communications and relationships were often direct and immediate, with members of the Washington community and society invited to state dinners, receptions, teas, and other White House occasions. As a descriptive representative, the first lady undertook to interpret and display nothing less than her own identity, securing support for her husband by tapping into deeply held beliefs about gender roles and gender power. The intimacy of this interpretation—its commentary on how lives should be lived, about what should be accepted or hoped for—made descriptive representation especially powerful and relevant to the president's message.

Because the passage of time, with historic events such as the women's movement and the adoption of new technologies, is important to understanding the first ladies as descriptive representatives, this chapter is organized, for the most part, chronologically. Because changes occurred from one administration to another, reflecting similarities or differences in gender, partisan ideologies, political capital, and organizational resources, the history is told with due regard for the priorities of each president and first lady. In the modern presidency, first ladies from Lou Henry Hoover to Jacqueline Bouvier Kennedy were effectively their own press secretaries. They confronted a relatively coherent and consistent set of societal expectations and had some leeway so long as they conformed to the prevailing standards of behavior for white, privileged women. This equilibrium was lost in the mid-1960s.

Lady Bird Taylor Johnson was the first president's wife with a press secretary and staff director independent of the social secretary and the social office. The creation of the new post was a significant investment in the first ladyship, drawing the president's wife much farther onto the public stage and into the public sphere. Lady Bird Johnson used her voice to enhance the popular appeal of the president's message and to build support for the administration. Specialization and departmentalization in the first lady's staffing continued and accelerated in the Nixon, Ford, and Carter administrations. At the same time, media scrutiny of the president, the first lady, and the presidency increased, and the societal consensus about women's gender roles fractured and was lost. In the later twentieth century, then, presidents' wives gained more organizational resources but confronted greater political and media constraints. From the Reagan administration onward, descriptive representation arguably became the definitive test of the first lady as a White House staff member with representation responsibilities. The how and why of the first ladies' achievements and failures are investigated below.

FROM LOU HENRY HOOVER TO JACQUELINE KENNEDY: THE FIRST LADY AS PRESS SECRETARY

With little consistent specialization among members of the White House staff until the Nixon administration, the first lady was simply another generalist in the White House Office. But media relations did emerge as an early specialization, and despite differences in White House staff structures and operations, media relations were an important and influential function throughout the modern presidency.[14] Presidents valued good press and invested staff resources in cultivating positive relationships with the media. Presidents also had ample opportunity to see the positive impact their wives could have in reaching out to the public. Yet it was not until the Johnson administration that the first lady was fully staffed by her own press secretary. Why this lag in providing expertise? Why didn't chief executives earlier in the modern presidency provide their wives with press secretaries, so that the first ladies could communicate more effectively?

The simplest answer is that the president simply did not see the first lady's need for staff, because he did not see the return that could be earned from investing organizational and political resources in her press relations. The first lady was a satellite, or so prevailing wisdom dictated, who reflected well upon her husband.[15] Her femininity threw his masculinity into high relief; her dedication in the private sphere drew attention to his sacrifices in the public sphere. Separate-spheres gender ideology was about contrast between two genders. If the wife was less feminine and crossed into the public sphere, then the husband was presumed to be less masculine and a weaker leader. This was especially a concern when the chief executive's personal and political strength was already in question. Bess Truman disavowed any role in her husband's decision making, her daughter believed, out of concern that her contributions would resurrect charges that he was easily influenced and lacking strength of purpose—charges originating in his early association with James Prendergast. In other words, Bess Truman believed (as Margaret Truman interpreted her mother's motives) that her descriptive representation—specifically, her performance of a gender ideology that politically empowered women—would impact the president's reputation. Mismanaged gender relations could carry a cost as high for President Truman as indebtedness to a political boss had for Senator Truman.[16]

The simplest answer, then, has both logic and evidence to support it. Providing the first lady with a social secretary conformed to prevailing gender norms, in that serving as a hostess was a well-regarded expression of femininity. It was also an accepted practice for society matrons—a gender-appropriate leadership role—to have this kind of staff support, which meant that the social secretary was a comparatively minimal innovation. But a press secretary would have overturned what one journalist named "the oldest tradition of the White House," namely, that the first lady "cannot be interviewed upon herself."[17] A press secretary signaled a first lady's rejection of well-established separate-spheres gender norms.

Yet first ladies were not silent during the five administrations in which they served as their own press secretaries. First ladies, like presidents, knew that political success depended upon their communications with the public. Roosevelt spoke and published extensively; her syndicated column was widely read. Although Hoover, Truman, Eisenhower, and Kennedy spoke rarely or infrequently in public, and did not publish as first ladies, they often lived by more self-expressive, individualistic standards in private. This makes their descriptive representation all the more intriguing: how did they balance conformity and resistance to popular expectations in their gender role modeling and press relations?

Hoover, Roosevelt, Truman, Eisenhower, and Kennedy exhibited varied responses to these questions. There was not yet a firm expectation that the press would have continuing or even regular access to the president's wife, so the women had some discretion in determining the extent and the character of their relationships with journalists. The result can best be described as an ebb and flow in the access that first ladies granted the media. Lou Henry Hoover and, much later, Mamie Doud Eisenhower minimized their press relations, conforming to separate-spheres conceptions of ladies as appropriately confined to the private sphere. In between these first ladies were Eleanor Roosevelt and Bess Truman, each with her own strategy for safeguarding and enhancing her personal autonomy. Roosevelt sought to achieve this goal by providing information through press conferences, interviews, and publications, at times and through outlets of her choosing. Bess Truman preferred not to divulge any information, in order to safeguard her privacy and create a life apart from the presidency. Jacqueline Kennedy was similarly self-protective, but was willing to reach out to the press when coverage would advance her efforts to restore the White House. This lack of a clear trajectory in first lady media relations may be confusing, but it should be understood as revelatory of these decades. From the 1920s to the 1960s, negotiations among gender roles were being conducted throughout the society, the economy, and the government. As gender role models, the first ladies reflected this changeableness and uncertainty; as descriptive representatives, the first ladies embraced very different strategies in communicating their gender ideologies.

Lou Henry Hoover and Mamie Eisenhower: The Power of the Private Sphere

Given the contrasts in their careers before they were first ladies, it is initially surprising that Lou Henry Hoover and Mamie Eisenhower evidenced such similarities in their descriptive representation during the White House years.

As the wives of formidably successful self-made men, Lou Henry Hoover and Mamie Eisenhower had taken very different approaches to the private and public spheres. Hoover had traveled extensively with her husband, even in war zones, throughout his years as a mining engineer. By one estimate, her oldest son had been around the world four times by the age of six. When her sons were in their teens, she and her husband became involved in relief work. Lou Henry Hoover then moved into executive positions in national not-for-profit organizations, establishing herself as a leader independent of her husband, though she continued to be a part of his career through various organizational partnerships. While Mamie Eisenhower joined her husband on many of his military postings, there were lengthy separations during the war years. Nor did Eisenhower partner with her husband in the public sphere. Instead, she controlled the private sphere, including the family finances. For Mamie Eisenhower, there were real boundaries between the private and public spheres, and neither she nor her husband crossed them. Hoover was committed to social development and improvement, and led women's organizations to achieve this goal. She was a product of her time, seeing women's and men's gender roles as distinct from one another, but she also foreshadowed the pressures for independence and autonomy that would come with the women's rights movement. Mamie Eisenhower was far more conservative in her gender ideology, embracing the separate-spheres dichotomy, claiming power for women as decision makers within the family.

In the White House, these differences almost vanished because Lou Henry Hoover changed her lifestyle to conform to the separate-spheres standards. A woman reporter remarked early in the administration that "Mrs. Hoover has a slight handicap . . . she has a reputation for being a brainy woman, to which she will have to reconcile the public."[18] But Hoover required the public to make few adaptations. She resigned her leadership positions and limited her organizational affiliations to honorary memberships. She virtually ceased publishing articles and essays, and rarely accepted speaking engagements. She did not consistently publicize her descriptive or her substantive representation. She did not speak on the record to the press, refusing interviews and limiting access to the White House. Her standards were so unbending that a member of the first lady's staff smuggled a reporter into the Christmas Eve reception, disguised in a Girl Scout uniform, so that there would be coverage of the event.[19]

Even so, Hoover and Eisenhower did communicate with the public. There was always the expected coverage in society pages and columns. Historian Lewis L. Gould maintains that Hoover did speak with the press on background and that she did engage in social outreach to the press. She did invite more than twenty women correspondents to Rapidan for a luncheon in July 1932.[20] Yet Hoover was never eager to draw attention to her politics, either at the grassroots or in Washington. When there were errors in the coverage, her response was tempered. When the media credited her with being fluent in seven languages, for example, she responded that this was more intellectual ability than she could hope to possess. When she was criticized politically, however, she lobbied the president's aides to issue statements that reflected her own understanding of the media as shaping public opinion. Defending her decision to invite the African American wife of a U.S. congressman to tea at the White House, for instance, she advanced a legal and constitutional argument that had already earned endorsements in the press and among letter writers.[21] Rather than using the power of the press, Hoover sought to avoid and deflect its forcefulness.

Though Mamie Eisenhower was mentioned in national newspapers such as the *New York Times* with a frequency that was similar to other first ladies, her homemaking focus was more suited to women's magazines, and she was featured in these publications on a regular basis. Mamie Eisenhower talked about inventorying the White House pantry, matching goods to menus. She became famous for saving the leftovers and for seeing that every meal was at once inexpensive and delicious. Yet because she did not neglect the glamour of her privileged station—the dresses and hairdos, the meetings with royalty and celebrities—she avoided linking the first ladyship to the mundane. Her supporters saw her as a princess who knew how ordinary people lived. And she had many supporters. In 1971, years after she had left the White House—years in which the woman's movement called into question the gender ideology that she endorsed—67 percent of respondents still responded that they had a "great deal" of respect for this first lady.[22]

As descriptive representatives, Lou Henry Hoover and Mamie Eisenhower amplified the statement that they made as symbolic representatives. These first ladies presented themselves as satellite wives, focusing the public's attention on the chief executive as the dominant figure in the public sphere. For Hoover, this entailed considerable sacrifice as she suspended her own career to support her husband and his administration. Her descriptive representation was performed more in silence than through words; she stepped away from speaking and writing, and limited her press relations. Eisenhower continued practices that she had accepted or adopted years before she entered the White House. If anything, she appeared more often before the public as first lady than she had as the wife of a five-star general or a university president. Like Hoover, Eisenhower exercised her voice strategically, performing descriptive representation that enhanced her husband's status in the public sphere. Both women earned public support for their descriptive representation as first ladies, though Eisenhower's popular appeal was more lasting.

Eleanor Roosevelt: Rejecting Public-Private Sphere Boundaries

Eleanor Roosevelt actively mediated with journalists on behalf of her husband's administration. Furthermore, she seized the initiative by publishing frequently in mass circulation publications, accepting innumerable public-speaking engagements, and traveling extensively and independently of the president. Unlike the first ladies who were her immediate predecessors and successors, she sought to control coverage by providing information. This first lady was as determined to establish her independence in her marriage as she was to prove her influence in the presidential administration. At the end of her first year in the White House, Roosevelt reported to her husband that she had earned a salary as a writer and lecturer that equaled his as president.[23] Talent and power, competitiveness and ambition drove Eleanor Roosevelt, qualities that were not associated with the private sphere and that were often considered unacceptable in a woman.

Those were, however, qualities that the first lady shared with many women, including those in the Washington press corps. When Eleanor Roosevelt instituted weekly press conferences exclusively for women reporters, and then proceeded to provide information and share her own judgments, media outlets found themselves forced to hire women journalists or sacrifice coverage. Roosevelt won this confrontation because she controlled resources—information and access—that her opponents valued and needed. And when she did win, she gained strong allies among women journalists. True, she had to continue to provide substantive information, giving the media reason to cover her press conferences, but the reporters in attendance were often sympathetic to her views or at least accepting of her activism.[24] The communication and the relationships she conducted with the reporters advanced her descriptive representation.

Roosevelt needed this support. She was well aware that her ideas and interests made her controversial. Roosevelt was somewhat similar to Lou Henry Hoover; Roosevelt, for example, did speak from a moral and ethical perspective, conforming to perceptions of women as moral guardians. But Roosevelt broke with separate-spheres beliefs in maintaining that women should speak in the public sphere, seeking to influence domestic and foreign policies. She was a loyal wife and mother, who stayed in a marriage often characterized by tension and infidelity. She also insisted on political and economic independence, contradicting separate-spheres thinking, which subordinated women to men in regard to family finances and political power.

Roosevelt tried to prove the coherence and value of her ideals by presenting them as directly as possible to the public. Her words in press conferences would be paraphrased, interpreted, and framed by the press, but she could hope that her own writings would be more lightly edited. The author of innumerable articles and several books, her most widely circulated publication was almost certainly her syndicated column "My Day."

"My Day" was published daily, from December 30, 1936, to September 27, 1962, the final column appearing less than six weeks before Roosevelt's death. It was, as its title promised, an account of the first lady's day, setting out her actions, encounters, and recollections for public consumption. To the extent that she was a leader within issue networks of women reformers, the column served as a motivational and organizational tool, reminding individuals of their priorities and consequent commitments. More generally, the daily columns, with their conversational writing style and eclectic mix of topics, simply engaged readers' curiosity and imagination. Roosevelt discussed books, movies, and radio programs that she had read, seen, or heard; commented upon policy battles and explained her positions on various issues, many relating specifically to women; described the minutiae of White House life; quoted from her public mail, with answers for the letter writers; and offered her assessment of current national and international events. The reader who wanted to know what the first lady was doing also learned what she was thinking.

Roosevelt did not hesitate to detail her daily discomforts, either. In 1944 she wrote, "I can hardly believe it, but I have received an anonymous letter which says nothing but pleasant things. That has never happened to me before." She became famous, however, for her more reflective political pieces. The August 1, 1939, column, written as the nation was preparing for war, exemplified her style, which was at once reflective and provocative: "It is wearisome to read of the balance of power. I would like to see somebody write about a balance of trade and of food for the world and the possibilities of so organizing our joint economic systems that all of us could go to work and produce at maximum capacity."[25]

As she observed the continuing displacement of New Deal priorities by preparations for wars in Europe, Asia, and Africa, and realized that social justice would become an increasingly elusive goal, Roosevelt likely was fearful of being irrelevant and determined to be bold. As more than one supporter remarked, the first lady had a willingness to share her ideas and a gift for inspiring trust.[26]

These were the qualities that characterized Roosevelt's descriptive representation. Notwithstanding her skill in framing an argument to her own advantage, she was remarkably forthright. Treating representation as a conversation, she listened to supporters and critics, and responded to questions and charges in print and on the record. Her positions on women, as constituents and as decision makers, were clearly articulated. There was little ambiguity about her gender role modeling. Women, Roosevelt argued, were as incisive and as analytic as men, and needed to use those abilities to achieve their political goals.

> How, then, can we bring the men leaders to concede participation in party affairs, adequate representation and real political equality?
>
> Our means is to elect, accept, and back women political bosses.
>
> To organize as women, but within the parties, in districts, counties and States just as men organize, and to pick efficient leaders—say two or three in each State—whom we will support and by whose decisions we will abide. With the power of unified women voters behind them, such women bosses would be in a position to talk in terms of "business" with the men leaders; their voices would be heard, because their authority and the elective power they could command who have to be recognized.
>
> Women are today ignored largely because they have no banded unity under representative leaders and spokesmen capable of dealing with the bosses controlling groups of men whose votes they can "deliver." These men bosses have the power of coordinated voters behind them. Our helplessness is that of an incoherent anarchy.[27]

Yet women were not and should not perceive themselves as being the same as men: "[W]omen are different from men. They are equals in many ways, but they cannot refuse to acknowledge their differences. . . . Their physical functions in life are different and perhaps in the same way the contributions which they are trying to bring to the spiritual side of life are different. . . . perhaps we are going to see evolved in the next few years not only a social order built by the ability and brains of our men, but a social order which represents the understanding heart of women."[28]

Roosevelt refused to separate the private and public spheres. She also refused to celebrate male leadership, insisting that women's knowledge be valued. She described masculinity and femininity not as mutually exclusive gender roles but as overlapping ("equals in many ways") but distinct (in "physical functions" and "spiritual" "contributions"). She believed that society needed women to participate in politics and in government, and that women who did so should be respected.

The clarity and lack of equivocation in Eleanor Roosevelt's voice made it easy for listeners and readers to decide whether they agreed or disagreed.

Many disagreed. By the standards of separate-spheres ideology, Roosevelt was undercutting and emasculating the president. Rather than reinforcing his message, she was setting out her own beliefs and judgments. From the perspective of social feminists and other reformers, though, Roosevelt was defending a democratic ideal that empowered men and women, masses and leaders.[29] It was a vision that Roosevelt refined and advanced across the years and decades, and the appeal of her gender role modeling increased as the women's rights movement gathered momentum into the early 1960s.

Bess Truman and Jacqueline Kennedy: The Private Sphere as Refuge

Lou Henry Hoover and Mamie Eisenhower tried to control their media coverage by denying or minimizing access, emphasizing their commitment to women's roles in the private sphere. Eleanor Roosevelt sought control by providing information and building alliances with journalists, rejecting the separation of private and public spheres in women's lives. Bess Truman and Jacqueline Kennedy had much in common with Hoover and Eisenhower, frequently and even routinely denying media requests for information. Yet Truman and Kennedy did participate in the public sphere, if not to Roosevelt's extent. Ultimately, these first ladies used the private sphere as a refuge, denying the media access except on rare occasions.

Bess Truman knew that good press relations were critically important to a presidential administration. She participated in Harry Truman's selection of a press secretary, and she was well aware that she was succeeding a first lady who had sustained positive relationships with the press for more than twelve years. In fact, press relations were among Truman's first and most worrisome concerns as a new first lady.[30] Sitting on the funeral train that brought Franklin Roosevelt's body back to Washington, DC from Warm Springs, Georgia, she said as much to Labor Secretary Frances Perkins. A friend and sometime mentor to Eleanor Roosevelt, Perkins recounted the conversation in her oral history.

> We talked about it for a while . . . I realized that she couldn't [hold press conferences], that if she did talk about [public affairs], of course she would make mistakes and that she'd be dreadfully unhappy and be half sick from the terrific pressure that even "the girls" can put on her.
>
> Well, Mr. Truman came back into the compartment then, and she said to him, "Now about this press conference . . ."
>
> He said again, "Mrs. Roosevelt just tells me that she'll sit with you or introduce you to a press conference on Tuesday if you wish."

She said, "Well, I just asked Miss Perkins about it, and Miss Perkins thinks it's not necessary."

He said, "Well, I don't know." He asked me to say what I had told her again. I did, and he said, "Well, I think she's right. There's no reason why you should do it, Bess."

I said, "There's no earthly reason why it should be established as an inalienable right of the press to interview the lady who happens to have married the man who happens to have become President. I'm speaking not only for you two, but for people for the next fifty years who will be President. Their wives are not selected for their publicity interest."

He said, "I think you're right. There's no reason why you should do it, Bess."[31]

The conversation moved from the personal—Bess Truman's own desire to avoid the press and the public discussion of policy—to the organizational—what demands the press could make of the president's wife. Not merely empathetic, Perkins was emphatic (even unequivocal) in defining a first lady's obligations. Ultimately, Perkins dismissed twelve years of first lady press conferences, 348 in all, as a matter of personal preference rather than a political or governmental responsibility.[32]

Bess Truman did cancel the press conference. She had not publicized her public-sphere contributions as a senator's wife and she refused to do so as a president's wife. Throughout her years as first lady, Truman avoided all possible contact with the press, almost never speaking on the record and refusing virtually every request for an interview. Her personal secretary, Raethel Odum, and her social secretary, Edith Helm, conducted her press relations. Neither enjoyed doing so. Helm quickly devised press releases to convey information about White House social outreach.[33] Odum delivered a list of the most frequently asked questions to the first lady, to be answered in writing. Among the questions, and the answers, were the following:

2. What qualities, innate or acquired, does she think would be the greatest asset for the wife of a President? For instance, good health, enjoyment of people, knowledge of languages, etc.

Good health and a well developed sense of humor.

4. Does she think there will ever be a woman President of the United States?

No.

Would she want to be President?

NO. [emphasis in original]

12. What would she like to do and have her husband do when he is no longer President? Travel, for instance, or return to Independence?

Return to Independence.

17. What experience since you have been in the White House do you consider Most Worth-While?

No comment.

25. Has living in the White House changed any of your views on politics and people? If so, how?

No comment.

28. Will you go to the Democratic National Convention in '48?

Expect to. Wouldn't miss a Democratic Con. if I could help it.[34]

The president remarked that there would doubtless be much press ink spent on her lengthy answer to the twenty-eighth question—and wondered what had provoked her optimistic response.

Equally telling were the questions that the first lady did not answer, even with a "no comment."

1. What is Mrs. Truman's conception of the role of First Lady?
10. What has been her most moving experience as First Lady?
27. How would you add up what being First Lady has meant to you?[35]

Truman had two strong reasons for choosing to be silent in the public sphere, even after she had overcome her resistance to being first lady. First, she was an intensely private person. That quality may have been set in her character when, as a young girl, she had to weather the layers of pain and intrusiveness that followed her father's suicide. She disliked being a spectacle for others— she refused to allow the Secret Service to accompany her while she was in Independence. Yet she also relished human contact, preferring small-town life and small gatherings to the anonymity of urban centers and large receptions. Second, Bess Truman was determined to protect her husband's reputation and prestige.[36]

Silence (or near silence) satisfied Bess Truman's desire for privacy and lessened her concern that she might adversely impact the administration. As a strategy, however, it did not allow her to capitalize on opportunities to strengthen the administration through her representation. Instead of moderating Roosevelt's practices, Truman simply stepped back and away from the press. Her descriptive representation was correspondingly muted.

When Bess Truman did reach out to the public, she emphasized her obligations as a daughter, wife, and mother. The press faithfully delivered this message. When she went to Independence, for example, she stressed that she was going home, not that she was leaving Washington, the White House, and her husband. In Independence, she redecorated and improved the family home, and cared for her mother and daughter.[37] In presenting herself as a private-sphere woman, Truman effectively dared the American public to criticize her priorities. And she did avoid negative press, in part because the president repeatedly and publicly endorsed her actions, never mind that in their private correspondence he asked her to spend more time in Washington, with him.[38] Her voice and his message were neatly in tune before the press and the public, and the gender role modeling of her private woman to his public man preempted challenge. Unlike Franklin Roosevelt, Harry Truman had a wife and first lady who was "genuine and gracious."[39]

Like Truman, Jacqueline Kennedy minimized her public-sphere contributions as a Senate wife; unlike Truman, Kennedy was willing to publicize her contributions as a president's wife, but on her own terms and to her own standards. Assistant social secretary Pam Turnure was assigned responsibility for the first lady's press relations, and Jacqueline Kennedy was very clear that Turnure was to serve as "a buffer—to shield our privacy—not get us into the papers." As she wrote in an early letter to Turnure, "I feel so strongly that publicity in this era has gotten so completely out of hand—& you must really protect the privacy of me and my children—but not offend them [the press]." Though Kennedy had allowed her daughter, Caroline, to be featured in both her husband's Senate reelection and presidential campaigns, as first lady, she was determined to deny virtually all requests for pictures or interviews. "My press relations will be minimum information given with maximum politeness. . . . I won't give any interviews—pose for any photographs, etc. for next four years. . . . [Press Secretary] Pierre [Salinger] will bring in *Life* & *Look* or Stan Tretwick a couple of times a year & we'll have an okay on it."[40] The private sphere was to be private.

In the public sphere, Jacqueline Kennedy monitored and regulated the release of all information relating to social outreach and to her substantive representation, which was focused upon the White House restoration. When *American Home* obtained an exclusive on the restoration by going through Pierre Salinger's office, Turnure's reprimand was swift and strong: "I am writing this merely to emphasize Mrs. Kennedy's wish that no articles or photographs concerning the household, i.e. furnishings, paintings, flower arrangements, Fine Arts Committee personnel are to be arranged by your office without Mrs. Kennedy's clearance through me."[41] Kennedy established a distinct sphere of expertise and influence by controlling her press relations.

Jacqueline Kennedy's descriptive representation and media relations were therefore more complex than Bess Truman's. Kennedy, like Truman, broadcast her commitment to the private sphere and its familial roles. That was not difficult. She delivered John Jr. a few weeks after the election and Patrick (who lived only a short time) just months before the assassination; for toddler Caroline, she organized a preschool class in the White House. But Kennedy also went on the offensive. She used her gift for languages to communicate with the public, both domestically and internationally. Her expressions of appreciation to voters in New Orleans and to the Cuban soldiers who returned from the Bay of Pigs generated extraordinary enthusiasm. In France, she spoke not only to the crowds but also with President Charles de Gaulle and several of his ministers. Her husband was obliged to concede that her public diplomacy was an asset to his administration. Her interest in the arts became a political advantage when the first lady conducted a successful campaign to restore the White House.[42] Arthur Schlesinger identified these qualities as setting a new standard for first ladies: "The things people had once held against her—the unconventional beauty, the un-American elegance, the taste for French clothes and French food—were suddenly no longer liabilities but assets. She represented all at once not a negation of her country but a possible fulfillment of it, a suggestion that America was not to be trapped forever in the bourgeois ideal, a dream of civilization and beauty."[43]

Others focused more immediately on her gender role modeling, concluding that as a descriptive representative, Jacqueline Kennedy moved, rejected, redrew, and even erased long-established gender boundaries.

> Jackie had these traditionally "masculine" qualities—she was smart and loved intellectual pursuits, she was knowledgeable about history and the arts, she wore pants, and she had big feet—yet she was still completely feminine, a princess, a queen. She knew how to take charge, and she also knew how to be gracious and ornamental. For those of us raised on Cinderella and Snow White, she suggested new possibilities for the princess role. Being educated, having some knowledge your husband didn't have, was glamorous, even enviable. This was important because women's magazines were still telling girls that the way to land a man was to pretend that you were dumber than he was. Jackie Kennedy told us all kinds of subterfuges and compromises were possible (as long as you looked like Jackie Kennedy, of course).[44]

Kennedy made mistakes as a descriptive representative—her enjoyment of fox hunting was controversial, and especially so when she went riding instead of keeping her White House commitments—but she succeeded in placing herself firmly on the Gallup Poll's "most admired women" list.[45] She also made compromises—working with American designer Oleg Cassini and understating her preferences for European art and culture; speaking in tones that were soft and childish, though her ideas were strong and mature—but she did alter public expectations of a president's wife.[46] Most significantly, she did not limit herself to reiterating the president's message. Instead, she expressed her self, and drew upon her talents, in ways that diversified and strengthened the administration's relationships with its constituents. Her voice was always on message, but not necessarily in ways that the president anticipated or even consistently embraced.

Kennedy may have shared some of Truman's desire for privacy; she definitely shared her predecessor's desire for a life that was not defined by the demands of politics, the presidency, and her husband's career. Kennedy refused to be a satellite wife. When her husband pressed her to do more, she made her resistance clear to him, to his staff, and to the press.[47] Notably, the president did not often directly confront the first lady on this matter, instead waiting until she was away from the White House to countermand her orders. Once while she was absent, the president brought Caroline and John to the Oval Office, and simply invited press photographers in for a picture-taking session. In this administration, the conduct of press relations was revelatory of the first lady's power within the White House and within her marriage.

Yet Truman and Kennedy were negotiating with the public as well as the president and the press. Their gender ideologies were of interest throughout the United States and, in Jacqueline Kennedy's case, internationally. The descriptive representation provided by first ladies had political and governmental consequences for the presidential administrations in which they served. Jacqueline Kennedy never forgot that the male strategists within the Kennedy family had given her negative reviews as a prospective first lady. Strong believers in gender hierarchies, the Kennedys "thought that the American people's idea of a First Lady was Bess Truman—a nice, matronly, dowdy, Midwestern American mother—and that someone like Jackie would just turn people off."[48] It was a decidedly backhanded compliment to Truman and a statement that reportedly angered Jacqueline Kennedy, but there was a large segment of the public that agreed with its sentiments. Truman worried that the public would find her uninteresting, passive, even ignorant. Kennedy was told that she was exotic, un-American, distant, and incomprehensible. The strategies of descriptive representation that each practiced through their media relations were designed as much (or more) in response to these fears and concerns, as to express the women's own priorities and creativity.

There was no single strategy for media relations in the Hoover, Roosevelt, Truman, Eisenhower, and Kennedy administrations, nor were these first ladies unified in their descriptive representation. The contrasts may be the most important aspect of their representation, highlighting the range of options that existed for these presidents' wives in defining themselves publicly, even when there was some agreement on what constituted "appropriate" behavior. For the first lady who was willing to pay the cost of controversy, and whose president would accept the associated losses of political capital, there was even more leeway. Still, the key words are "cost" and "losses." Descriptive representation was a critically important task for the first ladies, and controlling the media's presentation of their gender role modeling was essential to performing this task well. Eleanor Roosevelt and Jacqueline Kennedy, both of whom were familiar with the demands confronting journalists, were among the most successful in having their voices heard and in advancing the presidents' messages—though the latter was not always their first priority. Lady Bird Johnson, the third modern first lady with a media background, set a new and enduring standard for the provision of descriptive representation by the president's wife.

Lady Bird Johnson: The First Lady as Communicator

Among Lady Bird Johnson's earliest decisions as first lady was her selection of Bess Abell as social secretary and Liz (Elizabeth) Carpenter as her press secretary and staff director. Together they revolutionized the representation provided by the first lady.

Lady Bird Johnson's descriptive representation was presented to the nation through a comprehensive media campaign: the first lady advertised and facilitated the successes of her husband's administration through travel, speechmaking, and networking. Yet she framed this participation in the public sphere as an extension of her private-sphere relationships, presenting herself as a loyal wife and downplaying her politics.

> I do prefer to spend my life with personal interests and friends. I am, however, propelled by a genuine concern in my husband's life into learning about the things he is trying to do and the people who imple-

ment them. . . . But the net of it is that I am a private person extended into public life somewhat because of the opportunities and the impelling call of my husband's jobs through the years. The aspect of the role one doesn't forget is that it all hinges upon the man you've married. My needs are groomed into helping him.[49]

Johnson did not challenge the separate-spheres ideal. Instead, as this quote reveals, she used, bent, and manipulated its standards, seeking to mask the extent of her participation in the public sphere.

Lady Bird Johnson followed the lead of her predecessors in preferring to interact with the press on her own terms, generally avoiding administration controversies and failures (such as the Vietnam War), while promoting successes (especially educational and environmental programs). But Lady Bird Johnson was the first of the modern presidents' wives to adopt a media strategy designed to secure support for the administration's agenda throughout the full presidential term. Her press relations were so extensive that they must be characterized as aggressive. Consider her travel during the presidential term. Of her seventy-four trips, sixty-five (approximately 88 percent) were independent of the president. Each itinerary was packed with visits to local officials and program sites, speeches, and receptions.[50] Johnson was almost continuously available to the press during these trips, sharing meals and staying in the same accommodations. Establishing herself as an advocate for the administration, Johnson participated extensively in the public sphere. Yet she was careful to present herself as a satellite wife. This was a finely tuned performance, which stepped across the gender boundaries of separate-spheres ideals.

In many ways, Lady Bird Johnson resembled Eleanor Roosevelt, but Johnson was not as controversial as Roosevelt, in large part because Johnson diffused concerns that she was ambitious in her own right.[51] In Carpenter's words, "Mrs. Roosevelt was an instigator, an innovator, willing to air a cause without her husband's endorsement. Mrs. Johnson was an implementer and translator of her husband and his purpose. . . . She was first and foremost, a wife."[52] Johnson published little until after she had left the White House. As much as she traveled, she limited her press and public appearances, and her speaking engagements were unremunerated. Her words were calm and measured, focused upon the needs and hopes of others. Though she sometimes seemed distant in her private life,[53] she was lauded for her public approachability. Returning from a four-day trip to the intermountain West with Lady Bird Johnson, Interior Secretary Stewart Udall, and more than

fifty local and national journalists, Douglass Cater, special assistant to the
president, submitted the following assessment to Lyndon Johnson:

> 1. Mrs. Johnson represents a political asset for the campaign which
> is unique in Presidential history. She is highly appealing and effective on
> the platform. She comes across as intelligent and knowledgeable and *un-*
> *like* Eleanor Roosevelt thoroughly feminine. She maintains grace under
> the most hectic conditions. Politicians and reporters alike felt she would
> be more sought after than the Vice Presidential nominee for many occa-
> sions. The consensus was that she should make a number of treks apart
> from you—that she could give the extra push in critical states, visit-
> ing communities that lie outside the presidential circuit.[54] [emphasis in
> original]

Cater's compliments are telling: "appealing and effective on the platform . . .
intelligent and knowledgeable . . . maintains grace under the most hectic
conditions." In addition to these affirmations, Cater emphasizes that Johnson
does not evidence the strongest negative: "*unlike* Eleanor Roosevelt thoroughly feminine." Johnson strategically drew constituents' and analysts' attention to her private-sphere qualities and relationships—the other-directed,
gracious, generous wife—alleviating many of the concerns raised by her
public-sphere commitments and activism.

In devising and performing her descriptive representation, Lady Bird
Johnson had strong staff support. Her press secretary and staff director, Liz
Carpenter, had been a journalist before and during her marriage, becoming
the co-owner of a Washington news service. Carpenter was also a past president of the Women's National Press Club and had longstanding relationships
with a wide network of journalists. She was well known to the Johnsons, having been a congressional constituent of the president's, then a family friend,
and finally a campaign worker and unpaid member of the vice president's
staff. As a wife and mother herself, Carpenter's own gender role modeling
mirrored the first lady's in blurring the boundaries between private and public
spheres. "There is something in the modern superwoman that wants to do
everything at once—bear children, talk to Congressmen, and even dictate
news stories from her hospital bed. . . . Our children seemed to thrive on it.
They grew up from toddlers through their teens knowing how to answer long
distance phone calls and get the information right. . . . They are bright, sharp
kids and some of the credit must go to what the psychologists call 'healthy
neglect.'"[55]

The women who staffed Carpenter's press office similarly embraced a gender ideology that respected women as political and media professionals. Carpenter's assistant, Simone Poulaine, detailed from the State Department, had a strong background in broadcast journalism, complementing the press secretary's print expertise. Poulaine framed photo opportunities that consistently earned the first lady well-placed, positive coverage. Marta Ross and Marcia Maddox, who performed whatever task they were assigned by Carpenter, were in their early twenties. They were apparently chosen for their confidence, raw talent, and connections.[56] Carpenter augmented her staff with a far-flung network of women party members, with the president's encouragement.[57] Though the first lady's office did draw upon the talents of men in the Johnson network and among the president's aides and the party, women provided most of the staff support. Their presence and performance magnified the first lady's descriptive representation.

The gender role modeling of the first lady and of her staff, and their political resourcefulness and strength, were especially evident in Lady Bird Johnson's 1964 whistle-stop train campaign trip. A four-day journey from Alexandria, Virginia, to New Orleans, Louisiana, the trip was intended to court white southerners alienated by the president's support for the 1964 Civil Rights Act. Mixing nostalgia for the past with appeals to the future, and proclaiming both responsiveness to southern interests and support for racial equality, the whistle stop gave the first lady an opportunity to speak about the economic, social, and ethical obligations of the region and the nation.

High aspirations notwithstanding, the trip was a logistical nightmare. Train cars had to be located, then redesigned to provide a speaking platform and interior reception areas, as well as sleeping and working accommodations for the staff and press corps. Official visitors required White House hospitality, and staff and press needed at least the basic comforts, but the train cars had no air conditioning and limited running water. A series of train companies had to be consulted about the route and the stops. Local, county, state, and national political figures had to be persuaded to ride with the first lady.[58]

This was the year in which the twenty-fourth amendment went into effect, banning poll taxes. It was the summer of the Mississippi Freedom Project; of the murders of volunteers James Chaney, Andrew Goodman, and Michael Schwerner; and of race riots in Harlem and Philadelphia. Yet the first lady insisted that race relations could be improved if whites met their constitutional obligation to end segregation. Racial equality, she maintained, was an economic imperative for whites and for blacks. In this appeal to conscience and to pocketbook, the first lady mixed inspirational statements and utilitarian calculations. Separate-spheres gender ideologies had always respected women as moral guardians and as homemakers; Lady Bird Johnson expanded those roles into the public sphere, seeking to mask her power as a political actor by aligning herself with historic images of women as conscientious caregivers and consumers.

In her whistle-stop speeches, the first lady repeatedly described herself as a woman of the South who was determined to do what was right. She stressed her patriotism, speaking deferentially even as she asserted her values. She leveraged southern legends and imagery against her opponents, arguing that her visions were true to history and promising for the future. Her first speech, delivered in Alexandria, Virginia, set the terms and the tone of her campaign outreach.

> I wanted to make this trip because I am proud of the South, and I am proud that I am part of the South.
>
> I love the South. I am fond of the old customs—of keeping up with your kinfolks. . . .
>
> I am even more proud of the new South. . . . There are so many advances in the South—in its economy, in its interest in the arts, in its progress in education. . . .
>
> I am proud of what the South has contributed to our national life. . . .
>
> Yet in recent times, we recognize the strain in the South from national life as a whole.
>
> I have shared with many of you the concern that has come with this strain. I share the irritation when unthinking people make snide jokes about "corn pone" and "rednecks" as if the history and tradition of our region could be dismissed with ridicule.
>
> None of this is right. None of this is good for the future of our country.
>
> I asked for this assignment for many reasons. This trip takes me not only to the queen-like cities of the South, but to the small towns and rural areas—I was born in such an area and I am at home there. . . .
>
> To me, as to you, the South is not a place of geography, but a place of the heart. And so, it is with great joy that I undertake what is—for me—in every sense, a journey of the heart.[59]

Independence and strength, vulnerability and empathy, shared southern lives and racial identities were the themes of Lady Bird Johnson's whistle-stop speeches and of her descriptive representation. It was a communications strategy that earned qualified support from the media.

National news outlets provided the whistle stop with more positive coverage than did local outlets. National reporters focused on the first lady as the story, accenting her talent for outreach and often criticizing her opposition.

> Reception of the First Lady in the larger towns of South Carolina and Georgia was lukewarm. Throughout the countryside the little towns produced large, cheering, and often heavily Negro turnouts when the Lady Bird Special train arrived.
>
> There was heckling in both states, but always in the urban areas and mostly from rather rude teenagers who booed indiscriminately from beneath their banners for Barry. The reaction of the adult Southerners reflected moderate enthusiasm warmed by personal response to the first lady.[60]

For reporters for southern media outlets, however, local people and politics were the story. Their reporting bluntly defended racial inequities and rejected the first lady's descriptive representation.

> Mrs. Lyndon B. Johnson has come and gone, but the effects of her visit to South Carolina may last for a long time—well beyond Nov. 3, in fact.
>
> The chief effect, as we see it, was to introduce a new note of bitterness and division in this state. South Carolinians are accustomed to the rough and tumble of politics. They like a good political fight. But the arrival of the Lady Bird Special seems to have produced a flush of anger in South Carolina.
>
> For their part, the Johnson-Humphrey supporters are furious that the public didn't act as though a queen had arrived. The Goldwater backers, on the other hand, are indignant that they should be asked to give royal treatment to a lady who is a straightout political campaigner for an administration they believe is wrecking the country.[61]

Just one month later, electoral results suggested that the trip was, at best, a qualified success. Three whistle-stop states cast their electoral votes for President Johnson: Virginia and Florida, both of which had voted for Republican Richard Nixon in 1960, and North Carolina. The other six whistle-stop states voted for challenger Barry Goldwater. The drop in Democratic support ranged from 7.2 (Louisiana) to 23.4 (Mississippi) points. That drop continued in 1968, when the candidacies of George Wallace and Curtis LeMay of the American Independent Party drew considerable support from all the whistle-stop states.

The whistle-stop trip did have a lasting impact on the first lady and her staff. This first lady would not confine herself to a narrow agenda. Johnson wanted to reconcile different regions and different races, and to demonstrate the importance of the president's agenda for everyone. In campaigning independently of the president and addressing a region hostile to the administration, the first lady established herself as a representative rather than a satellite. Even as Lady Bird Johnson drew upon enduring, separate-spheres conceptions of femininity to mask her autonomy and her individuality, she implicitly supported the rights-centered agenda of the emergent women's movement.

Ultimately, the first lady's stated purpose of generating popular and media support for the administration limited her ability to work for change. This first lady gave new expression to well-established priorities but seldom pushed the president to new commitments. As a result, she avoided Roosevelt's fate of being marginalized within her husband's administration, but she also sacrificed some of her own credibility. No longer apolitical or nonpartisan, the first lady was now associated with all the ethical ambiguities of political compromise, as was to be expected of a "straightout political campaigner."

This quandary was most evident in Lady Bird Johnson's response to the war in Vietnam. Like most of her predecessors, she seldom spoke about foreign policy. As anti-war demonstrations became larger and more frequent from 1965 onward, and as she encountered more protesters while traveling, she appeared genuinely confused and upset by their practices. When anti–civil rights protesters interrupted her speeches on the whistle stop, she made an appeal for civility. These tactics did not calm anti-war protesters, and the first lady gradually shifted her itineraries to less accessible sites. A bunker mentality surfaced among her staff as well. In a memo to the president, recounting the successes of the first lady on a 1966 trip, press secretary Liz Carpenter wrote, "There hasn't been one ugly sign—the only sign was 'Welcome!'"[62] To describe the protests as "ugly" rather than as partisan or policy-based made them more intimate—this was the first lady who committed herself to beautification, and who had stated, "Ugliness is bitterness."[63] Yet it also ignored the policy and political concerns that were motivating the demonstrators. It therefore revealed the limits of the first lady's abilities and credibility as a proactive descriptive representative.

PAT NIXON, BETTY FORD, AND ROSALYNN CARTER:
SCRUTINY AND CONFLICT

The changes discussed at the beginning of this chapter—social, economic, technological, political—accelerated and became more volatile throughout the Nixon, Ford, and Carter administrations. Anti-war and multiple civil rights movements forced enduring changes in policy networks, giving motive force to backlashes and culture wars. Debates about the Equal Rights Amendment (ERA) made this very evident. As successful as the ERA supporters and critics were in mobilizing their allies, they were arguably even more effective in mobilizing their opposition. Meanwhile, the credibility gaps in the Johnson administration paled in comparison to those generated by the covert military operations, campaign finance obfuscations, and Watergate cover-ups of the Nixon administration. Greater suspicion and a more adversarial relationship with the president became the norm among the press and the public.[64] This combination of gender-role conflicts and heightened scrutiny created extraordinary difficulties for Pat Ryan Nixon, Betty Ford, and Rosalynn Carter as descriptive representatives. Support for their gender role modeling became increasingly elusive and their failures were well publicized.

Biographical profiles of these three first ladies often address similar issues—especially their campaign roles and their ERA politics—while stressing the women's differences. Pat Nixon is presented as rigidly self-contained, lacking warmth and spontaneity. Her marriage, similarly, is described as cold and emotionless, and she is presented as marginalized within her husband's administration. Betty Ford's candor is variously celebrated and critiqued, sometimes viewed as a joyful responsiveness to the public and sometimes disdained as a product of what she would later acknowledge as drug and alcohol addiction.[65] Ford undeniably ignored constraints that had been accepted by first ladies for generations, speaking about her parenting difficulties, admitting personal weaknesses, disagreeing with her husband's policies. Rosalynn Carter is indicted as scripted and packaged, and as incomprehensibly complex. Her participation in presidential politics and in policy making led to fears that her influence would be too great. Too contained, too open, too powerful—hardly flattering, these profiles are critiques that undermine the first ladies as gender role models and as political actors. Taken together, they suggest the difficulties confronting the presidents' wives as descriptive representatives of women in the unpredictable and uncertain times of the late 1960s and the 1970s. The balancing of the president's message and the

first lady's voice would be subjected to constant, critical scrutiny throughout
these years.

President Nixon and Chief of Staff H. R. Haldeman rejected the Johnson-
Carpenter approach to media relations, though there was a strong communications operation within the White House Office. Pat Nixon's first independent policy-related travel came six months into her husband's first term.
Insisting to reporters that the trip had no "political connotations," the first
lady visited relatively small social service programs in Washington and Oregon. These included a literacy program that was losing its grant from the
Office of Economic Opportunity and a neighborhood center that housed an
anti-war organization, which led a protest during the first lady's visit. There
were no ceremonies or meetings with elected officials.[66] The most favorable
coverage came in the *Ladies' Home Journal,* three months later.

> The focus for this, Mrs. Nixon's first solo endeavor, was volunteer-
> ism, self-help at the local level. Despite its political motivation, the cho-
> sen theme was an inspired one. Volunteers are ordinary but beautiful
> people who labor without pay in various vineyards of humanity and sel-
> dom seek or gain the spotlight. By adopting them as her own, Pat Nixon
> went a step beyond Jacqueline Kennedy's cultural endeavors and even
> Lady Bird Johnson's worthy beautification mission. This First Lady had
> chosen a human theme. She had discovered the power of compassion,
> and its dynamism not only gave radiance to her role but also seemed to
> nourish her inner sense of involvement and adequacy. The spirit so long
> imprisoned seemed to stir and flutter before our eyes.
>   Critics claim that the volunteer emphasis is an effort to strengthen
> the Nixon doctrine of letting the private sector shoulder the bulk of so-
> cial responsibility: But even Great Society supporters will admit that
> volunteers at the community level can work wonders, provided there is
> essential funding.[67]

Even this endorsement, in a magazine not known for its partisanship, included political assessments. Perhaps because other first ladies had claimed to
be nonpolitical while immersing themselves in presidential politics, the press
did not allow Pat Nixon to mask her participation in the public sphere. Also
affecting press coverage were the anti-war protests. Time and again, the first
lady was attacked as a member of the administration, held accountable for its
policies. As the Portland protesters chanted, "Mrs. Nixon, trouble's mixin';
money to kill, against our will; people at home, denied their own; brothers

Pat (Thelma Catherine) Ryan Nixon reaching out to the little baton twirler who led her motorcade during a reelection campaign trip to Atlanta, October 12, 1972. This photograph visually summarizes Nixon's performance of representation. Through public correspondence, spontaneous conversations with White House tour groups, and public diplomacy, this first lady consistently stressed personal contact in building relationships with presidential constituents. Journalists, engaged in mass communication, maintained that this strategy limited Nixon's influence and effectiveness. Photo by the White House Photo Office. Provided by the Richard Nixon Library at College Park, Maryland.

in jail, denied their bail; this hex on you will all come true; we'll all say no, your kind will go."[68]

For reporters socialized to Lady Bird Johnson's descriptive representation, to her mix of first lady voice and presidential message, Pat Nixon was a disappointment. She spent up to four hours a day on her public correspondence, but those letters went to private individuals. She spontaneously led White House tours, randomly intercepting tourist groups and guiding them through the mansion. Again, just a few people were reading or hearing her words. With the first lady's travel limited, domestically and internationally, journalists had few opportunities to hear the first lady's voice, to evaluate her delivery of the president's message, or to assess her political abilities.[69] Accordingly, the press corps began to develop its own narratives. In January 1970, a front-page *New York Times* article by Nan Robertson concluded that Pat Nixon's influence had not spread beyond the White House.[70] Leaked memoranda suggested that even this influence was minimal, and the first lady's staff was being regularly chastised and judged inadequate by Chief of Staff H. R. Haldeman, who described the first lady as "a prop" in his diary.[71] As the president remarked in a televised interview, "Once I make a decision, she supports it."[72] And the first lady, in her turn, stated, "[A] man has a right to make his own decision about his career. A woman should support that decision."[73]

Though the president and his chief of staff had largely defined Pat Nixon's descriptive representation, they were not pleased with the resulting press coverage. Relations between the "East" and "West Wing" staff, particular the president's chief of staff and the first lady's press secretary were strained. Constance (Connie) Stuart, the second press secretary to the first lady, was widely considered Haldeman's choice for the post. She was also the first lady's staff director, expected to bring order to the first lady's office and to improve relations with the "West Wing," in addition to securing favorable media coverage.[74] Though Stuart improved press relations, the president and the chief of staff's insistence on hierarchical, top-down management contributed to continuing tensions. Similar experiences were had by Stuart's successor, Helen McCain Smith. There were only intermittent efforts to publicly present the first lady as a valued member of the administration, mostly during the reelection campaign. The administration was seldom successful in conveying this message.

In March 1971, for example, a seventy-five-minute presidential interview conducted by nine women journalists resulted in articles describing the chief executive as highly defensive. Reporters quoted the president as concluding, "any lady who is First Lady likes being First Lady. I don't care what they say. They like it." Nixon added, "The wife has to be the stronger partner of the two . . . she helps the man. She complements him by shoring him up." Though he claimed to have a partnership marriage, reporters understood the president to favor subordination. As one wrote, "The thesis is that a President needs a woman of character and strength behind him. He [President Nixon] said Mrs. Nixon 'is in that tradition.'"[75]

Ultimately, there was not enough evidence and not enough interaction with the press to dispel enduring perceptions of this first lady as an outsider within her marriage, within the White House, and within her husband's administration.[76] Subtleties in Pat Nixon's descriptive representation, conveyed through correspondence and public diplomacy, were lost. Though journalist Helen Thomas described her as "the warmest First Lady I covered and the one who loved people the most," Pat Nixon was ultimately stigmatized as "Plastic Pat"—brittle and artificial, resentful of those with economic and social advantages, stunted by a lack of autonomy and power.[77] Members of the women's rights movement saw in Pat Nixon, as a gender role model, the tragedy of what Betty Friedan had termed "the feminine mystique." The lack of opportunities for intellectual growth and adventure, coupled with her dependence on men, led to a loss of creativity and strength.

Because Betty Ford had focused on her family throughout Gerald Ford's legislative career, many expected that she would follow Pat Nixon's lead in descriptive representation, with gender role modeling that presented the submissive satellite wife.[78] Instead, Ford publicly stated—and the president acknowledged—that she regularly lobbied her husband on behalf of women's appointments and other "women's issues."[79] This self-depiction as a political actor drew press attention and public controversy.[80] When Ford also publicized her policy disagreements with the president, some believed that the first lady threatened her husband's election. Phyllis Schlafly was mobilizing a grassroots movement that would defeat the ERA; Ronald Reagan was building the conservative coalition that would make him a formidable adversary in the 1976 primaries and a successful candidate in 1980; and Betty Ford was upholding an unqualified pro-choice position on reproductive rights and recommending the legalization of marijuana. Partisan disagreements were exacerbated by her gender role modeling as an independent, activist woman in the public sphere, though one who was intensely family oriented. Her descriptive representation was arguably more resonant with the Democratic than the Republican Party.[81]

The first lady's descriptive representation was perhaps most dramatically displayed during her *60 Minutes* interview in 1975. In addition to describing *Roe* v. *Wade* as a "great, great decision" and reiterating her arguments for legalizing marijuana, Ford delivered what many considered an endorsement of premarital sex.

> Safer: You've also talked about the young people living together before they've married.
>
> Ford: Well, they are, aren't they?
>
> Safer: Indeed, they are. Well, what if Susan Ford came to you and said, "Mother, I'm having an affair."
>
> Ford: Well, I wouldn't be surprised. I think she's a perfectly normal human being like all young girls, if she wanted to continue and I would certainly counsel and advise her on the subject, and I'd want to know pretty much about the young man that she was planning to have the affair with; whether it was a worthwhile encounter or whether it was going to be one of those—She's pretty young to start affairs.

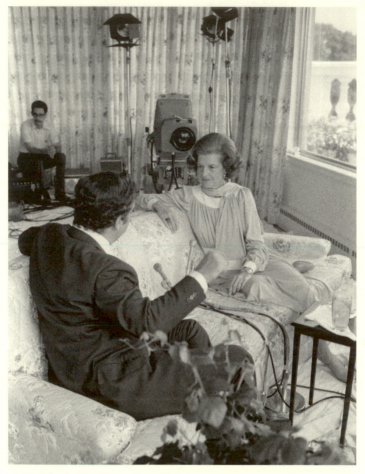

Betty (Elizabeth) Bloomer Ford taping her *60 Minutes* interview with
Morley Safer in the White House Solarium, July 21, 1975. The first lady's
easy posture suggests that her press secretary correctly anticipated that the
60 Minutes format, and Safer's own demeanor, would provide Ford with
the opportunity to present herself as poised and confident. The content of
the interview, however, drew significant criticism from conservatives in the
Republican base. Ford's descriptive and substantive representation routinely
placed her in the midst of the culture wars of the 1970s. Her claim that the
women's rights movement was as important to women in the private sphere
as to women in the public sphere earned little support. Photo by Ricardo
Thomas. Provided by the Gerald R. Ford Library, Ann Arbor, Michigan.

Safer: But, nevertheless, old enough—

Ford: Oh, yes, she's a big girl.

Safer: I mean would it surprise you, though, given the way the—
the way you brought these kids up, and the President brought them up,
would it surprise you if that happened?

Ford: No, I think there's a complete freedom among the young people now. And in some cases, I'm not so sure that, perhaps, there would be less divorce.[82]

The public response was immediate, with 8,579 critical letters (62.2 percent of the total) arriving over the next three months. Just 5,208 supportive letters (37.8 percent of the total) were received, most after the first lady's press secretary, Sheila Rabb Weidenfeld, mobilized women's movement networks. Critics castigated Ford for corrupting American morality, emasculating her husband, and undermining the Republican Party. Her words, they argued, gave conservatives a reason to vote against her husband. Supportive letter writers actually reinforced this view, stating that they wished the president shared the first lady's positions so that they could vote for him.[83]

Not surprisingly, Ford's independence did not bring her influence within the administration. Instead, she was often silenced. Though she participated in the campaign, her appearances were comparatively limited.[84] Ford was not so much refashioned as a satellite wife as she was removed from public life.

Betty Ford's openness with the press was a consciously chosen strategy, not merely an ad hoc practice. It was an expression of her commitment, shared with her husband, to make a clear break with the politics of the Nixon administration. As Betty Ford remarked to Helen Thomas, "I know I can't lie."[85] But her voice was about more than truth telling. Pat Nixon had been the submissive and obedient wife; Betty Ford was the assertive and activist wife. The 1975 Homemaking and Identity Conference provided her with an opportunity to showcase these qualities and to extend an olive branch to those who saw her feminism as dismissive of women whose lives were centered in the private sphere.

Let's face it—being a homemaker *is* a *profession*.

And just as a career woman finds an identity through her job, the homemaker needs to find that same sense of awareness—that same sense of self—through her job. . . .

And this is exactly why the subject of equal rights for women is every bit as important to the homemaker as to the "career" woman.

I'm in favor of the equal rights amendment. This is not only equal pay for equal work, but because I feel every woman should have the right to decide the direction of her life.

Whether a woman chooses a career in the home or outside the home, what is important is that she make that decision herself—without any pressures to restrict her choice. . . .

So what's all this about liberated women being career women?? Anyone who feels good about what she's doing in the home should have the same sense of liberation.

I think it all comes with this freedom of choice. And I hope that with the new emphasis on freedom of choice, the respect and stature homemakers deserve will be recognized.[86]

In this speech and many others, Ford presented women as united in their common need for self-awareness and self-realization, regardless of whether their lives were spent in the private or the public sphere. For women in the women's movement and in the Democratic Party, that made her descriptive representation appealing. Conservative women, however, found her less persuasive.[87] For these voters, some of whom expressed their views in letters to the first lady following her *60 Minutes* interview, Ford's descriptive representation was morally and politically unacceptable.

Given the endorsements that Ford's descriptive representation did receive from the women's movement and the Democratic Party, Rosalynn Carter's campaign promise to be a policy activist appeared strategically necessary. Yet Carter was careful to nuance her claims to independence and influence, identifying herself as a traditional military and southern wife. Though she sometimes reiterated or even clarified the president's message, she did not publicly disagree with her husband. In the White House, she and her staff referred to her attendance at meetings with the president and the cabinet as "learning" opportunities. Her advocacy on behalf of the ERA was measured.[88] As the term progressed, however, her work as honorary chair of the presidential commission on mental health-care reform, her continuing participation in presidential decision making, and then her extensive travel for the reelection campaign suggested that she was as much entrepreneur as wife.[89] These perceived shifts in her descriptive representation were evident in her media coverage, which changed dramatically across the presidential term. Initially dismissed as lacking influence, she was eventually challenged as too powerful.

Rosalynn Carter wanted the media to focus on her policy and political work so that she could effect tangible, measureable change—the passage of new laws, the provision of increased funding, the promulgation of rules to ensure full implementation. As would Hillary Rodham Clinton, Carter entered the White House expecting to express her descriptive representation through her substantive representation. Whether serving as the honorary chair of a presidential commission advancing mental health-care reform, leading a del-

egation to refugee camps along the border of Thailand and Cambodia, or recruiting volunteers for urban development programs, she measured success
empirically.

Rosalynn Carter had several advantages in seeking media coverage for
her descriptive representation. During the presidential transition, extensive
studies of the White House Office, including the first lady's staff, capitalized on the experience and wisdom of past administrations.[90] Reforms were
instituted to provide the first lady with a seasoned staff and to lessen tensions between the first lady's office and other units in the White House Office. Relations between the first lady and the press had stabilized somewhat,
and Betty Ford had not generated unduly high expectations of accessibility.
Rosalynn Carter presented what she believed to be a limited agenda, centered
on mental health-care reform, care for the aging, and volunteerism.[91] She was
convinced that her politics would make good copy. What Carter failed to
realize, or perhaps to consider, was that her gender role modeling would
generate criticism from all sides as the culture wars escalated. A woman who
claimed to be a traditional wife and to wield influence in the White House
was viewed by some as dependent upon her husband, by others as lacking accountability, and by still others as doing too little—or too much.[92]

Rosalynn Carter's early gender role modeling, however, met with almost
consistently negative reviews in the media.[93] In June 1978, a lengthy *Washington Post* article presented her as lacking personal strength, subsumed by
her husband's career, and a victim of White House image makers.

> As late as three weeks ago members of Carter's staff fed a story to the
> *New York Times* saying that she was "even more influential than Eleanor
> Roosevelt."
> . . . Rosalynn Carter . . . trying to help out and do the right thing,
> went along with it. She tried to act serious, tough, and determined, like
> the steel magnolia image that had been sold when, in fact, she was a
> wife and mother dedicated to her family, only unsure of herself as a
> politician.
> . . . What toughness can be found in her character is simply her
> natural fierce protectiveness of her family against any outside threat, in-
> cluding those to her husband's political career.

Also included were negative statements from Gloria Steinem—"there is no
independent thought"—and unfavorable comparisons to first ladies Jacqueline Kennedy and Lady Bird Johnson, and second lady Joan Mondale.[94]

Within two years, Rosalynn Carter had left behind these complaints and was being criticized for her political strength.

> A fluid blend of private life, public policy and pure politics has typi-
> fied Rosalynn Smith Carter's tenure in the White House—a baptism by
> total immersion from which she has emerged as probably the most in-
> fluential First Lady of modern times. As wife and mother she has stub-
> bornly protected her family from the merely curious; as First Hostess
> she has presided over ceremonies of state with plainspun aplomb. And
> although Eleanor Roosevelt loomed larger in the public eye and Edith
> Wilson more nearly controlled the executive branch for a short time,
> Mrs. Carter, 52, is an unmistakably full-fledged partner in her husband's
> earnest enterprise at the head of government. She is his confidante,
> sounding board, and trusted adviser, his surrogate before the nation and
> the world. . . . "She's more ambitious, tougher and less forgiving than
> Jimmy—everything that's characteristic of a politician," says one who
> knows her well.[95]

Though the article proceeded to defend ambition, toughness, and intol-
erance as requisite to success, these were not qualities that had previously
earned endorsements for first ladies. Rosalynn Carter's complexity, her "fluid
blend of private life, public policy and pure politics," did not win unqualified
support. In this piece, and in many others during the reelection campaign,[96]
the first lady's descriptive representation was portrayed as both threatening
and promising.

Carter herself was at varying points frustrated, bewildered, and angered
by her coverage. The media profiles, she felt, did not accurately depict her
work, her roles, or her contributions. Carter did her best to resolve the contradictions that seemed to constrain her coverage, but her blurring of private-
and public-sphere boundaries, her commitment to supporting her husband
and securing independence for herself, was not readily understood. As much
was evident in a favorable 1977 *New York Times* article, which followed Carter
through a dedication ceremony for a cruise-ship passenger terminal in New
Orleans to an interview on the flight back to Washington.

> Each of the speakers at the ceremony yesterday wrestled with the
> same problem of defining Mrs. Carter's role, trying to balance two essen-
> tially incompatible concepts: The First Lady as a stand-in for the Presi-
> dent and the First Lady as a distinguished guest in her own right, an
> influential member of the White House inner circle. . . .

In an interview later, as she flew back to Washington late yesterday afternoon, she implicitly denied that any contradiction existed, saying that "to me, I've always been able to do the things that are important to me and always helped Jimmy with the things that are important for him."[97]

By the reelection campaign, the first lady and her press secretary had almost come to expect press coverage that would offer "either/or" assessments of her gender role modeling: "'*It's really interesting,*' she [Rosalynn Carter] muses from across the aisle [to her press secretary], '*how I've gone from having a fuzzy image to being so powerful that I'm being muzzled by the President's men. You know as well as I know that I've done nothing differently from the day I walked into the White House.*'"[98]

Many reporters blamed Mary Finch Hoyt, Rosalynn Carter's press secretary, for the poor coverage. Hoyt was characterized as rejecting opportunities for "'natural' coverage in women's pages," as providing only a "fuzzy image" for the first lady, and as ignoring press deadlines.[99] Similar charges had been directed at press secretaries for Pat Nixon and Betty Ford, and their sheer consistency argues that deeper forces were at work.[100] Hoyt argued as much.

> Nobody has figured out what the public wants or expects from a president's wife. There's certainly no reason not to believe that Americans want to admire and respect, even love, their First Lady. Public opinion polls show that they do. For some, she is a model to emulate; for others, a sort of pen pal; and for many, she's a conduit to the "they" who control their lives and to the "he" who controls the "they." But even though Rosalynn is considered by many to be his closest adviser, she continues to be dismissed by those who believe a woman cannot claim worth or fulfillment just because she happens to be another person's mate. Moreover, because of the unusually equitable husband-and-wife relationship forged between the Carters over three decades, there is a concern that she might feel qualified to shape policy or exert power that she has not been elected to wield. And curiously, surrounded by an extended family which offers a support system that allows her to work a professional six-to-eight hour day, she's faulted not only for being too involved in too many projects for too much of the time, but for leaning on her family too much.[101]

Hoyt's defense of the first lady was doubtless somewhat self-interested, but her assertions resonate with scholarly analyses identifying a series of double binds confronting women in the public sphere. As Kathleen Hall

Jamieson has explained, double binds have their origins in theology, biology, and law.[102] Among those constraining the first ladies are the following:

- Women who speak out are immodest and will be shamed, while women who are silent will be ignored or dismissed.
- Women are subordinate whether they claim to be different from men or the same.
- Women who are considered feminine will be judged incompetent, and women who are competent, unfeminine.[103]

Though close media scrutiny affects all women in leadership positions, particularly those in elected office, the first lady's status as a gender role model means that these no-win rules are particularly influential. And yet, as gender politics scholars have stressed, these constraints are powerful because they are so often unnoticed—they are the unconsidered presumptions that slant perceptions, the unexamined norms that inform judgment.[104] As a descriptive representative, Rosalynn Carter forced a measure of reflection on the society: she claimed private- and public-sphere roles, responsibilities, and opportunities for women—wife and political actor, loyal supporter and decision maker, mother and policy entrepreneur. She named and confronted the reluctance of the Washington community and the wider society to allow a woman to be so complex in her relationships and so assertive in her politics. Carter herself did not seem to understand the extraordinary character of her descriptive representation. As she stated in interviews and reiterated in her memoir, she was simply following an example set for her by previous generations. The women in her family had always worked.

There were significant differences in the descriptive representation and media relations of Pat Nixon, Betty Ford, and Rosalynn Carter. Yet there were also underlying commonalities in the public challenges directed at their descriptive representation. With gender roles disputed, and an equal rights amendment awaiting ratification, it was hardly surprising that these first ladies found themselves periodically caught between contrasting standards of behavior. How much should a president's wife participate in the public sphere? How should she participate? How should she speak of her self, her marriage, her husband? How should she describe her roles and work as first lady? What should be her priorities? How should she act on those priorities?

For descriptive representation to secure support rather than engender criticism, a first lady needed to harmonize her voice and the president's message, reconcile polarized visions of women's gender roles, and educate the public to the constraints on her gender role modeling. The battle lines were now clearly drawn between those who endorsed separate spheres and those who insisted upon rights and equality. Finding a way to build consensus between these opposing ideologies would continue to be the principal challenge confronting the first ladies.

FROM NANCY REAGAN TO MICHELLE OBAMA:
OPPOSITION, SCANDAL, NEGOTIATION

The 1990 Wellesley College commencement generated a national debate about the first lady's descriptive representation when 150 seniors signed a petition that expressed disappointment and outrage at inviting Barbara Pierce Bush to deliver an address. "To honor Barbara Bush as a commencement speaker is to honor a woman who has gained recognition through the achievements of her husband. . . . [W]e propose extending an invitation to an additional guest speaker who would more aptly reflect the self-affirming qualities of a Wellesley graduate."[105] Yet Bush had made significant contributions to her husband's career and administration. In an ironic twist, her self-depiction and descriptive representation as a satellite wife, crafted to avoid controversy and garner public support, was generating conflict over women's gender roles and relationships.[106]

A speech also created difficulties for Laura Welch Bush, specifically her radio address defending U.S. military action in Afghanistan as a means of securing human rights for Afghan women. "The brutal oppression of women is a central goal of the terrorists. . . . The fight against terrorism is also a fight for the rights and dignity of women."[107] Many found the speech contradictory at best. A first lady and an administration who had not previously seemed to value women's rights or human rights was now claiming to have gone to war on their behalf. Often, this was considered a demeaning rationalization.[108]

Barbara Bush was accused of sacrificing her self to her husband's career. Laura Bush was viewed as having compromised her integrity for her husband's policies. And these were the first ladies whose approval ratings were generally high.

The political changes that extended from the 1980s and 1990s into the twenty-first century had profound consequences for the first ladies. Partisan polarization and a conservative backlash in the 1980s was followed by a

Laura Welch Bush with luncheon guests at Sheikha Fatima's Sea Palace in Abu Dhabi, United Arab Emirates, October 22, 2007. The administration identified the first lady as an emissary to women throughout the Mideast, to voice support for women's rights. In this photograph, however, the contradictions and difficulties of such descriptive representation are very evident. The clothing of the women dominates the portrait and showcases the contrasting definitions of gender that prevail in the women's cultures. As a result, a portrait that is meant to show the first lady at the center of change in the Middle East instead raises questions about the persuasiveness, even the relevance, of her gender role modeling. Official White House photo by Shealah Craighead. Posted at www.whitehouse.gov in 2007.

so-called Year of the Woman election in 1992 and a Republican revolution in 1994. The Republican Party made the most of its narrow partisan advantage by sustaining strong discipline. When Democrats were again in the majority in the House, late in the George W. Bush administration, conservative Democrats reemerged as a critical swing vote. Meanwhile, the postmodern women's movement was building, its attention focused on women's diversity. Embracing intersectionality, these feminists directly challenged the social conservatives' endorsement of gender hierarchies. First ladies found it even more difficult to win the support of both their party's base and its more moderate supporters through their descriptive representation.

This shared struggle was often hidden by the more obvious contrasts among the first ladies' descriptive representation. Nancy Davis Reagan, Barbara Bush, Hillary Rodham Clinton, Laura Bush, and Michelle Obama expressed very different gender ideologies and modeled very different gender roles for women. Hillary Rodham Clinton and Laura Bush manifested the greatest differences, though their race, religion, age, education, income, and family status were apparently similar. In actuality, Rodham Clinton, Bush, and Obama exemplified the postmodern contention that the intersectionality of multiple identities, experiences, and ideologies in women's lives precluded identifying a single essential woman—the cultural everywoman ideal was not merely challenged, it was wholly rejected.

Hillary Rodham Clinton was a committed and highly partisan participant in the public sphere, before, during, and after her years in the White House. Like Rosalynn Carter, she had campaigned extensively and independently for her husband's election to the presidency. Also like Rosalynn Carter, Rodham Clinton was determined to secure tangible policy change; both first ladies intertwined their descriptive and substantive representation. Like Jimmy Carter, Bill Clinton as a candidate and as a president repeatedly stated that Rodham Clinton's political expertise made her an invaluable resource. In brief, Hillary Rodham Clinton wanted to be and was valued as an effective policy entrepreneur. This gender role modeling was entirely congruent with the priorities of the women's rights movement, which had surged just as Rodham Clinton had come of age politically. Equal rights as the means to equal opportunities, individualism and excellence within established professional networks, activism that broadened the political agenda without overturning the political system were the hallmarks of that movement and of this first lady's descriptive representation.

Hillary Rodham Clinton pushed her gender role modeling further than other policy-oriented first ladies when she devoted herself to fulfilling a critical presidential campaign promise, health-care reform. As chair of the President's Task Force on National Health Care Reform, Rodham Clinton led an organization-cum-network that included senior members of the Executive Office of the President—including the White House Office—and cabinet officers. Including support staff, an estimated three hundred to four hundred individuals participated in or contributed to the work of the task force, at a cost to taxpayers of $13.8 million, as estimated by the General Accounting Office.[109] Eleanor Roosevelt had, also, held a formal appointment in her husband's administration, but she was never given a leadership position to equal Rodham Clinton's. Lady Bird Johnson's work—confronting the electoral significance of civil rights legislation, showcasing the success and appeal of domestic initiatives—drew considerable public attention, but in the context of generating support for the president. Rosalynn Carter did hold a leadership post and did claim the policy changes as her own, but the issue of mental health care was not on the presidential agenda. The descriptive representation provided by Hillary Rodham Clinton was that of the woman as executive—commanding, compelling, and comprehensive in her thinking and in her decision making.

When she was named to chair the president's health-care reform task force, Rodham Clinton's support seemed to be on the rise. Several national polls indicated that 58 to 59 percent of respondents felt that this was an "appropriate" role for the first lady.[110] Sustaining these polling numbers, however, became difficult. Having had an adversarial relationship with the press throughout the presidential campaign, Rodham Clinton was reluctant to reach out through interviews and press conferences.[111] She wanted the media to focus on the passage and implementation of her policies, but those innovations took time to unfold. Waiting, the press turned to other stories and issues, and the first lady lost the opportunity to control the framing of her representation. When the task force fell behind schedule and there were no initiatives to report, there were problems, tragedies, and scandals to cover.[112] Rodham Clinton's credibility was subsequently undermined by a series of investigations. Her role in firing the White House travel office staff, her actions after learning of Deputy White House Counsel Vince Foster's suicide, and the continuing investigations into her commodities and Whitewater investments suggested that the first lady was corrupt and dangerous, unethical at best. Her approval ratings dropped. In October 1993, 36 percent of respondents to a Harris poll thought she had done an "excellent" job "in developing and presenting the president's health plan" and an additional 38 percent described her performance as "pretty good." By July 1994, just 18 percent rated her work as "excellent," though 36 percent continued to say "pretty good."[113]

By late 1994, legislative proposals for health-care reform were stalemated; in November the White House announced that the first lady was no longer leading the task force.[114] Yet her favorability ratings continued to drop until June 1996, when a CBS/*New York Times* poll recorded her favorability rating at 29 percent, her unfavorability rating at 38 percent. A reversal in this trend was attributed to the investigations that revealed the president's adultery, and to public perceptions of the first lady as a faithful wife betrayed by a philandering husband. By 1998, Rodham Clinton's favorability rating was up, rivaling her numbers from the early weeks of the administration.[115]

As her numbers continued to drop in 1994 and 1995, however, Rodham Clinton was recrafting her descriptive representation. Shifting her policy focus to international relations, she delivered a series of speeches on women's rights as human rights. In 1995, she earned favorable international media coverage for her remarks at the plenary session of the United Nation's Fourth

World Conference on Women in Beijing.[116] The woman who had previously argued for comprehensive policy change behind closed doors and before Congress now stepped before an international audience.

Then, in 1998, appearing on the *Today* show as momentum gathered for the president's impeachment, Rodham Clinton asserted that her husband was the victim of a "right-wing conspiracy."[117] The first lady used a live interview, conducted in a "soft news" format, to express her partisanship and loyalty, taking advantage of the media's mass communication resources while avoiding intermediary frames. The contrast with her media strategies in regard to health-care was striking—Rodham Clinton was now using the media to amplify her voice.

A final example of Rodham Clinton's use of the media to convey her descriptive (and her substantive) representation was her 2000 campaign for the U.S. Senate. The campaign became famous for its "listening sessions," which were held throughout the state. The campaign also became infamous for its media relations. Rodham Clinton had learned the importance of courting the public and she was determined to soften the media's impact on the relationships that she was building. Her status as first lady, the constraints imposed by the Secret Service, and the sheer number of journalists covering the campaign did limit her availability. But these were contributing rather than determining factors. Reporters ultimately concluded that Rodham Clinton's White House experience had left her with an "incredible chemical aversion to self-revelation on any level," which resulted in constrained campaign press relations.[118] Though access did improve somewhat as the campaign progressed, Rodham Clinton resisted unguarded or spontaneous exchanges, preferring that more carefully crafted statements and events reveal her gender and partisan ideologies.

Throughout Rodham Clinton's eight years as first lady, her descriptive representation remained focused upon her leadership and her individuality. Even when she spoke on behalf of the president, she spoke with her voice. She softened her commanding style and incorporated an element of persuasiveness into her delivery in the second term, but she remained her own spokesperson and resisted media interventions that would limit her autonomy. Yet she did become more willing to use the media, as evidenced by her 1998 *Today* interview. Rodham Clinton focused effort and energy on her representation, and she was determined to maintain control over those relationships, the interpretive power of the media notwithstanding.

Laura Bush did not experience the volatile swings in public approval that Hillary Rodham Clinton had, largely because she did not present herself as an influential member of her husband's administration. In this regard, she was similar to her mother-in-law. Though Barbara Bush was famous for her forceful leadership during the campaigns and among her own staff, she publicly distanced herself from presidential decision making. This self-effacement freed her to exercise influence on a regular, if strategic, basis. Laura Bush had her own self-deprecating statements, which intentionally minimized her influence in her marriage and in politics. Her declaration—"I read, I smoke, and I admire"—offered in response to a question from her in-laws about what she contributed to her marriage—became, to quote Maureen Dowd, "legendary."[119] Yet there is evidence that her claims to be a satellite wife were more accurate than those of Barbara Bush. Though Laura Bush was credited with mitigating some of her husband's stances or counseling him on personnel matters, this was usually done in private.[120] Her influence was acknowledged by her husband in press interviews but rarely claimed by the first lady. Instead, the president did so: "I'll tell you this: She's not a shrinking violet. She doesn't get mad; she gets pointed. If I do something that needs to be toned down, she'll tell me."[121] When Laura Bush did grant an interview, as during the 2004 reelection campaign, her doing so was news in itself.[122]

There has been considerable disagreement about Laura Bush's descriptive representation. Journalists, analysts, and academics variously identify her as a social conservative, an antifeminist, and a postfeminist.[123] In other words, she has been perceived as embracing gender hierarchies that reserve the public sphere to men, as opposing women-centered initiatives, and as maintaining that women have achieved equality with men. Mixed messages can be expected of first ladies, given that they are expected to sustain the loyalty of the party base *and* win over unaffiliated and moderate voters. For Laura Bush, the mixed messages were virtually inevitable. She needed to reach out to the "religious right" (social conservatives) and to those who embraced laissez-faire market arrangements (economic conservatives), while distancing herself from liberal feminists and maintaining her commitment to such constitutional ideals as equal rights. As the president and vice president became polarizing forces, she was assigned greater responsibility for reaching out to moderates.[124] Still, this first lady was notable for the leeway that she reserved for herself. She did not follow the lead set by her immediate predecessors, each of whom had been active in their husbands' administrations as political advisors of one sort or another. Her descriptive representation was instead centered upon her self and her more personal relationship with the president.

Laura Bush presented herself as a reflective facilitator rather than as a commanding leader.[125] When she hosted White House conferences and summits, she modeled listening, sat in the front row, and concentrated on the speakers' words. As *Washington Post* reporter Ann Gerhart concluded,

> She learns by listening quietly. Rather than engaging others in a back-and-forth discussion, she needs a period of introspection to think through what she has heard. On top of that, she simply doesn't possess the dynamism to electrify a gathering, nor does she have any interest in doing so. And, as she did with her husband over and over again, she refuses to take any credit for what she might have accomplished by spending her personal capital as first lady. This is as startling as it is refreshing in Washington, a city where people fall over each other to take credit for things they didn't do. But it also diminishes her effectiveness. Quiet isn't sexy in a quick-cut, sound-bite, twenty-four-hour-news-cycle political culture. That's not fair, but it's reality.[126]

The description that Gerhart provides summarizes not only her reporting, but much of the coverage that Bush received.

Laura Bush consistently described herself as dedicated and devoted to others. She was a loving wife and mother, a thoughtful professional with expertise in child development and library science. She made it clear that politics was her husband's career, even as she campaigned extensively for congressional candidates. In her stump speeches, for the midterm and the presidential reelection campaigns, she referred to politics as defining her relationship with her husband, but not as defining herself.

> George and I first traveled together in 1978. He ran for Congress in West Texas, which was our home district. We had both grown up in Midland, Texas, together. It was quite a different campaign, needless to say. He—we drove together in his Oldsmobile Cutlass. And he was the person behind the wheel. And we drove up and down the panhandle of West Texas from Midland on the south to Hereford, Texas, on the north. Believe me, you learn a lot about your husband when you spend that much time in a car with him. (Laughter.) By the end of the campaign, he'd even convinced me to vote for him. This time, I don't need any convincing. (Applause.)[127]

> When your spouse is in politics, you're involved whether you want to be or not. (Laughter.) And we know that the politicians who do the very best are the ones whose families stand with them and are with them all the time.[128]

In each of these statements, there is a sense of separation between Bush and her husband, between Bush and politics. She tells the listener that she thinks and assesses—she "learn[s]"—so her judgments can be trusted. She also commits to being fully present and supportive of her husband. Her own preferences are set aside—"you're involved whether you want to be or not"—signaling that she is making a sacrifice, not acting on personal ambitions.

A satellite wife reflects and magnifies the attributes of her husband, setting herself aside on his behalf. As a first lady, Laura Bush fulfilled this definition, revealing more about her husband than about herself. Moreover, she dedicated herself to presenting her husband as a commanding and effective president: "September 11th was the defining moment for all of us. We'll never forget the bravery of our fellow Americans or the spirit of unity that spread over our country. And since that fateful day, I've watched as the President's leadership has not only made our world safer, but has also made people's lives better."[129] With this statement—delivered in a speech supporting a Republican congressional candidate—Laura Bush positioned herself as the observant insider, sharing her experiences in order to gain the voter's support. There is no sense that she inserted herself in presidential decision- or policy-making processes—she "watched." Here again Bush takes care to distance herself from the political process, presenting this as grounds for voters to trust and act upon her endorsements.

Reporters for national newspapers and magazines tended to view Bush's reflective advocacy with resignation, occasionally sliding into faint approval, as seen in Gerhart's statement above. When the first lady was more assertive, however, the coverage became less accepting and more skeptical. Then, reporters implied that Bush had adopted a false persona, and called her original and then-current gender role modeling into question.

These frames were not subtle. As other first ladies had learned, media coverage of the first lady's descriptive representation were routinely unequivocal. In a *People* cover story the week after the presidential inauguration, for example, Bush was presented to the nation as an "unpretentious Midland [Texas] girl." There were the statements that cautioned against seeing her as a "Stepford wife," that said Laura Bush was "the iron rod at her husband's back," and that predicted she would engage in policy making as a first lady. On balance, however, the article stressed her "traditional 1950s persona" and indicated that Bush saw her gender role as being centered in the private sphere, giving deference to her husband's power in the public sphere.[130]

> The new First Lady likes Irish singer Van Morrison and salt-rimmed margaritas on the rocks but is also a self-described introvert who, she

says, is "interested in politics because my husband is involved in politics."
She holds a graduate degree in library science but has not yet mastered
the computer. And when her husband met recently with National Security Advisor Condoleezza Rice and Dick Cheney at the Bush's 1,600-acre
ranch in Crawford, Texas, she retreated to the kitchen to whip up a
batch of chili. In short, as her husband, George W., 54, once said, "I
have the best wife for the line of work that I'm in. She doesn't try to steal
the limelight."[131]

This summarization suggests that the first lady is incompetent, not merely
bland. She lacks interests of her own, cannot access a principal resource of
the information age, "retreat[s]" to the kitchen, and "doesn't try" to assert
herself. Even her husband's endorsement is qualified, since he seems to imply
that if he entered a different "line of work," he would need a different wife.

Reporters dutifully recorded that Bush "bristle[d]" at the 1950s references, but further suggestions that the first lady was forceful were confined
largely to campaign coverage.[132] Those newspaper articles included "Go-
Along First Lady Shows She Can Go It Alone" and "The First Lady's Influence Is Starting to Reveal Itself."[133]

By 2005 Laura Bush was again being characterized as the consoler-in-
chief, as she had been described following the September 11th attacks four
years earlier.[134] Appearing in a Hurricane Katrina–focused episode of *Extreme Makeover: Home Edition,* she was praised by the executive producer:
"[W]hile we're certainly a nonpartisan show, I don't think she was there as a
politician or a politician's wife or even as the first lady. I think she was there
as someone who cares."[135] This statement encapsulates the problematic character of Laura Bush's descriptive representation as it was communicated by
the mass media. She was presented as other-directed, thoughtful, and caring.
By taking these private-sphere values into the public sphere, she provided
guidance and reassurance to the wider society. The most favorable coverage
depicted her as emotionally invested and insightful. As seen above, however, the least favorable presented Bush as passive and inadequate. This was
a well-rehearsed debate that applied more generally to judgments about the
separate-spheres ideology, as providing and protecting a sphere of influence
for women that was suited to their emotional and intellectual talents, or as
confining women to a limited set of opportunities for developing their abilities and realizing their potential.

Laura Bush seemed to endorse the gender ideology of the social conservatives among the Republican base, valuing the private sphere and self-
regulating her participation in the public sphere. Hillary Rodham Clinton

rejected the gender ideology of the separate spheres, as a first lady and as a U.S. senator, and later as secretary of state. Bush "watched" while Rodham Clinton led. The contrast in their descriptive representation and their media coverage was extraordinary. With Bush serving as first lady immediately after Rodham Clinton, it was also inescapable.

Michelle Obama is a generation younger than Rodham Clinton or Laura Bush, having come of political age after the women's rights movement had peaked and after ERA battles had quieted. Obama instead confronted the conservative backlash of the 1980s as a college and law school student, and as a young attorney and professional in the not-for-profit sector. As a first lady, her descriptive representation incorporated separate spheres and women's rights ideals, while holding to a black feminist gender ideology. In keeping with that worldview, she stressed the importance of self-definition: Obama has declared herself "mom-in-chief," insisted that women should value their health and well-being, and expressed a sense of pride in her identity as an African American woman.[136] To ensure that these values and judgments were accurately conveyed, she has made use of an extraordinary array of media outlets, while imposing significant constraints on her coverage.

Two years into her tenure as first lady, as this book was being written, Obama has made her role as "mom-in-chief" the hallmark of her descriptive representation, and often, of her substantive representation. It is a title that she has earned, her husband's career having caused her to effectively be a single parent at several points in her daughters' lives. But it is also a title that resonates well with separate-spheres adherents. This self-reference calls to mind Mamie Eisenhower's insistence that she was in charge of the home and the family. It is that echo that variously reassures, concerns, and bewilders observers. There is reassurance for those who feared the changes that Obama might bring to the first ladyship because of her youth, her race, her gender ideology, her profession, or her partisanship. There is concern from those who hoped for more change, because this first lady's identity and life experiences contrast somewhat with those of her predecessors. And there is bewilderment when these individuals actually confront Obama's descriptive representation in all its complexity.

The gender stereotypes for African American women are well known: mammy, Aunt Jemima, Sapphire, Jezebel.[137] Two of these have surfaced in media coverage of Michelle Obama. During the campaign, she was pilloried with Sapphire imagery, her comments framed as unpatriotic and emasculating. As an example of the former, reference was made to her comment, "For the first time in my adult life, I am really proud of my country, because it feels like hope is making a comeback."[138] As an example of the latter, there

Michelle Robinson Obama arriving at Pope Air Force Base on her first official trip as first lady, March 12, 2009. Historically, presidents have frequently been photographed from this precise angle, so that their welcoming salute to the crowd is set against the background of a jet, a leading symbol of American technological progress and power. Here, the president's wife delivers this message of optimism, strength, and resilience. It is a clear and unequivocal claim to authority by an African American woman whose descriptive and symbolic representation is profoundly intertwined. Official White House photo by Joyce N. Boghosian. Posted at www.whitehouse.gov on March 19, 2009.

were the statements that seemed to challenge Barack Obama as a husband and father. Though Obama refuted these criticisms, her polling numbers remained low.[139] During the presidential term, critics fastened on her fashion choices, and media coverage provided both anecdotal and analytic pieces on the first lady's body, exercise regime, and self-presentation.[140] Previous first ladies had been the focus of similar discussions—there had been Lou Henry Hoover's gowns (with or without trains?), Jacqueline Kennedy's clothing designs (sufficiently American?), Barbara Bush's weight (too much?)—and each first lady had acted to resolve the arguments to their advantage. Obama's claim to be the mom-in-chief was part of this strategy, desexing her self-presentation while highlighting her other-directedness and her thoughtfulness. In speeches and mailings, she constantly referred to her mothering, as evidence of her empathy, understanding, and critical insight.

     And let's face it: There are really just too many pressures on parents today.
     And I understand those pressures. I talk about this all the time. It's easy to live healthy when you live in the White House and you have

staff and people who are cooking for you and making sure that it's balanced and colorful, because I had a hard time doing it before I lived in
the White House and that wasn't so long ago. Barack and I were like any
working couple. I was a working mom with a husband that was busy, so
many times I was the one balancing that load and wrestling with many
of those challenges. And there were plenty of times, I tell you, that you'd
come home tired, you don't want to hear the kids fuss, and popping
something in the microwave or picking up a burger was just heaven. It
was a Godsend.

But we were fortunate enough to have a pediatrician, as I've mentioned, that kind of waved the red flag for me, as a mother, and basi-
cally cautioned me that I had to take a look at my own children's BMI.
Now, we went to our pediatrician all the time. I thought my kids were
perfect—they are and always will be—but he warned that he was concerned that something was getting out of balance, because fortunately he
was a pediatrician that worked predominantly in an African American
urban community, and he knew these trends existed, and he was watch-
ing very closely in his client population, his patient population.

. . . We always think that only happens to someone else's kid—and
I was in that position. We all want desperately to make the best choices
for our kids, but in this climate it's hard to know what's the right thing
to do anymore.

So even though I wasn't exactly sure at that time what I was supposed to do with this information about my children's BMI, I knew that
I had to do something, that I had to lead our family in a different way.

But the beauty was that for me over the course of a few months we
started making really minor changes. And I share this story because the
changes were so minor.[141]

This passage presents themes and stories that—as Obama herself acknowl-
edges—appear in many of her remarks. She presents her mothering and her
identity as a mother in terms that broaden her descriptive representation;
note the references to being a "working mom," a member of an "African
American urban community." Her biographical anecdotes then engender a
range of emotions, including weariness ("you'd come home tired"), relief ("It
was a Godsend"), gentle humor ("I thought my kids were perfect"), confusion ("I wasn't exactly sure at that time"), and strength ("the beauty was
that for me"). Finally, in giving advice, she is self-deprecating ("We always
think . . . and I was in that position") and confident ("I share this story").

Above all, she presents herself as a leader within the family, speaking to other leaders who are similarly determined to successfully effect change.

With her stress on mothering, Michelle Obama countered one set of stereotypes with another, and sold the more favorable frame to the media and to the public. Yet Obama was doing far more than merely leveraging positive against negative stereotypes. She was also changing race–gender role preconceptions and perceptions. For many whites, African American mothers were poor gender role models. Within the African American community, mothers were sometimes seen as too strong and too self-reliant.[142] In Michelle Obama, however, the polity confronted a woman who had achieved emotional strength and financial security, who acknowledged her worries as a parent but sought their solution through proactive conversations with teachers (about schoolwork), doctors (about health and nutrition), and coaches (about exercise). She presented herself as a professional woman whose career had and would evolve through several stages, who was now focused upon her family and her self, and whose husband was at ease with her assertiveness. While women's rights activists still hoped the first lady would emphasize her legal and executive credentials, most observers endorsed Obama's gender-race role modeling.

As will be seen in the next chapter, Obama has made linkages between the different facets of her descriptive representation, but perhaps more subtly and incrementally than some would wish. Among those who have praised and endorsed the mom-in-chief are several African American journalists, precisely because of the changes they see Obama effecting in long-held racial stereotypes.[143] While acknowledging that her descriptive representation is problematic for many feminists, these reporters see Obama's descriptive representation as having revolutionary potential. Certainly it is a strategy that has generated high approval ratings and positive media coverage for the first lady.[144] As the cover article of *New York Magazine* for March 23, 2009, proclaimed, "The Power of Michelle Obama: From Terrorist Fist-Bumper to American Icon in Eight Months Flat."

As a woman of the generation that came of age after the women's rights movement, the descriptive representation provided by Michelle Obama is interesting for what it suggests about the future of the first ladyship. As women of the World War II generation, the descriptive representation of Nancy Reagan and Barbara Bush reveals the impact of the twentieth century on this post and office. Nancy Reagan and Barbara Bush are also interesting for the cautions they offer in regard to historical generalization. Rather than highlighting generational contrasts with Michelle Obama, analysis of Reagan and

Barbara Bush suggests that there are important consistencies in the descriptive representation of these women.[145]

Ronald Reagan's presidential campaigns in 1976 and 1980 had mobilized conservatives throughout the country, from the "religious right" to the sagebrush rebels. Though Ronald Reagan, like Gerald Ford and Jimmy Carter, expressed support for the ERA, Nancy Reagan stressed the contrasts between her gender ideology and that of Betty Ford (in the 1976 primaries) and Rosalynn Carter (in the 1980 general election).[146] She seemed to promise the country a first lady who would limit her presence in the public sphere.[147] This commitment to stepping back and away from political decision making was extraordinary in its implications; the media relations of the first lady were apparently going to be curtailed, if not largely discontinued. Nancy Reagan would not raise issues of accountability, transparency, undue influence, or sexual manipulation. It was a promise that appealed to the voters targeted by the Reagan campaign.

Like Hillary Rodham Clinton, however, Nancy Reagan's media relations as first lady were almost consistently difficult. Reagan made a series of decisions that she deemed necessary and appropriate but which fixed a destructive image in the public's mind. The expenditure of over $800,000 to redecorate the White House residence, the White House china that cost over $209,000, the clothing and jewelry valued at more than $45,000—while the budgets of social programs were being cut and their constituents were suffering—suggested that the first lady was elitist, uncaring, even callous. The excuse that private and corporate donors provided the funds did not lessen the criticism, especially when there were reports of undue policy influence being exerted by the donors and taxation irregularities being practiced by the president's wife.[148] The contrast between her performance as a descriptive representative and her campaign commitments was glaring, and was emphasized repeatedly in the media.

Nancy Reagan's press secretaries devoted themselves to improving her media relations and enhancing her descriptive representation. The most successful of these corrections came at the 1984 Gridiron Club dinner, with her famous performance of a rewritten "Second-Hand Rose." Reagan's comedic timing and sense of political irony was attuned to her audience. Similarly, the "Just Say No" antidrug campaign was designed to generate press and public support by presenting the first lady as the gender role model she had promised to be throughout the 1980 presidential campaign. Though Reagan had demonstrated relatively little prior interest in the issue, her descriptive

Nancy Davis Reagan with her press secretary, Elaine Crispin, on Air Force One, June 30, 1986. Few published photographs depict the first lady as actively participating in the crafting of her communications strategy. In this official portrait, Reagan is framed as attentive and reflective, implicitly refuting critics' claims that she was overreaching and manipulative. Photograph provided by the Ronald Reagan Library, Simi Valley, California.

representation expressed a moral guardianship, not political entrepreneurship, in order to resonate with conservative gender ideologies. In this, her representation was successful. As Fred Barnes wrote in the *New Republic*, "Mrs. Reagan's crusade against drugs is a crucial part of one of the greatest political turnarounds in modern times. In fewer than three years, she was transformed from a frivolous clotheshorse and chum of the idle rich—the least popular president's wife in decades—into a compassionate friend of the troubled young and a trusted adviser to her husband. Now she is the most popular first lady of the last seven."[149]

Ultimately, however, Nancy Reagan did not establish herself as a descriptive representative distanced from political decision making but sensitive to the people's concerns. In significant part, she failed because her political priorities and actions contradicted her gender role modeling promises, and had done so throughout her husband's political career. She had always played a critical role in her husband's personnel decisions, for example. Chief of Staff Don Regan, whose firing was widely reviewed as indicative of the first lady's influence,[150] strongly and publicly objected to Nancy Reagan's participation in decision making. Regan's autobiography, published in 1988, was sometimes affirming of the first lady, albeit in terms critical of Ronald Reagan. "Her husband was all but incapable of firing a subordinate, and I suppose that she had become used to supply the missing determination. Her purpose was to protect the president from embarrassment and to insulate him from associates who might tarnish his reputation; in this she was above reproach."[151] This depiction resonated with enduring stereotypes that presumed strength in a president's wife would lead to weakness in a president.

More often, Regan provided an uncompromising critique of the first lady: "The First Lady's intense identification with her husband and his political fortunes was the random factor in the Reagan Presidency. Mrs. Reagan regarded herself as the President's alter ego not only in the conjugal but also in the political and official dimensions, as if the office that had been bestowed on her husband by the people somehow fell into the category of worldly goods covered by the marriage vows."[152] Regan's book, and its associated media coverage, presented Nancy Reagan as irrational and intrusive. Regan maintained that in addition to demanding that the president and his senior advisors follow astrological maxims, the first lady used her influence to marginalize or fire conservatives while rewarding and promoting moderates.[153] Meanwhile, also in 1988, the Internal Revenue Service determined that Nancy Reagan was again incorrectly stating her taxable income and claiming tax deductions. Also again, it was her designer clothing and jewelry that was at the root of her violations. A $1 million fine was imposed for back taxes, interest, and penalties.[154] Cumulatively, her descriptive representation seemed to express vindictiveness toward political opponents and disdain for the rule of law. These were not qualities that secured support among religious or economic conservatives, let alone those unaffiliated with the Republican Party.

Barbara Bush capitalized on her contrasts with Nancy Reagan.[155] A more classic style of dress, a body that had weight and curves, hair that was an undyed white, a purposeful manner—all were an abrupt change from her predecessor's Hollywood glamour, petite stature, salon grooming, and publicly performed soulful deference. Even more intriguing, it was descriptive representation that resonated with conservatives and with many liberal feminists, the latter seeing her as a gender role model for successful aging.[156] While Bush herself reportedly found this an unpleasant compliment, it was a perception that she turned to her advantage: "On some level, Barbara Bush recognized that women who appeared sexy or powerful could not get close to the president without unnerving Americans. Only asexualized matrons could serve their families and assert control without being threatening. Once defanged in public, Barbara could enter the Oval Office as often as she liked."[157]

Bush's media relations and public voice sustained the image of a woman devoted to the private sphere, obliged to enter the public sphere to support her family members.[158] Even when she had to defend this portrayal, as during the Wellesley College commencement, she sidestepped any reference to herself as ambitious, even denying the value of ambition. As she stressed in the speech that she delivered at the college, "We are in a transitional period right now, fascinating and exhilarating times, learning to adjust to the changes and the choices we, men and women, are facing. . . . Maybe we should adjust faster, maybe slower. But whatever the era, whatever the times, one thing will never change: fathers and mothers, if you have children, they must come first. Your success as a family, our success as a society, depends *not* on what happens at the White House, but on what happens inside your house."[159]

Yet Bush was extremely demanding of campaign and White House staff, requiring both loyalty and a competitive spirit. Her criticisms of individual staff members who failed to meet these standards were infamous.[160] During the 1988 presidential campaign, George W. Bush ran interference and remarked, "There were times when people did some things that I think upset my mother. Leaks, and staff siphoning off credit for ideas originating with the candidate especially infuriated her. I would then go talk to that person and inform them that they needed to amend their ways—and explain to them that if they weren't careful, the wrath of the Silver Fox would fall upon them."[161]

Barbara Bush admitted, "I think that people are slightly afraid of me."[162] Her husband agreed, reflecting, "She'll go to bat for me, sometimes more than I'm inclined to myself. She'll take 'em on head to head, dog eat dog. And that's fine. I'm glad to have her defending me. I'd rather have her on my side than not. She's been there for forty years."[163] Barbara Bush gentled this self-presentation to the general public, but very precisely: "Don't discount me. I've written two books. I've raised wonderful children. I've raised hundreds of thousands of dollars." In response to a question asking whether she regretted being a homemaker, Bush replied, "Do you think you'd say that to Arthur Miller, who wrote two plays? Would you say, 'You chose to be a homemaker' to him? I've written two books. I've done a lot more than raise a wonderful family."[164]

Here again were claims of confidence and of ability, as well as a continuing denial of personal ambition. The talents and accomplishments she listed only strengthened general perceptions that she, like many other mothers, had sacrificed for her husband and her children.[165] In the reelection campaign, some reporters began to challenge her self-presentation as "a cross between Mamie Eisenhower and Ethel Mertz,"[166] but she retained much of her control over the media framing of her descriptive representation until she left the White House. Critiquing the first lady became the equivalent of rejecting virtuous motherhood, as Hillary Rodham Clinton learned from the public's response to her own claim of ability and dedication: "I suppose I could have stayed home and baked cookies and had teas, but what I decided to do was fulfill my profession." From 1992 onward, the wives of presidential candidates have found themselves participating in *Family Circle*'s "cookie cookoff," presumably to allay concerns about their homemaker credentials.[167]

Nancy Reagan and Hillary Rodham Clinton had poor media relations, made political missteps and mistakes, and saw their descriptive representation become a vehicle for criticism. Both attempted to improve their media relations, win public approval, and give expression to descriptive representation that would win the support of their partisan base. Rodham Clinton was considerably more successful than Reagan in these endeavors. But Rodham Clinton had an advantage, in that her descriptive representation matched her substantive representation, whereas Reagan's contradicted her substantive priorities. Rodham Clinton's approval ratings turned sharply upward after investigations revealed Bill Clinton's marital infidelities, apparently because she was then a much more sympathetic figure. Sustaining significant support through the remaining five years of her first ladyship, while she returned to policy making and won a Senate seat, was a notable accomplishment. Ultimately, though neither of the women had much leeway, Rodham Clinton was more effective than Reagan in managing the media coverage of her descriptive representation.

Barbara Bush, Laura Bush, and Michelle Obama had relatively constructive press relations and attracted some support for their descriptive representation. They could not avoid all controversy; their gender role modeling did generate periodic debates about women's roles. Generally, however, these first ladies sidestepped the political controversies and scandals that dogged Nancy Reagan and Hillary Rodham Clinton. The three demonstrated that descriptive representation rooted in separate-spheres gender ideology could still be used to mask a first lady's political participation (Barbara Bush), express her political priorities (Laura Bush), or secure popular support (Obama), even in times that demanded greater transparency from the White House Office and that waged culture wars over gender roles.

CONCLUSION

First lady: "First," signifying eminence, and "lady," signifying a mannered, cultured conception of womanhood, a femininity that resonates with ideas of upper-class, white, female roles and responsibilities. The title awarded the president's wife gives a distinctive priority to her descriptive representation. When she is addressed as "the first lady of the land," her gender role modeling becomes an aspect of the nation's identity. It is no longer an individual expression of self, but a country's statement about the nature of its female citizens.

Descriptive representation, the gender role modeling provided by the first lady, is therefore integral to her post. And it makes good press relations critical for the president's wife. Gender is performed, and its performance must be seen, described, and interpreted. Mass communications do just this. Like it or not, and many first ladies have not liked it at all, the press mediates between the first lady and the millions who will never have an opportunity to meet her in person. The frames that press, broadcast, and electronic journalists place around the first lady's words and actions powerfully affect public perceptions and judgments. Samuel Kernell has observed that popularity is a presidential resource to be husbanded and expended with care, in securing policy initiatives, reelection, and other highly valued outcomes.[168] Similar circumstances prevail for the first ladies, especially as representatives for and to their husbands' administrations. Predictably, then, the first ladies (like the presidents) have sought to exert some control over their media coverage.

If the first ladies have shared a common goal in their media relations, they have still had widely varying motivations. The presidents' wives have sometimes sought to avoid controversy, either because they found conflict itself unpleasant or because they wanted to avoid costly political problems. They have sought to protect their privacy at some times, reached out to presidential constituents at others. They have exercised their voice to convey the president's message and to advance their own careers and agendas. Though all of these priorities—and many others—surface in the media relations and descriptive representation of every first lady, each has had her own first priorities.

Among those seeking to avoid controversy were Lou Henry Hoover, Pat Nixon, Nancy Reagan, and Barbara Bush. For Hoover and Nixon, this was part of a more general distancing of themselves from their husbands' presidencies. Though the Hoovers had had a number of professional partnerships throughout their marriage, Lou Henry Hoover limited her participation in her husband's administration. She presented herself as a woman whose life was centered in the private sphere, though extending into the public sphere, and followed past traditions in limiting press contacts. Whatever Pat Nixon's preferences, it is clear that she and her staff were marginalized, even denigrated, within the White House Office. Hoover's strategy of minimizing contact with the press generally succeeded in limiting controversy, but Nixon's adoption of this same approach embroiled her in difficulties. Social and political mores had changed by the Nixon administration. First ladies generated controversy when they avoided the press; they were supposed to act, providing good copy and fostering good relationships with journalists.

Nancy Reagan and Barbara Bush confronted a Republican Party base that included social conservatives, who wanted the president's wife to conform to the separate-spheres gender ideology. Both first ladies were extremely loyal to their husbands, whose political advancement they had facilitated. Their contributions continued in the White House, but with strong efforts to mask the extent of their participation in the public sphere. Nancy Reagan was not successful and found herself pilloried as a "dragon lady," her gender role modeling judged hypocritical, threatening, and dangerous. Barbara Bush was far less controversial. With some exceptions, including the Wellesley College graduation, she received strong public support for her gender role modeling. She presented herself as an older woman whose devotion to family obliged her to participate in the public sphere.

The first ladies who conducted press relations primarily to protect their own autonomy were Bess Truman and Mamie Eisenhower, though Eleanor Roosevelt, Jacqueline Kennedy, and Michelle Obama also acted with this motivation. Truman limited her participation in presidential politics, first to express her resistance to the presidency and then to stress her husband's independence. Eisenhower focused her attention and energy on the private-sphere aspects of the presidency, and following Truman's precedent, limited her press relations. These first ladies frustrated journalists that had benefited from twelve-plus years of Eleanor Roosevelt's accessibility, but there was not yet a societal expectation that first ladies, as gender role models, would seek press coverage. Their return to pre-war practices (though Eisenhower did grant some interviews and did allow herself to be quoted) seemed refreshing, especially to those who felt Eleanor Roosevelt had done and said far too much. Notably, this strategy was self-affirming, not merely defensive. Rarely speaking with the press allowed these first ladies to advance their own goals and interests while avoiding most criticism and controversy.

Eleanor Roosevelt, Jacqueline Kennedy, and Michelle Obama wanted to protect their interests and lifestyles. Roosevelt's published words stressed her desire to establish an identity independent of her husband; Kennedy evidenced a continuing concern for her own and her children's privacy; and Obama was determined to define herself to the nation and to the world. Yet all of these first ladies were quick to reach out to the press when they wanted to convey ideas and information to a national audience. Roosevelt's press conferences have become legendary. Her daily column set a standard that her successors have been called upon to mimic.[169] Kennedy insisted that she regulate all press access to information about the White House restoration, which allowed her to secure the best possible coverage through exclusives and timed releases. Obama similarly imposed strong constraints upon the press—the editors of *Vogue* were shocked by the limited discretion they were granted in their photo shoot for the magazine's cover—but then made far more extensive use of its resources for mass communication. Obama consistently presented herself as a woman who was a mother, a wife, and an individual. Although this mixture of gender roles had earned criticism in the past it now seemed to win widespread approval. Control of their press relations allowed these first ladies, at least to some extent, to select their audience and to tailor their performances as descriptive representatives.

Conducting press relations that showcased the first lady's voice were Lady Bird Johnson, Betty Ford, Rosalynn Carter, Hillary Rodham Clinton, and Laura Bush. Not all of these women would want to be included in this category. Johnson and Laura Bush, for example, might argue that this was an administration strategy that allowed the first lady to re-present the president's message (Johnson) or to deliver the president's message to audiences alienated by his partisanship (Laura Bush). Yet every first lady's press relations are reviewed and approved by the wider administration. Some presidents and presidential staff have capitalized upon the first lady's voice, while others have chosen not to.

What is interesting about these five first ladies is their historical timing and their extreme diversity in prioritizing the president's message. All of these women were first ladies after the women's rights movement had gathered momentum (Johnson, Ford, Carter), had established itself within the society (Rodham Clinton), or was viewed as having achieved many of its goals (Laura Bush). Women were politically recognized as having a voice, as well as potentially distinctive interests and ideas. The movement drew women into the public sphere as speakers and as leaders. Each first lady, in her own turn, made her own attempt at reconciling the opposing priorities of the separate-spheres and women's rights ideologies.

The dilemmas associated with descriptive representation are also evident in the first ladies' substantive representation. If anything, the quandaries become more difficult and divisive, as policy making and decision making firmly situate the president's wife in the public sphere, attracting scrutiny and stimulating criticism. The possibility of hiding or masking deviations from the separate-spheres gender ideology, of denying influence or power, seems slight. And yet, as with descriptive representation, first ladies have taken different approaches to claiming authority. In so doing, the presidents' wives have offered new insights on the ways in which partisan and gender ideologies are performed in the modern presidency.

GENDER AND POLICY:
The First Lady and Substantive Representation

Many of the modern first ladies have been substantive representatives. Lou Henry Hoover mobilized networks of citizens and organizations to provide social and economic relief during the Depression. Eleanor Roosevelt held a presidential appointment as assistant director in the Office of Civilian Defense, in which capacity she testified before Congress. Bess Wallace Truman successfully lobbied the president to increase funding for medical research. Jacqueline Bouvier Kennedy forged public-private partnerships, later formalized by statutory law and executive orders, to advance White House restoration. Lady Bird Taylor Johnson advertised administration policies and advanced a series of beautification programs. Pat Ryan Nixon conducted public diplomacy, improving north–south dialogues internationally. Betty Bloomer Ford lobbied for ratification of the equal rights amendment and for presidential appointments for women. Rosalynn Smith Carter effectively chaired the President's Commission on Mental Health and testified before Congress in support of its recommendations. Nancy Davis Reagan conducted a public and media campaign against drug abuse. Barbara Pierce Bush funded and facilitated a series of literacy programs in the private, not-for-profit, and public sectors. Hillary Rodham Clinton led the President's Task Force on National Health Care Reform and spoke internationally in support of human rights. Laura Welch Bush advocated on behalf of child development and youth mentoring initiatives. Michelle Robinson Obama led a media campaign and facilitated a series of initiatives to improve children's health and nutrition. The first ladies have had very different issue agendas, have concentrated their efforts in different policy jurisdictions, and have sought different outcomes. Mamie Doud Eisenhower's absence from this listing even encourages speculation about the extent to which a first lady may choose not to perform—or may be prevented from performing—substantive representation.

In the midst of this rich diversity, however, there have been consistencies. As one example, first ladies who endorsed a separate-spheres gender ideology, and whose partisan ideology led them to favor smaller and more limited government, conducted their substantive representation as moral guardians committed to private and not-for-profit initiatives. The strength of the relationships binding gender, partisanship, and policy making together are revealed by the strategies that first ladies have used to perform substantive representation.

Strategies of Substantive Representation

Like all successful policy entrepreneurs, first ladies committed to substantive representation have used multiple strategies to win support from the Washington community and the wider public. Each modern first lady, however, has tended to rely heavily on one approach while incorporating elements of the others into her advocacy. The result is a set of practices that are distinctive to each woman and yet susceptible to classification.

No public substantive representation independent of symbolic or descriptive representation. This approach to substantive representation publicly expresses a separate-spheres gender ideology because it (apparently) limits the first lady to her role as the nation's hostess. Bess Truman and Mamie Eisenhower were the most constant practitioners of this strategy.

Rhetorical substantive representation. First ladies who adopt this strategy rely on their words to convey their policy priorities. This approach has not been associated with a particular partisan ideology—the recommendations for change have been either conservative or liberal. Likewise, the gender ideologies have varied, depending upon whether the first lady used her voice as a moral guardian (a more conservative, separate-spheres interpretation) or as an autonomous advocate (a more liberal and feminist frame). Pat Nixon, Betty Ford, and Laura Bush consistently provided rhetorical substantive representation.

Nongovernmental substantive representation. First ladies providing nongovernmental substantive representation mobilized networks in the private and not-for-profit sectors. This strategy is most ideologically congruent with the partisan and gender priorities of Republican administrations. It reflects a conservative partisan ideology, which favors change driven by society or the market, and a conservative gender ideology, as the first lady models moral guardianship and caregiving. The first ladies who have implemented this strategy for substantive representation are Lou Henry Hoover, Jacqueline Kennedy, Nancy Reagan, and Barbara Bush.

Governmental substantive representation. This strategy draws the first lady directly into policy making, either as a semi-independent policy entrepreneur advocating her own agenda (e.g., Rosalynn Carter and mental health) or as a presidential advisor advancing administration priorities (e.g., Hillary Rodham Clinton and health-care reform). This strategy is associated with Democratic priorities: it is congruent with liberal partisan ideologies in its endorsement of an activist national government, and with liberal feminist gender ideology because it brings the first lady into the policy process as an individual determined to use (perhaps to reform) the existing system. Implementing this strategy requires presidential support, both to be effective within the government and to counter criticism from the public. The first ladies who have focused their efforts on governmental substantive representation are Eleanor Roosevelt, Lady Bird Johnson, Rosalynn Carter, and Hillary Rodham Clinton.

Eleanor Roosevelt's substantive representation reveals how a first lady relied heavily, but not exclusively, on one strategy to achieve her policy goals. Roosevelt committed herself emotionally, as well as politically, to governmental substantive representation. Her policy apprenticeship with political organizations, including the Women's Division of the New York Democratic State Committee, confirmed her belief in party-based, electorally driven change. Roosevelt's loyalty and devotion to effecting social justice through governmental policies and programs have been widely reported; they were the focus of conversations with the president, administration members, party officials, and legislators, among others. The first lady was also a journalist and lecturer, who pursued a rhetorical strategy to promote societal and governmental change. Beyond sharing information about her days and her responsibilities, Roosevelt's writings showcased her policy commitments, identifying the need for change and acknowledging the context in which the desired reforms would have to be sustained. To achieve this goal, Roosevelt allied herself with private and not-for-profit organizations. Though she saw the force and power of government as requisite to broad, lasting, national change, Roosevelt believed that nongovernmental networks could be invaluable resources. When an organization failed to meet her standards or contradicted her priorities, the first lady took strong and disciplinary action. Roosevelt was acting as a nongovernmental substantive representative when she publicized her decision to withdraw from the Daughters of the American

Revolution because they refused to allow Marian Anderson to sing in Constitution Hall. The only strategy that Roosevelt did not implement as a substantive representative, even when pressured to do so by the public and the president, was the one that limited her to symbolic and descriptive representation. Her longstanding commitment to reform, developed through decades of activism in state and national government, precluded her adopting that approach.[1]

Each of the four basic strategies, and its use by first ladies, is examined in the sections that follow. The reader will immediately see that there is no chronological progression. Lou Henry Hoover engaged primarily in nongovernmental substantive representation, Eleanor Roosevelt in governmental; Bess Truman and Mamie Eisenhower performed no public substantive representation independent of their symbolic and descriptive representation; Jacqueline Kennedy provided nongovernmental substantive representation, Lady Bird Johnson governmental—and the list goes on, with seemingly dramatic changes from one administration and first lady to the next. And yet, the first ladies did not have unfettered discretion in conducting their substantive representation. Like every other representative in governmental office, their strategies and agendas were a reflection of their gender and partisan ideologies, their organizational resources and constraints, public expectations, and their relationships with the president. There were very definite patterns to the substantive representation provided by the first ladies, and they were revealed through consideration of the political circumstances, priorities, and ambitions of the women. Accordingly, chronologies were set aside in this chapter, and the reader's attention was directed to the calculations, decisions, and actions of the modern first ladies as substantive representatives.

No Public Substantive Representation Independent of Symbolic and Descriptive Representation

Those who measure power in terms of influence over the policy process often presume that first ladies who do not publicly provide substantive representation are either lacking in ambition or have been disenfranchised. There is, however, a third, fourth, and even a fifth possibility—the first lady's ambitions may not be political, or she may be resisting or protesting prevailing political expectations and practices. A first lady who does not publicly engage in substantive representation may be powerless and politically isolated, or she may be individualistic and assertive. All of these descriptors apply, in varying combinations, to Bess Truman and Mamie Eisenhower.

Prior to becoming first lady, Bess Truman's public political participation was limited to her appearances as a loyal wife on the campaign trail. Yet she and her husband reportedly discussed political matters, nightly, throughout his years as a U.S. senator and as president. Bess Truman is credited with influencing a number of his personnel decisions, including his appointment of Charlie Ross as press secretary, a post that she considered critically important. She also affected a number of policy decisions, successfully lobbying on behalf of increased funding for the National Institutes of Health.[2]

Like Bess Truman, Mamie Eisenhower's most public political participation came during the presidential campaigns.[3] The documentary record for this first lady is extremely limited, but there is no evidence that she contributed to policy making during her husband's administration. She herself said, in specific reference to Dwight Eisenhower's decision to campaign for the presidency, "I was Ike's wife; he made his own decisions and I followed. I can't emphasize that enough."[4]

Bess Truman and Mamie Eisenhower were quite similar in the authority they wielded in the private sphere, suggesting a common commitment to the separate-spheres ideology. Harry Truman's references to "the Boss" were humorous but never ironic; he deferred to her on family matters. Dwight Eisenhower, in his turn, acknowledged his wife's authority by repeatedly observing that she had always handled their family accounts.[5] This was an exceptional practice, especially among military men of the time; military wives so consistently had financial problems with their husbands that a portion of servicemen's pay was ultimately mandated for family support. As Mamie Eisenhower remarked, in regard to her first ladyship, "I'm a housewife and I run my house."[6] Or, even more unequivocally, to the chief usher at the White House, "I run everything in my house."[7] Her descriptive representation as the nation's homemaker echoed the president's statements.

And yet there are also traces of other factors and motivations, especially for Bess Truman. Truman stated, on the record, that she would have preferred that her husband had not become president.[8] She was explicitly rejecting the office, not expressing sympathy in response to Roosevelt's death or doubt about her husband's abilities. She also rejected the activist, entrepreneurial approach that Eleanor Roosevelt had taken to being first lady. Instead, Truman left Washington regularly, traveling home to Missouri. These trips were important not only for the geographical distance they imposed and the personal affirmation they provided, but also for the control that they gave this first lady over her schedule. There was no assumption in the Truman administration that the first lady would be routinely available at the White House. Similarly, she did not publicize her substantive representation. Initially, this may have reflected her desire to disassociate herself from presidential politics, even from her husband's presidency. Later, however, her refusal to publicize her policy efforts seemed more expressive of her determination to live a life apart from politics, while supporting her husband. Margaret Truman offers another motivation: having seen her husband castigated for his affiliation with the Prendergast machine in Missouri, Bess Truman was determined that no action of hers would call his independence or his integrity into question.[9] For this first lady, not engaging in substantive representation was, in turn, self-asserting and self-sacrificing.

Mamie Eisenhower's marital and historical circumstances were quite different. The available evidence indicates that she rarely served as a substantive representative. Virtually the only indication that she made direct contributions to the substance of presidential decision making is found in the following comment made by her husband: "Mamie is a very shrewd observer. She has an uncanny and accurate judgment of people with whom she was well acquainted. I got it into my head that I'd better listen when she talked about someone brought in close to me."[10] Yet there is no evidence that the president requested these judgments with any regularity. Nor did the communication routines of the Eisenhower White House Office include the first lady.[11] Mamie Eisenhower's decision not to be a substantive representative is both an expression of her separate-spheres gender ideology and an indicator of her relative powerlessness in presidential politics.

With few written records or contemporaneous accounts, the motives behind Bess Truman's and Mamie Eisenhower's politics must remain largely unknown. The two first ladies appear similar, neither seeming to engage in substantive representation. After a difficult transition, however, Bess Truman did contribute to presidential decision making and did participate in the policy-making process. She did so quietly, even privately, through conversations with her husband. These actions speak to her sense of self-control and independence, as she refused to conform to the standards set by her charismatic predecessor or by the Washington community. Mamie Eisenhower focused her efforts on symbolic and descriptive representation, not substantive representation. Despite their apparent similarities, "the Boss" and the nation's first housekeeper were strikingly different in their ideologies, their marriages, their presidents, and ultimately, their politics.

Rhetorical Substantive Representation
With the established definition of substantive representation stressing action, assessments have tended to focus on deeds and outcomes. Success as a sub-

Bess (Elizabeth) Wallace Truman with her daughter, Margaret Truman, greeting President Harry S. Truman at Union Station following his return from a campaign trip, October 2, 1948. Bess Truman's dislike of campaigning was often evident in photographs; this is one of comparatively few in which she is smiling. This first lady preferred to take political action in the privacy of her home, through quiet conversations with her husband. In doing so, she blurred the boundaries between the private and public spheres, though she presented herself as agreeing with separate-spheres ideals. Photo by Abbie Rowe, National Park Service. Provided by the Harry S. Truman Library, Independence, Missouri.

stantive representative has been measured in federal dollars and programs, legislation and policies, formal offices and power. As valid as these standards are, they tend to focus on the later stages of the policy process. Also deserving of consideration are the earlier stages, when the salience of an issue is tested, the political and governmental agendas are developed, and priorities are set. At this time, success is measured by how well societal concerns are recognized and given expression. The task of giving voice to matters that have previously been ignored or set aside has been a hallmark of several first ladies' substantive representation.

Rhetorical strategies of substantive representation allowed first ladies to enter policy cycles at various points and with various goals. Though the federal government had funded cancer research for decades, Betty Ford increased public attention and awareness in discussing her breast cancer diagnosis and treatment. She contributed to removing the social stigma associated with the disease, along with lingering concerns that it was communicable or caused by poor hygiene. White House statements and the first lady's own speeches stressed the personal significance of the disease, recommended preventive care and medical consultation, and emphasized the likelihood of survival with high quality of life. Only some of these arguments had previously been widely heard; taken together, they began to challenge the medical expectations of average citizens.[12] Similarly, after serving as first lady, she spoke out on alcohol and drug addiction, calling on people to confront the impact of both on their lives and relationships. Her second memoir, *A Glad Awakening* (1987), public statements, and her outreach on behalf of the Betty Ford Clinic presented chemical dependency as a health crisis affecting individuals, families, and the wider society.

On other occasions, first ladies sought to shift public opinion in favor of particular alternatives making their way through the political system. This was a critical element of Lady Bird Johnson's substantive representation, which advertised the value of initiatives and programs sponsored by her husband's administration. She was so successful in gathering public support that Sargent Shriver personally recruited her to serve as the "national sponsor" for Project Head Start.[13] Cabinet members, who had observed the national media attention that Lady Bird Johnson could draw and were eager to advertise their own programs, proposed site visits and offered to travel with the first lady. And Johnson was not unique. Foreign policy makers in the Nixon administration lobbied to have Pat Nixon visit countries confronting humanitarian crises after she had shown her effectiveness as a public diplomat.

Numerous other examples of rhetorical substantive representation by the first ladies could be given. The presidents' wives receive so many invitations to speak, and speaking is so self-evidently a constitutive element of their representation, that their statements and their policy work are strongly connected. This was seen in the previous chapter, which considers how several first ladies used their voices to provide descriptive representation. While most first ladies have employed rhetoric to win public support, three have used it as their principle method and means of doing policy work. These three are Pat Nixon, Betty Ford, and Laura Bush.

Pat Nixon and Betty Ford have mixed records as substantive representatives. Nixon's contributions must be assessed with special care, as Watergate affected every aspect of her first ladyship. For example, Pat Nixon scheduled comparatively few events in 1974, which meant that she did not have the opportunity to perform the communications and relationship building req-

uisite to representation. With slightly over two years in office, including time
spent recovering from surgery, Betty Ford faced a different but equally imposing time constraint. These circumstances, added to the first ladies' organizational disadvantages and ideological commitments, unquestionably inhibited their performance as substantive representatives.

Pat Nixon shared certain similarities with Mamie Eisenhower, whom
she had understudied as "second lady." Both were married to men who perceived leadership as a masculine endeavor and who relied upon a hierarchi-
cally structured White House Office. These marital and political circumstances were reflected in the first ladies' descriptive representation, which
routinely endorsed the separate-spheres gender ideology. By extension, one
would expect a similarity in their substantive representation, with Nixon
rarely participating in decision making or policy making. To a very real extent, this proved to be the case. The Nixons seldom discussed politics or policy. Tensions among the senior aides to the president and the first lady were
pronounced. A first lady staff member concluded, "[I]t was like we were a
necessary evil, I guess. I think, in the back of their minds all Mrs. Nixon did
was tea parties or things like that. That really we didn't have much substance
to our activities."[14]

And yet there were also significant differences between Mamie Eisenhower and Pat Nixon, and these also were reflected in Nixon's substantive
representation. Pat Nixon had worked as a teenager to support her family,
had earned her way through college, and had been self-supporting before
she married. She continued to work throughout the early years of her marriage; her savings financed her husband's first congressional campaign. The
economic security that Mamie Eisenhower enjoyed, the support and gifts received from her family, were unknown to Pat Nixon. Reporters and first lady
staff members described Nixon as highly self-disciplined, devoted to duty,
refusing to complain, steadfast.[15] Senior presidential aides found that she
was loyal to her staff, defending them against criticism. She was willing to
reject the directives of her husband's chief of staff, H. R. Haldeman, taking
some disagreements directly to the president.[16] Similarly, personal intervention came to dominate her substantive representation. She devoted hours to
her public mail, instituted and led White House tours for the handicapped,
traveled to meet citizens rather than officials, and directed her praise to volunteers and community workers. Pat Nixon's gender and partisan ideologies
came together in her perception of government as "impersonal" and in her
conviction that "it takes people to change society."[17]

Pat Nixon's resistance to "impersonal" programs, her conviction that people had to assume responsibility for their own lives, and her own work ethic led her to focus on individuals. She modestly "described her principal attribute as 'personal diplomacy,' calling it 'my only claim to fame, both at home and abroad.'"[18] Her refusal to engage the public extensively, however, led some to describe her as a failure.[19]

Domestically, Nixon's substantive representation included advocacy for the equal rights amendment and voluntarism. Yet her ERA statements were always viewed with suspicion. As Janet M. Martin has detailed, President Nixon's support for the ERA was nuanced; it also evidenced a deference to congressional and then to state politics. When the first lady made the following statement in an address to the chairs of state and county commissions on the status of women, it seemed as if the Nixon administration was beginning to withdraw its support: "Women have equal rights if they want to exercise them. Women who are really interested should just go out and pitch [in]. I just don't feel there's any discrimination. I know my husband feels that way. He feels there are well-qualified women, and he wants them to serve in the Government."[20]

For many listeners, it seemed that Pat Nixon either blamed women for the discrimination they had been forced to endure or thought they imagined their disadvantages. Though the first lady subsequently and repeatedly endorsed ERA ratification, she never had great credibility with the women's rights movement. And in fact, the movement and the first lady had very different political priorities. The equal rights amendment promised top-down change, forcing new behaviors in the public and private sectors. Nixon's life experiences led her to embrace bottom-up change, with improvements predicated upon personal sacrifice. It was a philosophy that also led her to reject the student movement because "[t]hey think the world owes them a living."[21]

When individuals did need help and support, it was best provided by other individuals. Nixon made this point during her earliest visit to community centers in Oregon and California. It became a familiar assertion: "I have been a volunteer all my life. I plan to continue. If more people would get involved, we could change things. . . . I feel that if each person would give only 20 minutes a day to lend a helping hand, the quality of life could be enriched, and that's my plea."[22]

Nixon did not often meet with political leaders and officeholders on her travels. Her time, attention, and respect was given to the volunteers whose programs she visited. By all accounts, these were successful exchanges. While planning undoubtedly helped, even those who disagreed with her husband's policies credited the first lady with being an attentive and reflective listener. During her five-state tour of college volunteer programs, for example, students, many of them anti-war activists, found that "somewhat to their surprise, they had felt quite comfortable with the President's wife. One who guided her around Colorado projects said Mrs. Nixon was 'very, very interested in what we had to say.'"[23]

The first lady did conduct meetings with government officials while traveling independently to Ghana, Liberia, and the Ivory Coast. She worked to solidify relations with countries who had had constructive, if not enthusiastic, associations with the United States. Nixon met with chiefs of state and announced a new graduate school fellowship program for women, an undertaking that was congruent with her values of individual advancement.[24] Nixon's other major instance of independent travel was to Peru in 1970, following an earthquake that killed fifty thousand; this trip was even more reflective of her policy priorities. She took two planeloads of relief supplies, purchased with funds donated by "the White House and friends of the President." Stating, "I didn't come here to sit," she met with the chief of state and visited the devastated area, receiving very favorable media coverage. An editorial in *La Prensa* observed, "In her human warmth and identification with the suffering of the Peruvian people, she has gone beyond the norm of international courtesy and has endured fatigue in an example of solidarity and self-denial." Returning to the United States, she continued to work on behalf of the relief effort, with the Taft Commission for Peruvian Relief, the Peru Earthquake Voluntary Assistance Group, and Oxfam-America. In recognition of her efforts, Nixon was awarded the Grand Cross of the Sun by the Peruvian government.[25]

Betty Ford was more public, less interpersonal, in her substantive representation. Though her staff members wanted the first lady to be even more emphatic, she was generally considered to be unambiguous, even unequivocal, in her policy stances. As communications scholar Myra Gutin noted, "Americans did not always agree with her opinions, but by virtue of her many communication activities they knew exactly how she felt about issues of the day."[26] She was most closely identified with breast cancer and the ERA, though her officially listed interests were far more numerous. In the 1976 campaign, her "main concerns for America" included ERA ratification, social security benefits for homemakers, lighter sentences for marijuana use, handgun registration, and support for reproductive rights and women's health.[27] During the presidential term, she added advocacy on behalf of the arts and government appointments for women. Her leadership on breast cancer has already been discussed. She was less successful in working on behalf of ERA.[28]

As her principle argument for ratification of the amendment, Ford stated that equal rights for women were part of the American political tradition.

The long road to equality rests on achievements of women and men in altering how women are treated in every area of everyday life. . . .

Freedom for women to be what they want to be will help complete the circle of freedom America has been striving for during 200 years. As the barriers against freedom for Americans because of race or religion have fallen the freedom of all has expanded. The search for human freedom can never be complete without freedom for women.

By the end of this century, I hope this nation will be a place where men and women can freely choose their life's work without restrictions and without ridicule.[29]

Challenged for its radical content, this speech was a precursor to Hillary Rodham Clinton's argument that women's rights are human rights. Although Ford would maintain that she was advocating a universally beneficial change, she could not deny—or mitigate—the strong opposition of social conservatives. As one critic wrote, "What right do you have as a representative of all women to contact the legislators and put pressure on them to pass the hated E.R.A.?"[30] Meanwhile, Ford's public mail indicated that her ERA work was not building support for her husband: "You . . . have my unconditional support and applause for your good sense, honesty, and courage. If only you could have been the wife of one of the candidates I favor!"[31]

Laura Bush's speeches evidence the mix of issues that came to typify first ladies' speeches in the later twentieth and early twenty-first centuries; they range from ceremonial congratulations to congressional testimony. She and her staff, however, prioritized child development initiatives. These included an interagency working group focusing on at-risk youth, independent travel to observe and promote community-based mentoring programs, and leadership of the presidential initiative Helping America's Youth. As she had in Texas, the first lady founded a book festival, this time in the nation's capital with the Library of Congress as its official sponsor. As first lady, she was the honorary chair of the Laura Bush Foundation for America's Libraries. This private foundation, which awarded grants to public libraries throughout the United States, gave special recognition to the Gulf Coast following Hurricane Katrina. The first lady made several visits to the region, linking her foundation and the disaster relief efforts of her husband's administration.[32]

Throughout, Bush emphasized ideas and relationships as formative, and defended her recommendations by referencing her private and public sphere expertise: "My emphasis on making sure that preschool children are provided stimulating activities and interactions with adults and other children so they can develop strong language and pre-reading concepts from birth onward stems from my own experiences as a mother, a public school teacher, and a school librarian."[33] Bush was focusing specifically on an issue area—child development—that was widely accepted as a "woman's issue," in which she had professional credentials and work experience. Her substantive representation was framed to comply with the separate-spheres gender ideology. She presented herself as being drawn from the private sphere into the public sphere, in order to meet society's need for a woman's moral guardianship.[34] This frame was extended from domestic to foreign policy through her statements on behalf of children's, women's, and human rights. She delivered these addresses while traveling, often independently of the president, throughout Latin America, Europe, and Asia.[35]

Bush also made her point through the speakers she invited to White House and regional conferences, through the program leaders and clients whom she traveled to consult, and through the authors whose literary symposia she hosted. Having provided these individuals with the opportunity to express themselves to a national audience, Bush followed through by listening closely. When she canceled one reading—the authors having stated their anti-war views in advance—it made national news.[36] The first lady was forsaking her role as a listener and becoming an actor, favoring her partisan loyalties over her professional commitment to the free exchange of ideas. Laura Bush, however, maintained otherwise. As her press secretary explained, "While Mrs. Bush respects and believes in the right of all Americans to express their opinions, she, too has opinions, and believes that it would be inappropriate to turn what is intended to be a literary event into a political forum."[37] With this statement, Bush defended her credentials as a librarian, reiterated her love of literature, and distanced herself from politics. She also lost an opportunity to speak on behalf of the president.[38]

Laura Bush showcased a series of issues through conferences and other events, drawing public attention to successful programs. Yet she was focused on advertising the expertise and accomplishments of others, rather than engaging the political system in her own right. Pat Nixon had briefings from the national security advisor and private meetings with chiefs of state. Betty Ford lobbied state legislators. Though infrequent and limited, these interactions did require Nixon and Ford to understand themselves as political actors, managing conflict and pushing for desired outcomes. Laura Bush sidestepped these experiences and, it seemed, a public display of her self-awareness.

Pat Nixon and Betty Ford were first ladies during the height of the women's rights movement; both of their husbands endorsed the ERA. A wholly silent or silenced first lady would have contradicted presidential overtures to women. Nixon and Ford also followed two Democratic first ladies— Jacqueline Kennedy and Lady Bird Johnson—whose substantive representation had been favorably received. Republican administrations may well have been determined to equal the accomplishments of their Democratic predecessors. Societal, gender, partisan, and presidential factors aligned in favor of these first ladies performing at least some substantive representation.

Given the balance of resources and constraints for Pat Nixon and Betty Ford, their strategy of rhetorical substantive representation can be seen as a predictable compromise. Because speeches could be reviewed in advance, a rhetorical strategy allowed presidential aides to retain control over the gender and partisan messages delivered by the first lady. The rhetorical strategy also had the potential to appease two opposing sets of presidential constituents. A first lady who exercised her voice could appeal to the women's rights movement, who wanted an activist first lady, and a first lady who presented herself as a moral guardian, extending her role in the private sphere into the public sphere, had the potential to reassure social conservatives.[39]

Circumstances were not as clear for Laura Bush. Entering office after Hillary Rodham Clinton, Bush encountered highly polarized public responses to the first lady as a policy entrepreneur. Bush had to retain the loyalty of her partisan base, which was largely comprised of social and economic conservatives, neither of whom endorsed a women-centered policy agenda. As noted in the previous chapter, Bush responded to these contradictory expectations with descriptive representation that accented loyalty to her husband (which social conservatives could reinterpret as deference) and that expressed her own political interests (which economic conservatives could reinterpret as individualism). Substantively, the first lady focused on issues related to her professional areas of expertise—child development and reading, both historically recognized as "women's issues"—and performed representation that was, in significant part, directed at men and boys. Like Pat Nixon and Betty Ford, Laura Bush had to bridge disparate gender ideologies and agendas in her substantive representation. Unlike those earlier first ladies, however, Bush's substantive representation deliberately and explicitly crossed gender boundaries.

The substantive significance of a rhetorical strategy will likely always be debated.[40] On the one hand, the power of speech in policy making is incontestable. Persuasion is at once a presidential power and a singular talent, critical to the chief executive's success in a system of separated institutions sharing power. Well-timed appeals that mobilize the public and bring legislators into agreement exercise undeniable influence. On the other hand, the character and extent of the power exercised, gained, or lost through a rhetorical strategy is not easily measured. How much change can be caused through speech? How much is attributable to words and statements, as opposed to some other source, occasion, or event? Almost certainly, volunteers would have continued to serve their communities without Pat Nixon's endorsements. The breast cancer movement would have emerged without Betty Ford. Child development and libraries were continuing policy priorities, as evidenced by the administration's ongoing education reforms. Still, the argument that change was inevitable, that it would have occurred without the contributions of the first ladies, is all too neat, too clear. Each of these first ladies is widely credited with accelerating much-needed change by raising public awareness and by mobilizing and strengthening the relevant issue networks. These were contributions whose impact could only be judged years and decades later, but they were contributions nonetheless.

Nongovernmental Substantive Representation

Because representation is a political act, it is most readily associated with government. Legislators and presidential administrations have used government policies to court and win the support of influential publics. They have also acted as substantive representatives in advancing the national interest, through international as well as domestic policies. The association of substantive representation with government-driven change is understandable. Yet it often fails to give due consideration to the policy initiatives that are advanced in, through, and with the private and not-for-profit sectors.

Jacqueline Kennedy used private-public partnerships to achieve her policy goal of transforming the White House "from historic house to national monument."[41] In the same month that she became first lady, however, a full-color and lengthy *National Geographic* article advertised the beauty of the very rooms that the new first lady targeted for change. Effectively reconstructed during the Truman years, and redecorated during the Truman and Eisenhower administrations, the mansion seemed at once historic and new. There was neither money nor personnel for the innovations that Jacqueline Kennedy envisioned, and every expectation of considerable opposition. The first lady responded by stressing that she was seeking to restore, not redecorate, the White House. She rejected any notion that the White House was or should be, in the words of *National Geographic*, "unpretentious."[42] As she would later explain in her award-winning televised tour of the mansion,

Jacqueline Bouvier Kennedy with (left to right) Senator Everett Dirksen, Vice President Lyndon B. Johnson, Senator Mike Mansfield, Maureen Hayes Mansfield, and Archivist of the United States Wayne C. Grover, opening the renovated White House Treaty Room, June 28, 1962. This photograph interweaves the first lady's descriptive and substantive representation, revealing the ambiguities of her gender role modeling and ultimately highlighting her substantive achievements. Descriptively, the first lady's hands are behind her back as she smiles, listening to Dirksen. Her body, however, faces the audience in a poised and confident stance. Perhaps more obviously, the artifacts in the room—the chandelier, painting, and desk—diminish the first lady, relegating her to the background. This photographer focused upon the evidence of the first lady's accomplishments as a substantive representative. Photo by Abbie Rowe, National Park Service. Provided by the John F. Kennedy Presidential Library and Museum, Boston.

It's so important, the setting in which the presidency is presented to the world, to foreign visitors. And American people should be proud of it. We had such a great civilization, yet so many foreigners don't realize it. This little table, for instance; it's by Lannuier, a French cabinetmaker who came to America. Not many people know of him. But he was just as good as Duncan Phyfe or as the great French cabinetmakers. All the things we did so well, pictures, furniture—I think that this house should be the place where you can see them best.[43]

On this and many other occasions, the first lady mobilized support by tapping into the pride and the insecurity that gave American nationalism its distinctive tone. Her commentary was simple and direct, asserting that the United States had the proud history of a "great civilization," which must be impressed upon other, now disdainful nations. To ensure that her voice was heard, the first lady maintained control over all related press and communications initiatives.

Jacqueline Kennedy began her restoration work by recruiting individuals who could provide resources, from funding to knowledge to artwork. The Fine Arts Committee for the White House, created one month after the presidential inauguration and chaired by Henry du Pont, was charged with fundraising. Its members had extensive curatorial and collecting experience, but they were also prospective donors with connections to other development prospects. A "Special Advisory Group," also chaired by du Pont, had a membership of eminent museum curators, directors, and scholars. Later, the Special Committee for White House Paintings (established November 1961) and the Library Committee (established May 1962) provided even more expertise. Policies were set for the receipt of gifts. The White House was legislatively declared a museum administered by the National Park Service, and donations were made tax deductible. The White House Historical Association was chartered by Congress in November 1961 and assumed responsibility for reviewing White House publications. In 1964, by executive order, President Johnson established the White House curator's post, which secured the status of the White House as a museum.[44] Subsequent first ladies continued Kennedy's mix of fundraising and collecting. Rosalynn Carter, for example, established the not-for-profit White House Endowment Fund to cover restoration costs; the $25 million goal was met in the Clinton administration.[45] Even after White House restoration had been formalized as a governmental policy, then, there remained a real and heavy dependence on the private and not-for-profit sectors.

Jacqueline Kennedy turned to the private sector for utilitarian reasons. It was highly doubtful that she could have accessed the money and the expertise to achieve her goals if she had appealed only to the public sector. In the Hoover, Reagan, and George H. W. Bush administrations, however, the first ladies' nongovernmental substantive representation expressed an ideological commitment to a smaller national government, fostering citizen self-reliance while decentralizing power to states and localities. In these administrations, the first ladies' policy initiatives were intended to showcase both awareness of needs, and confidence that the society could and would act. Nancy Reagan's "Just Say No" antidrug campaign, for example, affirmed the values of strength and autonomy. Her policy arguments identified individuals and families as key to halting the demand for drugs and facilitating an addict's recovery, while her husband's drug policies focused upon stopping the major suppliers. It was an approach that argued for reserving government dollars for police and military operations, in keeping with Republican priorities.[46] The first lady's substantive representation was meant to forestall Democratic criticisms that the administration was uncaring or lacking in compassion for those suffering from addiction.

There was also a gender ideology being put into practice, and it too was associated with conservative administrations. For those who held to the social conservative ideal of the separate spheres, a woman's involvement in government policy making was unacceptable, unless she was supporting women's performance of their private-sphere responsibilities.[47] A Republican first lady who framed her substantive representation in these terms could provide social and religious conservatives with descriptive and substantive representation that they would welcome. This was the strategy pursued in the "Just Say No" campaign. Previously described as a "dragon lady," the first lady was now reframed as a madonna, a role model for mothers and teachers.

Though the numbers vary, they indicate that Nancy Reagan invested considerable time and effort in "Just Say No." The initiative began in 1981, and the first lady was traveling for this initiative by mid-1982. By late 1985, communications scholar Myra Gutin found that Reagan had appeared on twenty-three television programs, ranging from sit-coms (e.g., *Diff'rent Strokes*) to a PBS documentary (e.g., *The Chemical People*). In 1986 she addressed the United Nations on the issue, becoming the first sitting first lady to do so. Michael Deaver, a strong ally of the first lady, wrote that she ultimately "took her crusade to sixty-five cities in thirty-three states, to the pontiff's side in Rome, and to capitals the world over." Joseph Califano, President Carter's secretary of health, education, and welfare, and later the president of Columbia University's National Center of Addiction and Substance Abuse, concluded that "parents needed backup, and 'Nancy filled that role as a national parent when it came to drugs.'"[48]

Nancy Reagan's substantive representation was not limited to "Just Say No." She was and is widely credited with effecting significant shifts in the president's agenda.[49] Biographer James G. Benze Jr. maintains that Nancy

Reagan, after studying Richard Wirthlin's public opinion polls, came to believe that moderate conservativism would win continuing electoral support. The first lady established alliances with individuals who shared her perspective, lobbying the president on behalf of their priorities and policies, while marginalizing and ousting their opponents. In foreign policy, Nancy Reagan allied herself with James Baker and George Shultz against William Casey.[50] But this was not the policy work that the first lady or the administration wanted to advertise. Though Helen Thomas unreservedly complimented Reagan for her part in facilitating the summit meetings with Gorbachev, the first lady's participation in the policy process was more often viewed as evidence that she was pushing the president to betray the conservative cause, or that she was unaccountable and therefore threatening.[51] Her continuing participation in political and governmental decision making put her at odds with the separate-spheres gender ideology that was embraced by her husband's social conservative supporters.

Barbara Bush was more proactive and more convincing than Nancy Reagan in her gender role modeling as a family-oriented satellite wife. Bush set her descriptive and substantive agenda early. As her scheduler explained to reporters during the 1988 Iowa caucuses, "Mrs. Bush doesn't talk on issues. She talks on literacy, on voluntarism, and on the family. She doesn't talk about the deficit. For her, speaking on the issues is not her thing. She doesn't want to be misquoted."[52] The reference to misquoting could have been linked to Bush's infamous 1980 reference to Geraldine Ferraro, which had driven down her approval ratings.[53] More likely, however, it reflected her determination to avoid any public association with policy making. This had to be a disheartening assertion for the literacy policy network. Though Bush only started working on literacy in the buildup to the 1980 primary campaigns, anticipating questions that would be asked of her as a prospective first lady, she hosted over five hundred "literacy events" as the vice president's wife and by her own account had come to be accepted as a member of that policy network.[54] Now, however, literacy was being identified as something other than a policy issue. Worse, the clear implication was that literacy was *less* than policy.

In actuality, literacy was a constant in Barbara Bush's substantive representation, though she also devoted time to other issues. The first lady announced the establishment of the Barbara Bush Foundation for Family Literacy in early 1989, with an initial endowment of $1 million raised from corporate, foundation, and individual donors. She continued to host literacy events, which received more attention because they were now associ-

Barbara Pierce Bush with members of the Martin County Literacy Council in Stuart, Florida, May 6, 1991. Pictures of first ladies with people of color typically present the presidents' wives in privileged leadership roles. This photograph, however, suggests a somewhat more complex interplay of identities and power. Though Bush and the white women dominate the picture visually, they are listening to the African American man, who is speaking with apparent intensity. Deference, confidence, and knowledge are all on display, and race, class, and gender intersect in an explicitly nongovernmental setting. Photo provided by the George Bush Library, College Station, Texas.

ated with the president's wife. And though the first lady's influence in the policy process may never be fully documented, her aides maintained that she contributed to initiatives, programs, and legislation throughout her husband's administration. The National Adult Literacy Survey was "the largest assessment . . . funded by the Federal government . . . designed to assess the English-language literacy of the adult population living in households in the United States." A federal agency, the National Institute for Literacy was established to provide leadership and to serve "as a national resource on current, comprehensive literacy research, practice, and policy." The National Literacy Act of 1991 established the National Institute for Literacy, to provide leadership and to serve "as a national resource on current, comprehensive literacy research, practice, and policy." It also increased authorizations for state, local, and municipal programs. The Even Start Act authorized intergenerational and family literacy programs, focusing on preschool and the early grades, and specifically responding to those for whom English is a second language. And the momentum continued into the next administration, as a 1989 educational summit, led by the president and attended by the nation's governors, generated goals and standards that were implemented during the Clinton presidency.[55]

Though literacy was receiving more attention from the government, the first lady continued to stress its social and familial character. This intermixing of her descriptive representation as a mother and grandmother, and her substantive representation as a literacy advocate, was nationally broadcast through the ABC radio series *Mrs. Bush's Story Time*. Bush read aloud from children's books and enhanced the program's appeal through her recruitment of other readers. Reba McEntire performed *Possum Comes a-Knockin'*, Ossie Davis and Ruby Dee read *Flossie and the Fox*, and George H. W. Bush played himself in *Arthur Meets the President*.[56]

The impact of Barbara Bush's publicized substantive representation was evident throughout the 1992 presidential campaign. As Democratic pollster Celinda Lake commented, "The strongest part of [George] Bush's domestic issues is being supportive of family values. She is key to that. He has very little credibility right now, so he says, 'Barbara and I care.'"[57] The first lady's substantive representation gave expression to the president's compassionate conservativism. In keeping with separate-spheres ideology, her moral guardianship and his strength complemented one another. This presentation was carefully designed and precisely executed. Barbara Bush effectively presented herself as an updated Mamie Eisenhower, who had been a beloved gender role model long after her husband's administration had left the White House. Bush further, subtly denounced first ladies' involvement in presidential decision making. In the following statement, for instance, Bush echoed Eisenhower and implicitly critiqued Nancy Reagan: "If I thought something was hurting George, I would certainly say to him, 'George, I think Jane Smith is doing you a disservice.' I wouldn't say, 'Fire her or fire him.' That's not the way we work. We have a good marriage. One reason it's good, maybe, is I don't fool around with his office and he doesn't fool around with my household."[58] As her son Neil observed, "I think Americans want a First Lady who won't be active in policy-making but will use her leverage and clout to enhance the lives of others."[59] Substantive but not political, well-positioned but not partisan, decisive but not demanding—Bush escaped the constraints imposed by Republican conservatives and by a general public suspicious of a powerful first lady.

Jacqueline Kennedy, Nancy Reagan, and Barbara Bush focused on different issue areas and sought to achieve different goals. Yet each of these first ladies advertised their substantive representation, seeking public support to ensure the success of their programs. Lou Henry Hoover, however, explicitly refused to publicize her substantive representation. Like Pat Nixon, she believed that substantive representation was about responding to the needs of average citizens. Answering the requests of those individuals did not require—and sometimes could not be accomplished in the midst of—public pronouncements and credit claiming.[60] As an underlined passage in the Herbert Hoover administration's report on its "accomplishments in the first fifteen months" stressed, *Leadership is not to be judged by the noise it makes. Leadership is to be judged by results.*"[61]

Hoover employed several full-time staff members (all but one at her own expense) and had well-established routines within her office. As the economic crisis extended through her husband's term, and the volume of her correspondence grew, she refined her organizational routines. There were form letters—seventy-one, by one count—to ensure quick and consistent responses.[62] When the first lady could not respond affirmatively to a request, the tone was apologetic but firm: "Unfortunately, it would not be possible for Mrs. Hoover to help you personally, though she would sympathize with you in your present problem. But her resources for assistance are not adequate to meet the vast number of demands upon them."[63] Other requests were referred to specific organizations, such as the Red Cross or the General Federation of Women's Clubs, or were forwarded to departments or agencies. Hoover's office then did a follow-up, to make sure that the letter was answered and action was taken. When the first lady believed a response was necessary, but could not identify an organization or government agency to provide one, she relied on the Women's Division of the President's Emergency Committee for Employment. The first lady had recruited women with national reputations to serve in the division, to draw attention to women's needs and to ensure that they would be met.[64] Her correspondence pushed this mobilization even further. She described the process and character of this communication in the form letter sent to correspondents who might benefit from the network.

> I want to tell you of a committee, with headquarters in Washington, whose means for assistance and advice are far-reaching. It is composed of sympathetic and understanding members,—many of them women,— who are well equipped to advise and find means for assisting to solve just such problems as yours. Though they endeavor to carry out their efforts in such a way as to avoid unnecessary publicity . . . strict secrecy is impossible.

Would you not feel that your emergency is such that you would like me to refer your difficulty to a member of this committee, on the chance that she might be able to help you? If she could find a solution for your problem, would not your relief be great enough that it outweighs any possibility that your friends might learn of the fact? For it is not a disgrace to have misfortune which one could not prevent oneself.[65]

Once the letter writer gave permission, Hoover forwarded the original letter to a woman who had the network (organizational, social, or otherwise) to investigate the situation, assess what resources might be available, and act as an advocate, if appropriate, for the letter writer. When there was no one on the committee to do this work, the division's own investigator stepped in.[66] To ensure consistency, reports were filed and cases were cross-referenced. Establishing and sustaining these practices, coordinating paid and voluntary workers, required considerable managerial skill on the part of the first lady and her staff.

They confronted hard decisions. Repeatedly, the notation appears in reports that the letter writer and her family are living in conditions that are typical for the locality. As one investigator noted of a letter writer, "[S]he is far better off than many."[67] Resources had to be conserved for extreme cases. When these did surface, the aid was secured. If it was not available from the community, it was provided by Hoover's network or by anonymous donors. Hoover included herself in the fundraising, even though the stock market crash had depleted the Hoover family fortunes and the costs of the presidency were an ongoing financial drain.[68] This also reflected her policy priorities and partisan ideology. Earned advantages and inequalities—Herbert Hoover had amassed his fortune through mining, prospecting, and investing—did not mean that the suffering and needs of others could be ignored. Thoughtful, well-managed philanthropy was an obligation, with society taking care of its people and government attentive to the national well-being.[69] As biographer Nancy Beck Young concluded, Hoover saw "the nation's spiritual crisis . . . as a larger concern than the economic one," with "small-town values under attack by urbanization and modernization."[70]

This expression of partisan ideology and policy priorities is the point at which the similarities are most pronounced between Hoover and the other Republican first ladies who engaged in nongovernmental substantive representation. Nancy Reagan and Barbara Bush advanced policies and programs that supported their husbands' ideological and partisan agendas. Like Lou Henry Hoover, they wanted to change citizens' perceptions of government as the source of expertise and funding, while increasing personal and social efficacy. Nancy Reagan's "Just Say No" campaign stressed personal strength as the primary counter to drug addiction. Barbara Bush's literacy fundraising maintained that society could achieve desired ends with accountability and without government. Both first ladies built social and economic capital in individuals, in order to meet societal needs.

Also like Nancy Reagan and Barbara Bush, Hoover's substantive and descriptive representation were closely interwoven. Though Hoover did not necessarily prioritize women or "women's issues" in her substantive representation, the Women's Division of the President's Emergency Committee for Employment did provide both access and voice for women leaders and citizens. It recognized women as presidential constituents. This acknowledgment was reinforced on every occasion that an organization was contacted about the concerns or needs of the first lady's letter writers, the vast majority of whom were women, as were the members of her network.

Descriptively, Hoover presented herself as apolitical and nonpartisan, as upholding the dictates of the separate spheres. She seldom stepped far onto the public stage as a first lady, unless doing so could be justified as an extension of private-sphere duties. Her work was excused and masked as a woman's duty to care for those in need. But she coordinated an extraordinary nationwide effort, endorsing her husband's political ideals in every arena of domestic policy. A formidable manager and executive, Lou Henry Hoover chose not to advertise her substantive representation. Instead, she advertised her adherence to the separate-spheres gender ideology, avoiding criticism even though her actions gave form to a gender ideology that identified women as credible and effective actors in the public sphere.

Organizational talents, partisan and political acumen, and the skilled use of descriptive representation to garner support are qualities possessed in some measure by all the modern first ladies. What sets apart the presidents' wives who focused upon the not-for-profit and private sectors in their substantive representation is that they forged political relationships outside government. Each took a public policy issue—economic relief for Hoover, White House restoration for Kennedy, drug addiction for Reagan, and literacy for Barbara Bush—and turned to society for action and reform. During the Hoover and Kennedy administrations, when the first lady's staff had yet to be fully coordinated or integrated into the routines of the White House Office, the initiative came from the first lady, and the support was painstakingly mustered through social networks. Later, this substantive representation was done with the full support of the White House Office (Nancy Reagan), or with the endorsement of senior presidential aides and a specialized staff (Barbara Bush). Even so, and without denying that these first ladies made qualitatively different investments in their substantive representation, their work revealed their political priorities and abilities. For Kennedy, it was government change driven by rapid innovation and public-private initiatives. For Hoover, Reagan, and Bush, it was small government, private and not-for-profit responsiveness, and individual self-reliance. Their nongovernmental substantive representation was rooted in their partisan and gender ideologies.

Governmental Substantive Representation

Eleanor Roosevelt, Lady Bird Johnson, Rosalynn Carter, Hillary Rodham Clinton, and Michelle Obama were all Democrats who evidenced important strategic similarities as substantive representatives. Yet they also were very different in their policy priorities, gender ideologies, marital relationships, and White House staff resources. Those differences make the similarities all the more intriguing.

Throughout the three-plus terms of Franklin Delano Roosevelt's presidency, Eleanor Roosevelt's first priority was social justice. It caused her to oppose her husband on a number of critical issues, including civil rights, when war forced Franklin Roosevelt to focus on military and international policy. This divergence in the agendas of the first lady and the president was, however, attributable to more than historical circumstance. This first lady and president consistently disagreed about the goals that should be sought through the presidency, especially in national crises.

For Eleanor Roosevelt, presidential leadership was appropriately exercised when it upheld liberal constitutional ideals. Responding to immediate demands was insufficient; she maintained that government had an obligation to provide for citizens' long-range needs, protecting the minority against the majority. Civil rights for African Americans were an important concern for the first lady, whose domestic agenda encompassed shelter, health care, and food policy.[71] The first lady stated her case repeatedly, but she was unusually pointed in a March 1941 article published in *Common Sense*.

> I feel very strongly that no one today, looking at our own country and really knowing it, can be satisfied. If you ask me if I want to merely "maintain" under the defense program, gains we have made in various lines of social service to the country in the last few years—or of social justice—I will say that I will not be satisfied just to maintain those gains. I feel that we still have many things to do before we can even begin to feel that we are really a democracy.
>
> I do not see why, under the defense program, we cannot move for-

ward. It seems to me that in housing alone there is a great opportunity for experiment in the next few years. . . . One thing which I am very much interested in . . . is not merely whether we shall provide shelter but whether the government hasn't an obligation . . . [to] work out opportunities for good living. . . .

Under the defense program we are, of course, confronted with the need for emphasizing certain kinds of production, and to certain people that production is a paramount obligation. We all acknowledge that that must be achieved. But I think it will be better achieved if at the same time we achieve for human beings a constantly increasing satisfaction in their way of life. . . .

Only with equal justice, equal opportunity, and equal participation in the government can we expect to be a united country—a country that is prepared to win out in any battle, the battle of economic production and of solving of our social questions, or the battle of ideas. . . . It is only the knowledge that you are fighting for a better future which makes life worth living.[72]

The ways in which "unmet human needs interfere[d]" with the war effort was a focus of Roosevelt's congressional testimony, which presented her work as an assistant director in the Office of Civilian Defense as devoted to improving civilian morale in order to increase industrial productivity.[73]

For Franklin Roosevelt, presidential leadership was exerted in an environment of limitations and constraints. Coalition building was essential, especially in dealing with Congress. It was even more necessary in preparing for war, when the president modified his policy agenda to sustain the support of conservative southern Democrats.[74]

This first lady and president, then, had continuing ideological and policy disagreements, which the president had good reason to advertise. Drawing public attention to the contrasts between his priorities and those of the first lady marked the limits of her influence—she had failed to persuade the president to adopt her agenda. At the same time, the president did periodically and quietly adopt a number of the first lady's recommendations. Anna Rosenberg reflected, "I remember him saying, 'We're not going to do that now. Tell Eleanor to keep away; I don't want to hear about that anymore.' And then 2–3 weeks later he would say, 'Do you remember that thing Eleanor brought up? Better look into it, maybe there's something to it—I heard something to indicate that maybe she's right.'"[75] The president could have his cake and eat it, too. By publicly circumscribing the first lady's influence, he protected his own reputation and prestige; by quietly acting on her policy recommendations, he advanced the policy interests of his administration.

Ultimately, Eleanor Roosevelt's record as a substantive representative was mixed. She was very effective in providing allies with access to the president, helping them to achieve their political goals as government officials and policy entrepreneurs. She was also successful in lobbying for various changes in the New Deal programs. These included founding women's divisions within the Federal Emergency Relief Administration and the Civil Works Administration, and leading White House conferences. Her influence was also felt in the National Youth Administration and the Public Works Arts Project. Yet congressional critics forced her resignation from the Office of Civilian Defense. And though the first lady's advocacy on behalf of civil rights for African Americans drew considerable media coverage, it resulted in little change. Her opposition to more forceful antisegregationist acts, such as a march in front of the White House to protest discrimination by defense contractors, led to strong criticism from African American leaders and citizens.[76]

Of all the modern first ladies who practiced a governmental strategy of substantive representation, it is Lady Bird Johnson who seems most similar to Eleanor Roosevelt. In both the Roosevelt and Johnson administrations, there was an early convergence of first lady and presidential agendas, which focused on an ambitious set of domestic programs to promote economic recovery (Roosevelt) and development (Johnson). The first ladies then continued to focus on domestic policy, while the presidents became progressively more involved in foreign policy. The distinction is one that fits with the dichotomizing of gender roles recommended by the separate-spheres ideology, with the women devoting themselves to the home front while the men waged war.

Yet this is where the similarities stop. Unlike Roosevelt, Johnson acted primarily as an emissary on behalf of her husband's administration. Though she sometimes disagreed with the president in private, she was publicly loyal. Rather than advancing her own agenda, she dedicated herself to the president's, showcasing the value and effectiveness of his administration's programs. Her own early interest in abortion, and what would later be identified as reproductive rights, was not publicly stated, silenced by the potential for controversy. Instead, the first lady associated herself with beautification, an issue area that she defined as encompassing national parks and wilderness, rural development and poverty, and urban redevelopment and race relations.[77] The breadth of beautification was a match to that of the War on Poverty, but its framing offered a feminine counterpoint to the masculine aggression of the War on Poverty.

> Our immediate problem is this: How can one best fight ugliness in a nation such as ours—where there is great freedom of action or inaction for every individual and every interest—where there is virtually no artistic control—where all action must originate with the single citizen or group of citizens?
>
> This is the immediate problem and challenge. Most of the great cities and great works of beauty of the past were built by autocratic societies. The Caesars built Rome. Paris represents the will of the Kings of France and the Empire. Vienna is the handiwork of the Hapsburgs, and Florence of the Medici.
>
> Can a great democratic society generate the concerted drive to plan, and having planned, to execute great projects of beauty?
>
> I not only hope so—I am certain that it can.[78]

In this address, Lady Bird Johnson states her commitment to a process as well as to a goal, identifying consensus building as a democracy's greatest challenge. This would be an extraordinary accomplishment, which the first lady described in nonpartisan terms but wanted to claim for a highly partisan presidency. This was also a goal that allowed the first lady to present herself as a moral guardian rather than as a policy entrepreneur, though she was an active participant and leader in the public sphere.

As an issue and as a strategy, beautification can best be assessed through consideration of initiatives and programs in Washington, DC, and of the 1965 Highway Beautification Act. Though beautification encompassed many more issues, these were given special priority by the first lady and the White House. They are correspondingly revealing of the first lady's strengths and weaknesses as a substantive representative.

As a site for beautification programs, Washington, DC, served several purposes. As the nation's capital, it was a showplace for the nation's culture. Collaborating with longtime policy entrepreneur and philanthropist Mary Lasker, the first lady facilitated improvements to the parts of the city that were on display to tourists and other visitors. Washington, DC, was also notable for its class divisions, its segregation, and its poverty. When Lady Bird Johnson had visited its neighborhoods with Eleanor Roosevelt in the 1930s, she had been overwhelmed: "Accustomed as I was to rural poverty and poverty among blacks, I hadn't seen anything like urban poverty."[79] Thirty years later, she worked with Walter Washington from the National Capital Housing Authority (Lyndon Johnson later named him the first African American mayor of the city), philanthropists Laurence Rockefeller and Brooke Astor, and Democratic activist Peggy Shackleton to create employment programs for the city's African American youth, underwriting the hard work of rebuilding devastated neighborhoods. This included creating play spaces, reconstructing buildings, removing waste, exterminating rats, and landscaping.[80]

As different as the Lasker and Washington efforts were, they had a similar reliance on private-public partnerships for leadership and financing. Lasker, with the first lady, established the not-for-profit and tax-exempt Society for a More Beautiful National Capital to facilitate her fundraising. Rockefeller contributed financially to employment programs in the summer of 1966 and took full responsibility for a program that employed 110 youths from 1967 to 1968. Funding from the federal government was sought, but it became more limited as the presidential term progressed, as domestic programs were cut and the Vietnam War escalated. Unlike Jacqueline Kennedy's partnerships, which became more governmental, Johnson's partnerships became more dependent on the private and not-for-profit sectors. Losing support within Congress and among the white majority after the urban riots of the late 1960s, the long-term consequences of the Washington, DC, programs fell short of the consensus-building celebration of American civilization that the first lady had envisioned.

The Highway Beautification Act resulted in similar outcomes. Strongly opposed, its passage required the efforts of senior aides to the president and to the first lady, with the first lady and president personally contacting legislators. The final bill included numerous compromises and some criticized it as too weak, others as too strong. Low appropriations inhibited its implementation until 1968, when it was effectively abolished by the Federal Highway Aid Act.[81] Lady Bird Johnson focused her substantive representation on the government, but she was more successful in drawing public attention to her husband's administration programs than in creating programs herself.

The reasons for Johnson's failures are partly partisan and historical. Increasing opposition to the administration throughout the country and in Congress cut the support and the funding for her initiatives. Jacqueline Kennedy, in contrast, had had the Johnsons to continue and formalize her restoration of the White House and her historic preservation initiatives in the capital city. Escalating racial tensions further contributed to a white rejection of programs whose primary clients were perceived to be people of color. Reinforcing these biases and prejudices was a strong resistance among senior presidential aides and in the wider Washington community to the first lady as a political actor. During the House floor debate about the Highway Beautification Act, Republicans cited the first lady's support for the bill as sufficient

Lady Bird (Claudia Alta) Taylor Johnson with President Lyndon B. Johnson and congressional leaders at the signing of the Highway Beautification Act, October 22, 1965. Although the first lady is standing and is a strong presence in this formal portrait, her lesser status is evidenced by the president's control of her hands. This depiction is congruent with prevailing perceptions that "her" act would not have passed without presidential intervention. Photo by the White House Photo Office. Provided by the Lyndon B. Johnson Library, Austin, Texas.

grounds to vote against it. Notwithstanding Lady Bird Johnson's effort to present herself as a gender role model acting in accord with separate-spheres gender ideology, her presence in the public sphere was deemed unacceptable—even threatening—by many decision makers. Her success as a substantive representative was tied to her relative powerlessness and her advertised subordination to the president. She could earn public support by re-presenting her husband's accomplishments, but she generated opposition when she was perceived as influencing her husband or his agenda.

Rosalynn Carter was the next first lady whose publicly announced substantive representation focused on the government. She evidenced similarities to both Eleanor Roosevelt and Lady Bird Johnson. Like Johnson, Carter accepted a responsibility for explaining presidential programs and interpreting the presidential message, in an effort to gain public support for the administration.[82] In the 1976 campaign, Carter had proven her willingness and her talent for retail politics, so much so that the president described her as "an extension of myself" shortly after the inaugural. Early in the administration, the president indicated that she would continue this work internationally, as well as domestically.[83]

Rosalynn Carter inaugurated her international substantive representation in 1977, traveling to Latin America. It was her third visit to the region, though her first as a president's wife. The trip went beyond public diplomacy to consultations with chiefs of state, addressing issues that included international loans and U.S.-Cuban relations (Jamaica), beef exports (Costa Rica), arms sales and reductions (Ecuador, Peru, and Brazil), human rights (Brazil), drug trafficking and criminal prosecutions (Colombia), and preferential trade status and oil exports (Venezuela). Traveling with the first lady, in addition to members of her own staff, were Robert Pastor (director of the National Security Council's Office of Latin American and Caribbean Affairs), Terrance Todman (assistant secretary of state for inter-American affairs), and Gay Vance (wife of the secretary of state), all respected individuals but not high-ranking officials. This circumstance, and the presence of the first lady rather than the president, led to considerable criticism in advance of the trip, expressed in partisan and gender terms. Summarizing the response of Brazilian officials, a reporter for the newsmagazine *Veja* concluded, "They say that for years Latin America has been in the backyard of U.S. foreign policy, and now we're being promoted to the kitchen." Similar statements and challenges were issued domestically. Press Secretary Jody Powell described the trip as a "goodwill gesture," taking a significant step back from the president's statement that the first lady would "conduct substantive talks" with national leaders. Rosalynn Carter unequivocally rejected Powell's characterization; she stated the trip would "be more than a goodwill trip. I want it to be valuable to the countries."[84]

The interplay of sexism and policy continued throughout the trip, with questions constantly raised about the "feminist aspect of her diplomatic mission" and the policy significance of the consultations. As Peruvian foreign minister José de la Puente remarked, "She's won us all by her sympathy, sweetness, simplicity and with the frank manner she treats us. At the same time she's a very well prepared woman. Her interview with president Francisco Morales Bermúdez went off very smoothly—I'd even say professionally." The trip achieved its goal of initiating relations between her husband's administration and a select group of Latin American countries, stressing the new president's commitments to human rights and democratic processes. If there had been protests (in Ecuador) and rejections (Brazil refused to sign the American Convention on Human Rights), there had also been much-needed consultations. Rosalynn Carter—who had felt obliged to declare, "I like being a woman," in response to reporters' questions—could claim to have contributed to foreign policy.[85]

It was not a success that was repeated, however. Mary Hoyt, the first lady's press secretary, readily conceded that the itinerary had been too ambitious. It lasted too many days, visited too many countries, included too many meetings. It had also consumed too much political capital, as the administration found itself countering critics at home and abroad, in the general public, the media, and among elite decision makers.[86] Lacking a record of past achievements in foreign policy making, this first lady could not defend her credibility as a substantive representative in this arena.[87]

Rosalynn Carter's next independent international travel, of similar consequence, did not occur until 1979, and it was a very different enterprise. Rather than elite consultations with chiefs of state, the first lady visited relief workers and displaced people in the Cambodian refugee camps along the Thai border. Rather than politics and economics, the focus in 1977, her substantive representation in 1979 was centered on humanitarian need. Rather than traveling with White House staff and subcabinet members, she was accompanied by bureau chiefs and policy experts—the director of the Centers for Disease Control and the U.S. surgeon general, public health officials from the State Department, and members of relief and refugee policy networks. After her return, she received continuing support from such well-positioned individuals as the Reverend Theodore Hesburgh. Using these relationships, the first lady successfully petitioned the public, the Congress, the president, and the United Nations for funding.[88] The direct impact of the second trip may well have been greater than the first, but the second trip accepted the gender boundaries that had historically been imposed on first ladies. Like Pat Nixon in Peru, Rosalynn Carter in Thailand communicated acceptably feminine ideals of selfless compassion and care. Like Lady Bird Johnson, Rosalynn Carter found that she was most accepted as a substantive representative when her influence was directed at "women's issues."

Rosalynn Smith Carter at the public hearings conducted by the President's Commission on Mental Health, January 17, 1978. Prioritizing her substantive representation, Carter was determined to keep the campaign promise she had made to reform the mental health-care system. Even so, she listened more than she spoke at commission hearings and meetings, apparently limiting her participation in the public sphere. In this portrait, however, her commitment to the issue is evident in her solemnity and focus. Photo from the Carter White House Photographs Collection. Provided by the Jimmy Carter Library, Atlanta.

As an independent policy entrepreneur, Rosalynn Carter's substantive representation was epitomized by her work for mental health-care reform, which she linked to her advocacy on behalf of the elderly and to her efforts to advance voluntarism. As honorary chair of the President's Commission on Mental Health, Carter attended public hearings and commissioners' deliberations. Transcripts indicate that she seldom contributed to the questioning or the negotiations, but she was insistent that the final recommendations be well-grounded, feasible, creative solutions that would contribute to removing the stigma associated with mental illness and to alleviating the difficulties of receiving care. Carter could also be quieter in public because she had ready access to Dr. Peter Bourne, the president's special assistant for health issues, who coordinated the mental health policy initiative in the White House. Kathy Cade, director of projects, issues, and research for the first lady, also devoted a significant portion of her time to the issue.[89] Notwithstanding various setbacks, the commission's recommendations were given legislative form in the Mental Health Systems Act of 1980, its budget secured through intensive lobbying.[90] In four years, Rosalynn Carter took a campaign promise from commission recommendations to statutory law.

Commenting on this work, Cade remarked, "Mental health was viewed as a first lady issue around the White House. . . . It was sometimes annoying because we had to carry it all."[91] Yet this had its advantages. Because mental health-care reform was distinct from the president's agenda, the first lady could not be perceived as influencing his judgment or reordering his priorities, as some had worried about her Latin American travel. The concern to respond to individual need, to care for the weak, and to show respect for the powerless resonated with conservative conceptions of women as nurturers and moral guardians, values that Carter had also modeled in visiting the Cambodian refugee camps. Finally, throughout the campaign for mental health-care reform, the first lady's public persona was that of the attentive listener or, during the media campaign and congressional hearings, the soft-spoken woman determined to provide for others. She was the advocate without ego or ambition.[92] Issue framing, partisan politics, and gender role modeling allayed concerns that this first lady was an aggressive political actor. Rosalynn Carter succeeded in her substantive representation by using enduring public expectations as resources—she did not accept them as constraints—to facilitate issue-based, governmentally driven change.

But Rosalynn Carter was not consistently successful as a substantive representative. When her policy goals were not precisely articulated, as in her substantive representation for the elderly or for volunteers, skillful framing and tactics could not compensate. She was most effective in issue areas in which she had past experience; her apprenticeship in mental health policies provided the first lady with an understanding of how her efforts would be perceived and judged. These are hardly surprising qualifiers—clear outcomes and prior experience routinely improve the likelihood of success in any endeavor. What is also required is an appreciation for the way in which descriptive representation can advance or undermine substantive representation. Carter's domestic and international successes occurred when her substantive representation could be linked to both the separate spheres and to women's rights gender ideology. In working for mental health-care reform and in responding to the Cambodian refugee crisis, the first lady could present herself as a moral guardian and as a policy entrepreneur, reconciling opposing gender role priorities.

Hillary Rodham Clinton understood that substantive representation was complex and multifaceted—she had been a staff member on the House Judiciary Committee, researching impeachment procedures as the articles were voted against President Nixon. She also appreciated that communication was integral to policy making—as the first lady of Arkansas, she had facilitated sweeping and controversial education reforms by conducting public hearings throughout the state.[93] But there is little evidence that Rodham Clinton comprehended the power that could be wielded through still-enduring conceptions of the first lady as a gender role model whose credibility was rooted in the private sphere. This president's wife seemed to epitomize the individualist praised by the women's rights movement. She was determined to realize her potential and viewed gender as an artifact of discrimination. For instance, she claimed an office in the "West Wing" so that she could continue to serve as a policy maker, in Washington as she had in Arkansas. Rodham Clinton and her staff felt the associated responsibilities could not be fulfilled without access to similarly situated decision makers, hence her claim to an office in closer proximity to the president's. The idea that countervailing historical practices and gender ideologies could refute this logic seemed to surprise the first lady and her staff.

As first lady, Hillary Rodham Clinton was determined to be an effective, innovative substantive representative. More than a professional commitment, this determination to act was intrinsic to her own sense of self. As she stated in an interview given shortly after her husband was elected governor, "We realized that being a governor's wife could be a full-time job. But I need to maintain my interest and my commitments. I need my own identity too."[94] She was fundamentally a problem solver, with a firm belief that governmental interventions could improve lives.[95] During the eight years that she was first lady, Rodham Clinton addressed an extraordinary range of domestic and foreign policy issues. (See chapter 4 for a discussion of her gender role modeling via her issue advocacy throughout her husband's two presidential terms.) Her work as chair of the presidential task force for health-care reform from 1993 to 1994 and her U.S. Senate campaign in 2000 provide the greatest insight on her priorities—not merely because they come at the start and end of her first ladyship, but because they reveal her deeper partisan and gender ideologies as a substantive representative.

When Hillary Rodham Clinton committed herself to sweeping change in the health-care system, she set a goal of developing a program that would meet the widespread need for accessible and affordable medical care.[96] To achieve this end, she conducted most of her consultations in closed-door meetings with more than three hundred participants. (Some estimates have run as high as six hundred.[97]) When interest groups found themselves excluded, some sued and many became critical. Members of Congress were sim-

Hillary Rodham Clinton, chair of the President's Task Force on National Health Care Reform, testifying before the Senate Labor and Human Resources Committee, September 29, 1993. Rodham Clinton's presentation earned her the legislators' respect but not support for the proposed reforms. Here the first lady's posture displays the intensity of her descriptive and substantive representation, which was then wholly focused on policy making. Photo from the White House Photograph Office (Clinton Administration). Provided by the William J. Clinton Library, Little Rock, Arkansas.

ilarly resistant, notwithstanding Rodham Clinton's expert testimony before five House and Senate committees. The final bill was 1,342 pages long and submitted two months after her testimony. When Rodham Clinton resisted compromises that many considered both appropriate and necessary, the opposition increased. No bill was ever reported out of committee. Continuing (and multiplying) scandals contributed to this resistance by weakening the public standing of the first lady and the president.[98]

The task force was charged with keeping a campaign promise and it relied upon campaign techniques in seeking to achieve its ends. But campaigning and governing are different, a lesson that the first lady—like many presidents—learned through failure. As Lawrence O'Donnell remarked, "When your purpose is to pass legislation, you don't set up war rooms and you don't believe that you are going to vanquish the opposition." Senator Daniel Patrick Moynihan (D-NY) was even more pointed: "You simply had to have modesty instead of arrogance. Not any loss of idealism or loss of ambition. But modesty in the face of a guy named Bob Dole, who I knew could beat me when [he] wanted to, when he had to. So going up against that kind of force and saying, 'I can beat it,' was a recklessness of arrogance that ended up destroying the party's control of government. And that, to me, is unforgivable."[99] There were many reasons for the 1994 "Republican revolution," and observers believed that one was the first lady's substantive representation.[100]

In 1999, as Hillary Rodham Clinton considered whether to run for the retiring Senator Moynihan's seat, she met with New York political and party leaders, and conducted a "listening campaign" focused on citizens and local officials throughout New York State. "[T]he off-the-record goal," *New York Magazine* columnist Michael Tomasky reported, "was twofold: first, to show voters that she wasn't the scheming harridan of their imaginations; second, to bore the press into submission, thus beginning the process that the *New York Observer*'s Tish Durkin would later name the first lady's 'controversectomy.' "[101] When the first lady and Senate candidate subsequently stated her issue positions, she referenced these sessions. She was, as her campaign advertisements proclaimed, "Hillary"—no reference to "Rodham" or "Clinton." Repeatedly, the first lady stressed her willingness to meet with and learn from the public.

When Rodham Clinton won, defeating Congressman Rick Lazio by twelve points, she could claim a victory for both her substantive and her descriptive representation. Substantively, she had allayed concerns about her status as a carpetbagger and had demonstrated a responsive fluency to voters throughout the state. She had focused her attention on a finite set of issues that polled well with middle-class voters and the resulting turnout for the election was extraordinary, the vote total surpassed only by the 1964 election of Robert F. Kennedy and the 1988 reelection of Daniel Patrick Moynihan. Descriptively, she successfully mobilized women despite early and continuing resistance in a state that had not elected a woman to statewide office in over fifty years. Ultimately, 60 percent of the women voting, voted for her; the percentage was higher for working women (65 percent) and for New York City women (75 percent) though even 55 percent of the more conservative upstate women gave her their vote.[102]

Five days after she became first lady, Hillary Rodham Clinton was named to lead a major presidential task force. Seventeen days before she ceased to be first lady, she was sworn in as a U.S. senator. In the eight years between these two achievements, her substantive representation underwent various changes, was sometimes successful and sometimes failed, and drew both bitter criticism and strong support, internationally and domestically. What remained constant was Rodham Clinton's determination to lead by effecting change through the government. As her chief of staff remarked, in language that echoed Lady Bird Johnson, "Hillary . . . is a doer, a worker who gets things done."[103] She measured herself by her performance as a substantive representative.

Though Michelle Obama committed herself to several constituencies and programs when she became first lady, her campaign for childhood health and nutrition emerged as the focus of her substantive representation in her first two years in the White House. In March 2009 an eleven-hundred-square-foot kitchen garden was planted in the south lawn of the White House with the help of the National Parks Service and students from nearby Bancroft Elementary School. A few months later, the first lady announced that the $180.00 in seeds and fertilizer yielded an early harvest of over 740 pounds of produce, which was shared with the schoolchildren, with a nearby food pantry and soup kitchen, and with White House guests. Featured on the *Iron Chef, The Biggest Loser,* and innumerable other programs and articles, the garden generated extensive and supportive media coverage.[104] Health-care reform was controversial, but good nutrition for children and families was not.

The second stage in this initiative began early in 2010 with the announcement of Let's Move!, a public awareness campaign against childhood obesity. It is important to note that the kitchen garden, and the first lady's associated presentations, were framed in terms of health and nutrition. Obama's speeches consistently stressed positive opportunities for good eating, such as seasonal and local foods. Let's Move!, however, tipped the balance. Though avoiding any suggestion of criticism, Obama was now identifying a problem and calling on people to solve it. Specifically, she identified childhood obesity as an "epidemic" and offered parents four routes to its elimination. Let's Move! provided information to parents on nutrition and pushed to improve labeling for foods. It advocated on behalf of improved nutrition in the school breakfast and lunch programs. It expanded and modernized the President's Physical Fitness Challenge. And it advocated on behalf of greater access to food through farmers' markets and grocery stores. Here was the first lady as a moral guardian, a gender role that first ladies had modeled for a very long time with widespread support.

> [I]t's clear that we need a comprehensive, coordinated approach. But we also have to be clear that that doesn't mean it requires a bunch of new laws and policies from Washington, DC. I have spoken to many experts on this issue, and not a single one of them has said that the solution to

this problem is to have government telling people what to do in their own lives.

It's also not about spending huge sums of money, particularly during these times, when so many communities are already stretched thin. Instead, it's about doing more with what we already have. . . . [W]e can do what's good for our businesses and our economy while doing what's good for our kids and our families and our neighborhoods at the same time. We can do it all.

. . . We know it won't be easy to solve this obesity crisis, because these big problems are never easy. . . . We're going to have to work together. But if there's anyone out there who doubts that it can be done, then I would urge them to come here to Philadelphia and see what you've done here. I would urge them to see the difference that we can make when government and businesses and community groups and ordinary folks come together to tackle a common problem. It's a powerful thing. . . . Just imagine how many jobs we can create. Just imagine how many neighborhoods we could revitalize and how many lives could be transformed. You are all seeing that now.

So let's move. That's really the point. If we know it can be done, let's move, let's get it done. Let's give our kids everything they need and everything they deserve to be the best that they can be.[105]

The claims and promises made in this passage appear repeatedly throughout Obama's Let's Move! speeches. The first lady stresses that this is a program that respects individuals and honors their choices, and that will not expand the government or increase its spending—anticipating and countering criticisms that were then being directed at the proposed health-care insurance reforms. But she also reprises themes from the 2008 presidential campaign with her insistence that much can be accomplished if "government and businesses and community groups and ordinary folks come together to tackle a common problem." "We know it won't be easy. . . . If we know it can be done, let's move, let's get it done." These imperatives are just a short step away from the "Yes, we can!" calls of 2008, which mobilized so many volunteers and voters. This program is designed to do the same.

Obama has gone further than moral suasion. She has sought to reform the school breakfast and lunch program through private-public partnerships with approximately forty of the major corporate suppliers. This has been a collaborative effort, meant to reflect well on an administration whose relationships with the business sector have been somewhat uncertain. Within the government, meanwhile, a presidential task force has reviewed existing programs and initiated needed improvements and updates. Proposals to modestly increase the budget for key programs have been advanced.[106]

Obama's early substantive representation is centered in the government: the kitchen garden is part of the White House landscape, "Let's Move!" is a government website, the corporate dialogues are about a government program, and the presidential task force spans the executive branch. Yet the first lady has been strategically incremental in her substantive representation. Her speeches have evolved only gradually from inspiring to problem solving, and the shift was made so deftly that it earned widespread approval. She has kept her appeals purposefully vague, avoiding association with organic food controversies, for example, and sidestepping charges of elitism with plantings that are familiar to everyone. And the first lady has consistently presented her work in the public sphere as an extension of her commitments in the private sphere, so that her descriptive and substantive representation have become mutually reinforcing. As the mom-in-chief, she shares experiences, frustrations, and wisdom with other moms and dads.

Eleanor Roosevelt, Lady Bird Johnson, Rosalynn Carter, and Hillary Rodham Clinton each pursued a policy agenda that was broad, ambitious, and controversial. Michelle Obama, in contrast, has advanced a focused and tightly controlled agenda whose potential is only gradually being revealed. Like many others, all of these first ladies found the most success when pursuing comparatively specific proposals, through processes that facilitated compromise and ownership. The Mental Health Systems Act, the focus of Rosalynn Carter's substantive representation, may epitomize this strategy. Yet in addition to the workings of separate institutions sharing powers, and the systemic preference for incremental change, first ladies seeking to mobilize the government have had to confront a formidable gender bias against their participation. As each first lady learned, sometimes through failure, success came at the price of publicly denying personal ambition, claiming to be apolitical, and emphasizing a commitment to "women's issues." A skilled strategist in domestic politics, who routinely masked the activist character of her descriptive representation, Johnson was widely accepted as a substantive representative until the Highway Beautification Act was advanced in her name. Her participation then became a rallying point for the bill's opponents. Though legally recognized during the Clinton administration as de facto public officials, at least in some advisory contexts, first ladies have been routinely and profoundly marginalized when as substantive representatives they sought to direct the exercise of government power.

CONCLUSION

For most appointed and elected members of the government, substantive representation is a responsibility that brings opportunities to exercise power by meeting constituents' needs and by advancing the nation's interests. In return, officials are rewarded, promoted, or reelected. First ladies have been among those experiencing these exchanges of power and affirmation. Yet first ladies have also encountered difficulties as substantive representatives, and their failures have carried high reputational and electoral costs. Because the first lady's power is derived from a relationship, her performance as a representative is viewed as deeply revealing. Then, too, as a substantive representative in the public sphere, she is overturning longstanding conceptions of women's gender roles. Cumulatively, these circumstances ensure that the first lady will be closely scrutinized. She will earn some support as a successful substantive representative—and she will encounter strong criticism if she fails. These risks notwithstanding, there is a general expectation that the first lady will engage in at least some substantive representation, dealing well enough with the contradictions that she is able to respond to presidential constituents. As Nancy Reagan learned, first ladies can no longer limit their representation to the symbolic and the descriptive.

As substantive representatives, first ladies have exercised what control they could in meeting popular and presidential expectations, linking partisan and gender ideologies, and establishing themselves as political actors. Their strategies for substantive representation—rhetorical, nongovernmental, and governmental—have facilitated their exercise of power. These were not simplistic coping mechanisms for dilettantes who amused themselves with "projects" while their husbands held presidential office.

There are also more precise lessons to be learned from the modern first ladies' substantive representation. As Janet M. Martin and Kira Sanbonmatsu have discussed, Democratic and Republican party platforms and candidates have endorsed equal rights for women, among other feminist priorities, during the modern presidency. Though the parties have taken distinct positions on abortion and reproductive rights, gender issues relating to "a woman's place" in the public sphere have received less attention from the parties, in part because electoral responses have been so changeable.[107] This is a circum-stance with which first ladies are acutely familiar. And yet, precisely because first ladies are before the public as representatives of and to their husband's administrations, their actions express judgments about women's roles in the private and public spheres. Their descriptive and substantive representation is interwoven, and they are most definitely making statements about wom-en's "place" in the society, the market, and the government.

The Republican pollster Richard Wirthlin concluded that "[i]n most cases values can be communicated more effectively by symbol, through anec-dote, by nonverbal communication, and they have little political worth un-less they are rooted in something that is concrete: policy or the attributes of an administration." This has been the communication that first ladies have facilitated as representatives. As gender role models, they perform and voice an ideology that privileges a particular interpretation of a critical aspect of human identity. Their value-laden judgments are conveyed through their so-cial outreach and symbolic representation, as well as their descriptive repre-sentation and press relations. And those judgments are expressed concretely, to use Wirthlin's phrasing, through their policy work, their substantive rep-resentation. Though party platforms may have sidestepped gender issues re-lated to women's "place," first ladies have not been allowed to do so.

If the first lesson to be learned from the first ladies' substantive repre-sentation accentuates the gendered facets of their representation, the second emphasizes the partisan elements. Though the Democratic and Republican party ideologies are not mutually exclusive in their issue positions or in their underlying ideologies, the two have evidenced different visions of govern-ment and society. Democrats have typically seen the need for a more activist government and Republicans have favored a more limited government. This contrast has surfaced in first ladies' substantive representation. Democratic first ladies, including Bess Truman, have commonly pushed for government action. (In restoring the White House, Jacqueline Kennedy turned to the private and not-for-profit sectors because government action was not forth-coming. Still, her innovations were later formalized as governmental poli-cies.) Republican first ladies have favored rhetorical and nongovernmental strategies, mobilizing individuals, networks, and organizations in the private and not-for-profit sectors. (This could also be said of Mamie Eisenhower's symbolic representation. Her endorsement of social equality among the races and her rejection of McCarthyism modeled a standard of social behavior for the wider society.) These partisan ideologies have correlated with the wom-en's gender ideologies. Support for a more activist government was paired with gender role modeling that endorsed women's activism in the public sphere, while reliance on the private sector was linked to gender role modeling that prioritized women's commitment to the private sphere. Partisan and gender priorities were mutually supportive, the first ladies' representation giving expression to a coherent political ideology.[108]

The third lesson relates to the presidential marriages. Without discounting the nuanced differences among the presidential couples, this study of substantive representation has found that presidents' support for first ladies' substantive representation is routinely qualified. Even when a first lady is acting in furtherance of the presidential agenda, or has benefited from the president's provision of staff support, or is successful in effecting change, chief executives have often distanced themselves from their wives' substantive representation. And yet, there is some evidence that constraints on the first ladies' work in the public sphere are lessening, as voters now ask what these women will be doing while they are in the White House. "Projects" and policy work are now more often expected of the presidents' wives.

The fourth lesson relates to the power that may be exercised by first ladies. Presidents' wives are granted the luxury of a more incremental start to their substantive representation, in part because neither the Washington community nor the public necessarily expects them to be influential decision makers. The irony of that circumstance comes in the realization that time itself is a resource, allowing for a wiser and more effective allocation of personnel, crafting of strategy, and selection of issues. The constraints, however, are formidable. First ladies are limited by formal law (anti-nepotism and anti-deficiency statutes) and by informal mores (gender ideologies and marital status). As elections have become more volatile and polling more sophisticated, the informal mores have become more influential and more contradictory. As the balance between resources and constraints has shifted, first ladies have only sometimes been able to manage these conflicts to their advantage or ignore them without great cost. As policy makers, first ladies have found that every opportunity to exercise power has carried significant limitations, forcing them to justify their credentials, agendas, and decisions. This burden is great enough, and distinctive enough, that it is a defining element of the first lady's substantive representation.

CONCLUSION

First ladies confront extraordinary responsibilities. They are expected to use, interpret, and make symbols that will facilitate communications and relationships among the public and their husbands' administrations. They are perceived as gender role models and charged with winning the support of moderates, while sustaining the loyalty of their own party's base. They are critiqued as policy and political entrepreneurs, expected to facilitate change in social norms and government priorities. Being first lady is difficult, exhausting, and meaningful.

Contributing to these challenges is the intense sense of identification that the general public—women, especially—express in regard to the presidents' wives. Among other pieces of evidence, the public correspondence collections in the presidential libraries contain innumerable letters, notes, and telegrams whose authors convey their thoughts with an easy familiarity. Whether requesting help or guidance, commenting on the first lady's recent actions, or advising her on impending decisions, these correspondents write as if they are personally acquainted with the president's wife. That same comfortable intimacy surfaced repeatedly in conversations about my research. Almost invariably, people would volunteer which first lady was their "favorite" and would then proceed to tell stories about that particular woman. The president's wives are known; the public feels that they are known well.

Perhaps not surprisingly, the presidents' wives have found themselves with bewildering coalitions of supporters and critics. Modern first ladies have negotiated gender through several women's and civil rights movements; partisanship through realignment, dealignment, and polarization; and presidential politics through institutional shifts in the White House, social and economic upheaval, and war. Even so, their communication and relationship building has consisted of more than coping strategies in contentious and difficult times. Their political expertise has evidenced considerable self-awareness, prioritizing responsiveness while strengthening the connections between gender and partisanship.

THE WOMEN WHO HAVE BEEN THE MODERN FIRST LADIES

The wives of the modern presidents have, as discussed in the second chapter, entered the White House with significant political expertise. Most commonly, they have exhibited a hard-won strategic understanding of campaigning and governing, having participated in their husbands' campaigns and then closely observing (if not continuing their participation in) their husbands' governance. Only Lou Henry Hoover and Mamie Doud Eisenhower were introduced to political campaigning when their husbands ran for the presidency, and their experiences are unlikely to be repeated in the future. With governors and U.S. senators considered the strongest prospects for the Oval Office, first ladies will likely have experiences and credentials similar to those of Eleanor Roosevelt, Rosalynn Smith Carter, Nancy Davis Reagan, Hillary Rodham Clinton, and Laura Welch Bush, all first ladies in their home states, or Bess Wallace Truman, Jacqueline Bouvier Kennedy, Lady Bird Taylor Johnson, and Michelle Robinson Obama, all senators' wives. States' first ladies have tested their skills and strategies of representation, especially in regard to substantive representation, before coming to Washington. Senators' wives have often been more knowledgeable about the Washington community and Washington society.

The different kinds and degrees of knowledge possessed by the women have been evident in their successes and their failures. Carter and Rodham Clinton epitomized the experiences of the governors' wives who became first ladies. Carter's facilitation of mental health-care reform could be attributed to her lengthy apprenticeship in its policy networks, and to her experiences in seeing policy change negotiated in a state with a will to effect change, despite its past reputation for poor care and its limited financial resources. Rodham Clinton's failure in health-care insurance reform, similarly, was attributed to her lack of familiarity with the associated networks and negotiations. As first lady in Arkansas, she had conducted extensive public outreach and acquired significant policy expertise, but her husband in the capital had conducted the negotiations that resulted in programmatic change. Among the senators' wives, Kennedy and Johnson were particularly illustrative. Kennedy used White House resources to reach out to cultural elites, including donors and museum curators, and Johnson used White House resources to contact officeholders and voters. These were constituents with whom the first ladies had previous relationships and with whom they could cultivate a shared identity. As these examples demonstrated, the women whose husbands became president did have to learn to be first ladies, but they brought experiences and expertise into the White House that eased that learning throughout the presidential term.

Quite clearly, then, *who* is first lady has mattered in particular eras and years. It has also mattered to the first lady's post as it has emerged throughout the modern presidency. Political science, however, looks for patterns that extend and hold beyond the individual. This book, therefore, has investigated the more systematic influences on and consequences of the first ladies' decisions and actions. Acknowledging the kinds and the extent of the first ladies' expertise has been a starting point in this analysis, which argues that the first ladies are informed political actors—not disinterested observers, amateurs, or dilettantes. But then, having recognized these women as possessed of political expertise, how do we study the more systematic influences on and consequences of their actions?

I have argued in favor of studying the first ladies as representatives, analyzing their contributions to the presidency through symbolic representation, descriptive representation, and substantive representation. For those who associate representation exclusively with elections, this will be a controversial presentation, for the same reason that the first lady's post has been controversial. The president's wife is designated for her post, not elected or appointed, and her power is earned in part through marriage. Formally, her status has yet to be fully determined, though a federal appellate court has ruled that she is a de facto public official for the purposes of the Federal Advisory Committee Act. Informally, her status is contingent upon societal judgments about gender, autonomy, and power. The first lady will always be a problematic figure for those who believe that power should be reserved to those who are autonomous, whether because their singularity testifies to their fitness for office or clarifies their accountability while in office.

Such a firm and radical commitment to individuality, however, would render every senior member of the White House staff questionable and few have taken the critique this far. Criticisms of the first lady are tied to her marital relationship with the president, with characterizations of the first lady ranging from oppressed (e.g., Pat Nixon) to self-interested and manipulative (e.g., Nancy Reagan). If the first lady is oppressed, then she cannot be held accountable for her actions because she is a victim, doing what she must in order to survive. Even so, she may well be a dangerous political actor, her lack of accountability undermining the democratic republic. If the first lady is self-interested and manipulative, she may well avoid being held accountable because the public's knowledge of her marital relationship will be limited. The husband, not the wife, can be held accountable. Consequently, the president, not the first lady, should exercise power. Thus, a gendered critique of marriage, a commitment to individual agency and autonomy, and a perception of the political system as an electoral meritocracy all combine to marginalize the first lady and to limit her performance of representation.

As historically weighty as these concerns are, the theories and empirical studies of representation provide thoughtful and important counterarguments. These intellectual resources make possible a broad and yet wellfocused examination of the first ladies' roles and responsibilities. They also facilitate an assessment of the factors that affect these roles and responsibilities, in their historical and political contexts. Representation thus helps us to take the step from the individual to the institutional that political science recommends and requires.

The Performance of Representation and the First Lady

At its most basic, representation is the making present of that which is absent. When "that which is absent" is the people, accountability is a concern. In a country that claims to be a democratic republic, with its legitimacy judged and determined by the quality of its responsiveness, the accountability of the representatives is even more important. Elected officials are tested by campaigns and elections. Unelected officials—whether appointed, nominated-and-confirmed, or designated—answer to elected officials in congressional hearings, presidential meetings, and impeachment proceedings, among other exchanges. The accountability of United States representatives is constantly being assessed, directly and indirectly, by democratic and republican standards.

These undertakings are well suited to the constitutive tasks of representation, communication, and relationship building. The representatives' democratic intent are preliminarily revealed by the varying types of communication and the diversity of the relationships in which they engage. More telling is the content of their communication and the character of their relationships. This book has analyzed the following three facets of representation:

- *symbolic representation,* with communications and relationships centered on the use, interpretation, and making of symbols that give tangible expression to complex abstractions (for example, the presentation of the White House as a symbol of leadership, honor, national purpose, and power);
- *descriptive representation,* with communications and relationships centered on the expression of the identities shared by the represented and the representative (for example, the provision of role modeling, or the securing of civic equality and inclusion); and
- *substantive representation,* with communications and relationships centered on establishing and meeting the needs of the represented, as those needs are understood and mediated by the representatives.

As these definitions make clear, the communication and the relationship building that together constitute representation require effort on the part of the representative and the represented. Whether focusing on symbols, identities, or interests, representation involves consultation, conflict management, and decision making. Ultimately, representatives determine which symbols (and then which meanings), which identities (and then which ascribed roles), and which policies (and then which programs) will be invested with the power of the government. It is because of this power that the members of a democracy are so determined to hold their representatives accountable. And it is because first ladies do wield this power as representatives that they merit close study.

Presidents' wives are constantly engaged in public dialogues, meeting with different publics and trying to persuade them to adopt the administration's priorities as their own. The first ladies' representation is intended to win support for the party and its candidates, for initiatives and policies, and for the administration and the president. Because these goals are obvious to the public, the first ladies' accomplishments and failures are also obvious. This holds even when the means to achieve the goals are uncertain or unknown, as during volatile election campaigns (e.g., Laura Bush's extensive, independent campaign travel in 2004 and 2006) or in the midst of polarized political debates (e.g., Eleanor Roosevelt's commitment to social justice during the buildup to World War II).

As representatives, first ladies have used correspondence, media relations, travel, public awareness campaigns, public-private partnerships, presidential commissions and task force hearings, public diplomacy, and various other mechanisms to communicate with the public. In response, the public has, at various points in the modern presidency, affirmed or constrained the first lady. In other words, the public has held the first lady accountable. And the presidents' wives have responded accordingly. They have, for example, undertaken more extensive communications with the public (e.g., Lou Henry Hoover and Nancy Reagan), altered their social outreach (e.g., Bess Truman and Mamie Eisenhower), changed their campaign strategies (e.g., Betty Bloomer Ford and Barbara Bush), and recast or developed their policy agendas (Hillary Rodham Clinton and Michelle Obama).

Recognizing the first ladies as representatives reveals the significance of gender in the presidency and in the democratic republic. The public continues to assess first ladies by standards that, routinely, are more reflective of the separate-spheres gender ideology. Greater support has been given to the first ladies' descriptive representation when the presidents' wives have modeled women's gender roles centered in the private sphere, presenting women's activism in the public sphere as an extension of private-sphere commitments. Similarly, the first ladies' substantive representation has been more widely endorsed when it advanced policy initiatives linked to "women's issues" or "women's interests," both defined through reference to the private sphere.

These responses cannot be categorized by party affiliation or political ideology. Throughout the modern presidency, the Democratic and Republican party platforms have sometimes taken similar positions on "women's issues" (including the equal rights amendment), have sometimes taken contrasting positions (as in regard to reproductive rights), and have sometimes avoided taking a position (generally declining to comment on women's "place" in the public sphere). The gender ideologies of the various women's movements have been no less conflicted in their assessments of women in the public sphere and of political wives. Social conservatives, while embracing the separate spheres, have concluded that women must sometimes enter the public sphere in order to advocate on behalf of the private sphere. Women's rights and postmodern feminists have endorsed the activism of political wives, when those women were advocating on behalf of changes endorsed by their movements. The coalitions that have supported or opposed each of the modern first ladies have therefore been principled and practical, strategic and philosophical. Consistently, however, they have considered gender an important aspect of the first lady's representation and have relentlessly held her accountable for her gender ideology, as well as her partisan politics.

LOOKING AHEAD: FIRST LADIES, GENDER, AND REPRESENTATION

Modern first ladies have made contributions that have extended across in-dividual administrations to encompass the modern presidency. These con-tributions have been neither linear nor cumulative—the factors influenc-ing the first ladies' decisions have been far too numerous and diverse to be readily summarized as a single trend, but there are ideas and practices that have lasted throughout the decades and the generations. A first lady may have little in common with her immediate predecessor or successor, and yet be quite similar to more chronologically distant figures—with due allow-ance made for historical and political contexts. As much is seen in the non-governmental substantive representation performed by Lou Henry Hoover, Nancy Reagan, and Barbara Bush, or the governmental substantive represen-tation performed by Eleanor Roosevelt, Lady Bird Johnson, Rosalynn Carter, Hillary Rodham Clinton, and Michelle Obama. Identifying and investigat-ing these patterns in first lady representation, delineating how and why they exist, has been a critical feature of this book.

Granting that patterns exist, but that there is no consistent trajectory to the first ladies' representation, what questions should be placed on a research agenda? Every scholar will have her or his own answer to this question. The following are just a few suggestions, offered from the perspective of a re-searcher who sees the first ladies' performance of representation as their criti-cal contribution to the presidency.

In regard to symbolic representation, greater consideration needs to be given to the power that is wielded by the first lady in her use, interpreta-tion, and creation of symbols. Symbolic representation is influential not only because the first lady's social outreach targets influential decision mak-ers, or even because White House events and occasions make significant claims on the time of the president. What matters most is that, through symbolic representation, the first lady is expressing (as distinct from exer-cising) the power of the presidency. Lou Henry Hoover's public receptions on New Year's Day, Eleanor Roosevelt's teas, Bess Truman's lunches, Mamie Eisenhower's invitations to Mahalia Jackson and Lucille Ball, Jacqueline Kennedy's abolition of "the season," Lady Bird Johnson's use of the Johnson ranch, the reinstitution of white tie events during the Nixon administration, Betty Ford's state dinner just one week after her husband took the oath of office, the increase in events for ethnic groups throughout the Carter administration, the decline in gender-segregated events through the Reagan and G. H. W. Bush administrations—in each instance, the first lady and the administration were recognizing presidential constituents, prioritizing their needs, interests, and values. Recent presidents, not surprisingly, have given considerable attention to the first lady's symbolic representation and social outreach, integrating the social secretary and the social office more comprehensively into the "West Wing" staff operations. Political scientists should follow their lead in order to gain greater insight into the dynamics of presidential leadership.

In regard to descriptive representation, further thought needs to be given to the gender roles of the first lady and to their intersection with various other facets of her identity. A number of scholars prefer to speak of the "president's spouse." However, being a wife is presently a critical component of the first lady's descriptive representation; under these circumstances, the reference to "spouse" hides her responsibilities and her contributions, complicating rather than facilitating research and analysis. The ways in which the "first lady" title is interpreted by the public and by the presidents' wives merits close study, promising further insights on the ideas and ideals that inform their descriptive representation. Yet gender analysis is only the beginning of this work. The first lady's post has been structured around many other facets of a person's identity, and the women who have been first ladies have indicated as much. Class, race, religion, and ethnicity especially have received significant commentary by the presidents' wives. The ways in which these identities interact through the first ladies' post, person, and performance must be analyzed if we are to comprehend the role modeling and the leadership of these women.

In regard to substantive representation, detailed analysis of the first ladies' entrepreneurship is required if we are to understand the ways in which gender and partisan politics are intertwined in the first ladyship. Little is currently known about the lobbying that a number of the first ladies have conducted in the private, the not-for-profit, or the public sectors. Also neglected has been the process by which the presidents' wives have set their issue agendas. As gender outsiders in the branch judged most masculine, as political actors subjected to close scrutiny, and as persons-in-relationship in a political culture that honors the self-reliant individual, the first ladies have little presumptive credibility as advisors or as decision makers. And yet, time and again, they have effected significant change. How they have done so— how they have crafted their rhetoric, built their coalitions in the society, and transformed their proposals into government programs—is of corresponding interest and significance.

A discerning reader will object that the facets of representation must be examined in relationship to one another, not as distinct endeavors. Symbolic representation provides opportunities for communication about substantive matters; the role of "nation's hostess" is highly gendered and closely tied to descriptive representation. In presenting a gender identity, the first ladies articulate the substantive needs and wants associated with that identity. In listing these and other relationships, however, we only draw more attention to the importance of further and close examination of the first lady's actions. We need to know more about how the first ladies are performing representation, if we are to acquire a better understanding of gender and power in the United States presidency.

Gender, representation, power. There is ample evidence that the first lady is perceived and judged as a gender role model, that she is recognized and accessed for her talents in communication and relationship building, and that her influence is examined and critiqued—and that all of this is done by average citizens as well as by policy makers. Acknowledged as a member of government, the first lady is among those who create (and may be tangled in) the relationships that bind the political system and the society together. Ultimately, this is why these women have been so interesting as individuals and so important as representatives: from them, we learn about ourselves. It is a lesson that we can never learn too well—or too thoroughly.

Notes

Chapter 1

1. Gil Troy has extensively investigated the gender-related controversies surrounding the first ladies. His class- and gender-based analysis led him to conclude, in marked contrast to this author, that the first lady's power is rooted in her celebrity status. Consequently, her power is significantly determined by her public approval ratings. Her collaboration with the president should therefore be focused upon image making, not upon policy making, in order to maximize her effectiveness and to minimize the likelihood of "lasting damage." Troy, "Image-Making Not Power-Sharing." See also Troy, *Affairs of State*.

2. On the public expectations directed at political wives, see Arvonne S. Fraser, "Political Wives Strike Back," *New York Times*, April 28, 1989; Schultz, *And His Lovely Wife*. See also Bostdorff, "Hillary Rodham Clinton and Elizabeth Dole."

3. On the masculinity of the presidential office, see Duerst-Lahti, "Reconceiving Theories of Power" and "'Seeing What Has Always Been.'" On the increasing emergence of the presidency as an institution, see Ragsdale and Theis, "Institutionalization of the American Presidency."

4. Duerst-Lahti, "Reconceiving Theories of Power," 21–22.

5. Friedan, *Feminine Mystique*.

6. See, for example, Schlafly, *Feminist Fantasies*. See also Klatch, *Women of the New Right*.

7. Borrelli, "Competing Conceptions of the First Ladyship," 399–400.

8. Laura Bush, "Remarks at the 6th Regional Conference on Helping America's Youth."

9. White House Office of the Press Secretary, "Presidential Memorandum—Establishing a Task Force on Childhood Obesity," February 9, 2010; [Michelle Obama], "Remarks by First Lady Michelle Obama at the White House Garden Harvest Party," June 16, 2009; "Let's Move!" letsmove.gov; [Michelle Obama], "Remarks of First Lady Michelle Obama," February 9, 2010. See also [Michelle Obama], "Remarks by First Lady Michelle Obama at a 'Let's Move' Event," March 3, 2010; [Michelle Obama], "Remarks by the First Lady at Event on Surgeon General's Report," January 28, 2010.

10. Elshtain, *Public Man, Private Woman;* Templin, "Hillary Clinton as Threat to Gender Norms"; Borrelli, "Competing Conceptions of the First Ladyship."

11. When Betty Ford responded to press questions by stating that she shared a bedroom with her husband, she was denounced as "disgraceful and immoral." Ford, *Times of My Life*, 173.

12. As quoted in Patterson, *White House Staff*, 284.

13. Dovi, *Good Representative*. See also Dovi, "Theorizing Women's Representation in the United States": Mansbridge, "Should Blacks Represent Blacks and Women Represent Women?"

14. Pitkin, *Concept of Representation*, 92–111.

15. For a contrary argument, see Pitkin, *Concept of Representation*, 107.

16. Pitkin, *Concept of Representation*, 61–90.

17. Pitkin, *Concept of Representation*, 83.

18. Pitkin, *Concept of Representation,* 80.

19. Pitkin, *Concept of Representation,* 220–22.

20. Ritter, "Gender as a Category of Analysis in American Political Development."

21. Weldon, "Beyond Bodies."

22. Dovi, "Theorizing Women's Representation in the United States," 156–58.

23. See West, *Upstairs at the White House,* 191–282; Baldrige, *Of Diamonds and Diplomats,* 154–276; Perry, *Jacqueline Kennedy,* especially 15, 76–81.

24. Klatch, *Women of the New Right,* 142–47.

25. Borrelli, "Competing Conceptions of the First Ladyship."

26. Hult and Walcott, *Empowering the White House;* Walcott and Hult, *Governing the White House.*

27. First lady scholar Lewis Gould similarly observed, "First ladies are not a leading indicator. They are a lagging indicator. Social change will happen and about 15 years later, we'll say it's ok for first ladies, too." As quoted in Krausert, "From Baking Bread to Making Dough."

28. The ideological debate has also generated a significant legal debate. For example, see Broyde and Schapiro, "Impeachment and Accountability."

29. On the challenges associated with presidential transitions and start-ups, see Kumar and Sullivan, *White House World.*

30. In her memoir, Barbara Bush reported that she was surprised at the escalation of press coverage when she transitioned from the second lady's to the first lady's office. Bush, *A Memoir,* 253.

31. Betty Ford encountered especially heavy demands with regard to symbolic representation. A state dinner was to be held within a week of her becoming first lady. On the one hand, there was the need to provide continuity; on the other, this occasion was to be the first statement of the new administration's priorities in social outreach. See Ford, *Times of My Life,* 177–84.

32. Postal Revenue and Federal Salary Act of 1967, Public Law 90–206, Section 221; Edwin S. Kneedler to John M. Harmon, February 17, 1977, Memorandum, "FG 287 1/20–77—1/20/81" Folder, Box FG—216, White House Central File—Subject File, p. 15, Jimmy Carter Library; Rosalynn Carter, "Remarks of the President and Mrs. Carter at the Signing Ceremony of Executive Order 11973" and "Executive Order 11973."

33. Scharrer and Bissell, "Overcoming Traditional Boundaries."

34. *Association of American Physicians and Surgeons, Inc., et al. v. Hillary Rodham Clinton,* 813 F. Supp. 82 (1993), 997 F. 2d 898 (1993).

35. On the integration of "West Wing" and "East Wing" operations, see Eksterowicz and Paynter, "Evolution of the Role and Office of the First Lady."

36. It is important, however, not to overstate the "orientation time" granted first ladies, even earlier in the twentieth century. A series of responsibilities, which receive little acknowledgment and yet require considerable attention, have fallen to the president's wife. These include managing the move into the White House, ordering the private residence, and establishing family routines.

37. Bernstein, *Woman in Charge;* King, *Woman in the White House;* Rodham Clinton, *Living History,* 143–55, 190–92, 247–49, 369–70; Clinton, *My Life,* 482, 499.

38. On the significance of the presidential term and timing in decision and policy making, see Borrelli, Hult, and Kassop, "White House Counsel's Office."

39. On the particular significance of gender issues in health-care insurance and finance, see Guy, "Hillary, Health Care, and Gender Power."

40. "White House Study Project: Report on the Functions and Organization of the Of-

fice of the First Lady," January 6, 1977, "ADP—First Lady's Staff" Folder, Box 1, Staff Offices—Administration—[Dan] Malachuk, Jimmy Carter Library.

41. Brinkley, *Unfinished Presidency,* 167; Kaufman, *Rosalynn Carter,* 42–48, 83–85. Kaufman also discusses the negative impact that followed Peter Bourne's departure from the White House, when there was no individual charged with advancing the commission recommendations into legislation. Hoyt, *East Wing,* 191–92.

42. Kneedler to Harmon, February 17, 1977, White House Central File—Subject File, Jimmy Carter Library; Krausert, "From Baking Bread to Making Dough."

43. White House Personnel Act of 1978, Public Law 95–570, 105(e).

44. *Association of American Physicians and Surgeons, Inc., et al. v. Hillary Rodham Clinton.* See also Carl David Wasserman, "Firing the First Lady"; Patel, "First Lady, Last Rights?"

45. Duerst-Lahti, "Reconceiving Theories of Power," 23.

46. On the president's staff, see Walcott and Hult, *Governing the White House.* On the first lady's initiatives, see Young, *Lou Henry Hoover.*

CHAPTER 2

1. A fifth type of expertise already existed within the White House. These were the careerists who understood how the White House Office works and were able to think "institutionally" across administrations, and who were willing to share their expertise. See Kumar, "White House Is Like City Hall," 88.

2. For the four-part classification schema, see Kumar, "White House Is Like City Hall," 84–87. See also Kumar, "White House World."

3. Rodham Clinton, *Living History,* 465. On Pat Nixon's similar trust in her husband, see Thomas, *Dateline,* 202.

4. Clinton, *My Life,* 802.

5. Ruth Marcus, "First Lady 'Committed' to Her Marriage," *Washington Post,* August 19, 1998.

6. Rodham Clinton, *Living History,* especially p. 470. For an example of a supportive response from the public, see Stephen P. Titus, "Don't Rush to Judge Mrs. Clinton," *New York Times,* August 28, 1998.

7. Joyce Howard Price, "Meanwhile, Hillary's Approval Numbers Get Better," *Washington Times,* August 23, 1998.

8. Guy Friddell, "Hillary Stands Tall," *Virginian-Pilot,* August 22, 1998; Sarah T. Connell Campbell, "Don't Rush to Judge Mrs. Clinton," *New York Times,* August 28, 1998; Maureen Dowd, "Stop the Babble," *Pittsburgh Post-Gazette,* August 21, 1998; Nicole S. Urdang, "Hillary's Support of Bill Sends the Wrong Message to Chelsea and American Women," *Buffalo News,* August 30, 1998; Susan Whitney and Elaine Jarvik, "He Done Her Wrong: What's She To Do?" *Deseret News,* August 22, 1998; Ron Siebel, "Letters from the People," *Anchorage Daily News,* August 25, 1998; Wendy Wasserstein, "Hillary Clinton's Muddled Legacy," *New York Times,* August 25, 1998; Kathryn Wenzel, "A Woman Must Be Weak, Pitied to Win Approval," *Oregonian,* August 24, 1998.

9. [Lyndon Johnson], "Annual Message to Congress on the State of the Union," January 8, 1964.

10. Dale and Virginia (Scooter) Miller interview, 24.

11. Dale and Virginia (Scooter) Miller, interview, 13.

12. The women referenced were Mrs. Donald S. Russell (first lady of South Carolina, 1963–1965), Mrs. Carl E. Sanders (first lady of Georgia, 1963–1967), and Mrs. Dan K.

Moore (first lady of North Carolina, 1965–1969). Memorandum, Katie [Louchheim] to Liz [Carpenter], "Proposed Whistle Stop through the South for Mrs. Johnson," August 24, 1964, "Whistle Stop 10/13–16/64," Box 11, Liz Carpenter Subject Files, Lyndon B. Johnson Library.

13. An exception to this general practice may have been Eleanor Roosevelt. See Hoffman, interview by Soapes, October 13, 1977, p. 3.

14. Carter, "Remarks of the President and Mrs. Carter at the Signing Ceremony of Executive Order 11973"; U.S. Senate, "Examination of the Recommendations of the President's Commission on Mental Health"; Borrelli, "The First Lady as Formal Advisor to the President."

15. For a discussion of these programs from the first lady's perspective, see Carter, *First Lady from Plains,* 302–23.

16. "Presidential Salary Correspondence" Folder, Box 257, Post-Presidential Papers— Subject File, Herbert Hoover Library.

17. Social Functions [Scrapbooks], [Vol. 1] March 4, 1929 to November 18, 1930, and [Vol. 2] December 2, 1930, to March 4, 1933, Herbert Hoover Library; "Groups Received by Mrs. Hoover" compiled by Archivist Mildred Mather, Herbert Hoover Library.

18. Vylla Poe Wilson, "Mrs. Hoover at Reception Wears Train," *Washington Post,* October 13, 1929, "Clippings, 1929: Social, October—December," Box 40, "Lou Henry Hoover" Subject File, Herbert Hoover Library; Randolph, *Presidents and First Ladies;* Hoover, *Memoirs of Herbert Hoover: The Cabinet and the Presidency,* 323.

19. This statement appears in virtually every biography of Mamie Eisenhower; this particular passage is excerpted from David and David, *Ike & Mamie,* 66.

20. Betty Ford, *Times of My Life,* 132.

21. This pattern of gendered experiences was examined in detail by Friedan in *Feminine Mystique.*

22. For a historical overview of the contributions and responsibilities of the first ladies, see O'Connor, Nye, and van Assendelft, "Wives in the White House."

23. Robert A. Caro's biographical series focusing on Lyndon Johnson is one of the few accounts that challenges the veracity of this image of autonomy and singularity. It is interesting to note, however, that Lady Bird Johnson distanced herself from Caro's work as his research and writing progressed. See Caro, *Years of Lyndon Johnson: The Path to Power.*

24. Pfiffner, *Character Factor,* 64.

25. Holt, *Mamie Doud Eisenhower,* 49–50.

26. For an extended analysis of this perspective, comparing public responses to several presidents, see Pfiffner, *Character Factor.*

27. Caro, *Years of Lyndon Johnson: The Path to Power.*

28. Caro, *Years of Lyndon Johnson: The Path to Power,* 56–57, 114. See also Russell, *Lady Bird.*

29. Russell, *Lady Bird,* 143.

30. Though compulsory heterosexuality is a comparatively new analytic construct in academia, generations of political wives have been well schooled in its precepts.

31. Perry, *Jacqueline Kennedy,* 52.

32. As quoted in Marton, *Hidden Power,* 90.

33. Margaret Truman, *Bess W. Truman,* 183.

34. Caro, *Years of Lyndon Johnson: Means of Ascent,* 70–71.

35. Edmondson and Cohen, *Women of Watergate,* 220.

36. For an extended and comparatively even-handed discussion of the "name issue," see

Bernstein, *Woman in Charge,* 140, 157, 160–61, 165–67. For a critical perspective, see Olson, *Hell to Pay,* 83–97, 188–93.

37. Margaret Truman, *Bess W. Truman,* 183.

38. When Jacqueline Kennedy did join the campaign, she drew the attention of the press. See "Kennedy Team Hard to Beat," *Boston American,* October 8, 1958.

39. Betty Ford, *Times of My Life,* 103–04.

40. Lee Kelly, "Laura Bush Wants to Help Texas Authors," *Austin American-Statesman,* January 17, 1995; Anne Morris, "First Lady Reveals Plans for Texas Book Festival," *Austin American-Statesman,* March 26, 1996; Michael Holmes, "First Lady's Program Gives Financial Boost to Literacy in 10 Cities," *Austin American-Statesman,* July 10, 1996; Don McLeese, "Book Event Was Too Noble for Cynicism," *Austin American-Statesman,* November 19, 1996; Texas Book Festival, www.texasbookfestival.org (accessed June 25, 2008).

41. It is interesting to note that Gerald Ford described his own opportunity to observe his predecessors in office as relevant to his service as president. See Gerald Ford, "Remarks on Taking the Oath of Office," 2.

42. Clark Clifford has also stated that Bess Truman was an important advisor to the president on personnel matters. As quoted in Marton, *Hidden Power,* 100–101. For Gerald Ford's acknowledgment of Betty Ford, see "Remarks on Taking the Oath of Office," 1.

43. Hoover, *Memoirs of Herbert Hoover: Years of Adventure,* 210–12, see also 117–209; Clements, *Hoover, Conservation, and Consumerism,* 26–38; Nash, *Life of Herbert Hoover,* 252–53; "Lou Henry Hoover Chronology," Subject File, Herbert Hoover Library.

44. See "Girl Scouts of the United States of America, Mrs. Herbert Hoover, From Mrs. Dermady of the NY Hdqrs, July 1965," Subject File, Herbert Hoover Library; Sefton, *Women's Division, National Athletic Federation;* Hoover, *Memoirs of Herbert Hoover: Years of Adventure,* 272–74, see also 217–427; Smith, *An Uncommon Man,* 80–96; "Lou Henry Hoover Chronology," Subject File, Herbert Hoover Library. On Lou Henry Hoover's use of her connection to the Girl Scouts to advance administration interests, see Gould, "Neglected First Lady," 67, 76. More generally, see Young, *Lou Henry Hoover,* 30–40; Mayer, *Lou Henry Hoover.*

45. Russell, *Lady Bird,* 210.

46. Barbara Bush, *A Memoir,* 130–35.

47. Schweizer and Schweizer, *The Bushes,* 142, 158, 224, 243, 259, 272, 276.

48. On the need for women to be activists and to actively participate in politics, see Mrs. Roosevelt, as told to Catharine Brody, "What I Want Most Out of Life." On the need for women to "organize as women" to work within the system and see that their interests are served, see Mrs. Franklin D. Roosevelt, "Women Must Learn to Play the Game as Men Do," *Redbook,* April 1928, 78–79, 141–42. More generally, see Perry, "Training for Public Life"; Ware, "ER and Democratic Politics"; and Zangrando and Zangrando, "ER and Black Civil Rights," all found in Hoff-Wilson and Lightman, eds., *Without Precedent.*

49. Bill Clinton, "Remarks and an Exchange with Reporters on Health Care Reform," 14; Rodham Clinton, *Living History.*

50. State of Georgia, Governor's Commission, *Helping Troubled Georgians Solve Their Problems,* 30; Rosalynn Carter, *First Lady from Plains,* 93–95.

51. Phillips Brooks, "First Lady Stakes Out Political Ground," *Austin American-Statesman,* June 23, 1999. On later controversies associated with Head Start funding, see Brooks, "Day Care or Education? Head Start Debate Reignited," *Austin American-Statesman,* September 12, 1999.

52. For evidence of Hoover's coalition building across gender boundaries and her leadership in women's athletics, see "National Amateur Athletic Federation: Women's Division"

files, Clubs and Organizations, Box 40, Lou Henry Hoover Subject File, Herbert Hoover Library. See also Sefton, *Women's Division, National Amateur Athletic Federation,* 1–9.

53. Prior to her years as a first lady, Barbara Bush was also an accomplished fundraiser. Following the death of their daughter Robin, Barbara and George H. W. Bush founded the Bright Star Foundation to raise awareness and funding for cancer research. Barbara Bush later created a second foundation, focused on literacy, which may be more widely known. Bush, *A Memoir,* 144–47.

54. Bernstein, *Woman in Charge,* 315–16.

55. Hillary Rodham Clinton repeatedly contrasted policy and protocol. For a general discussion of the implications of this assertion, see Patterson, *White House Staff;* Helm, *The Captains and the Kings;* Gretchen Poston, exit interview conducted by Emily Soapes, January 2, 1981, Jimmy Carter Library.

56. Cook, *Eleanor Roosevelt,* vol. 1; Eleanor Roosevelt, *Autobiography,* 75–87; Lash, *Eleanor and Franklin,* 184–92, 210–11.

57. Margaret Truman remarked that her father had little patience with social outreach during the war years, viewing it as an inappropriate distraction for elected officials. Bess Truman acknowledged that a great deal of politicking was undertaken at social events, but she limited her own participation for financial and personal reasons. She was also protective of her daughter, allowing her to attend very few society events. Truman, *Bess W. Truman,* 217. See also Robbins, *Bess and Harry,* 46–64.

58. Bradford, *America's Queen;* Anderson, *Jack and Jackie;* Klein, *All Too Human.*

59. See, for example, Ford's description of the Mount Vernon dinner during the Kennedy administration: Ford, *Times of My Life,* 107–10.

60. Notably, Rodham Clinton's memoir stresses her career before her marriage, and then her professional and electoral relationships as first lady of Arkansas. See Rodham Clinton, *Living History,* 56–98. This presentation was subsequently reiterated and assessed for its social outreach implications in Bernstein's biography, *Woman in Charge.*

61. Perry, *Jacqueline Kennedy;* Russell, *Lady Bird.*

62. Eleanor Roosevelt, *Autobiography,* 163.

CHAPTER 3

1. Eisenhower, *White House Years,* 260.

2. Randolph, *Presidents and First Ladies.*

3. RG 130, General Accounting 597, Payroll Records Box 1225, Chief Disbursing Agent's Files, White House Office of Budget and Accounting, Herbert Hoover Library; Philippi Harding Butler, interviewed by Raymond Henle, November 6, 12, 1966, pp. 26–27, Herbert Hoover Library.

4. The addition of a train to Lou Henry Hoover's gowns was considered especially noteworthy because she had resisted this standard of formal White House dress throughout her years as a cabinet wife. See Wilson, "Mrs. Hoover at Reception Wears Train," *Washington Post,* October 13, 1929, "Clippings, 1929," Herbert Hoover Library. On the spontaneity and generosity of the Hoovers' hospitality, see Ava Long, with Mildred Harrington, "Presidents at Home," *Ladies' Home Journal,* September 1933, 8. See also Jean Eliot, "Hoover Doubles White House Social Program," *New York Times,* November 10, 1929, "Clippings, 1929: Social, October–December," Box 40, Lou Henry Hoover Subject File, Herbert Hoover Library.

5. Randolph, *Presidents and First Ladies.* See also Susan L. Dyer interview by Raymond Henle, September 29–30, 1966, pp. 52–53, Herbert Hoover Library.

6. Herbert Hoover estimated that he covered the cost of 140,000 meals each year; the federal government paid only for the major diplomatic receptions. "Presidential Salary Correspondence" Folder, Box 257, Post-Presidential Papers—Subject File, and Herbert Hoover to James L. Wright, May 18, 1945, "Hoover—Secretaries and Aides" Folder, Herbert Hoover Library.

7. At least one reporter identified this practice of welcoming women's and girls' organizations to the White House as a continuing tradition, previously practiced in the Harding and the Coolidge administrations. Margaret Wade, "Washington Society Is Gay Preparing Spring Event," *Buffalo Evening News,* March 24, 1929, "Clippings, 1929: Social, January–March," Box 40, Lou Henry Hoover Subject File, Herbert Hoover Library.

8. Hoover, *Memoirs of Herbert Hoover: The Cabinet and the Presidency,* 323. Herbert Hoover, however, did limit his more routine availability to the public. For example, he cut the "handshaking lines" outside his office—when the president was available to all members of the public with an introduction from their member of Congress—to just Mondays and Wednesdays. Criticized in the press, he claimed the previous practice was "undignified." Carlisle Bargeron, "Hoover Makes Change in Reception Methods," *Washington Post,* March 12, 1929; "Hoover At-Homes Become Just That," *New York World,* March 12, 1929, "Clippings, 1929: Social, January–March," Box 40, Lou Henry Hoover Subject File, Herbert Hoover Library.

9. Herbert Hoover, "In Praise of Izaak Walton," *Atlantic,* June 1927, 813–19. See also Hoover, "Business of Boys," in *Addresses upon the American Road,* 238–40.

10. "The President's Mountain School, History to May 10, 1931," by Ruth Fesler, "Rapidan School History" Folder, Box 77, Lou Henry Hoover Papers—Subject File; Ruth Fesler to William Hutchins, November 4, 1929, [William] J. Hutchins to Ruth Fesler, November 13, 1929, Ruth Fesler to W. J. Hutchins, November 22, 1929, all in "President's School—Teacher Candidates" Folder, Box 77, Lou Henry Hoover Papers—Subject File; Christine Vest to Miss Fesler, Fall 1930, and Christine Vest to Miss Fesler, May 7, 1931, both in "Enrollment Statistics" Folder, Box 77, Lou Henry Hoover Papers—Subject File; Memo, ca. 1956, "Presidential Salary Statement by Herbert Hoover" Folder, Box 257, Post-Presidential Papers—Subject File, Herbert Hoover Library. See also Mayer's "Introduction: A Quick Review of a Busy Life," in Mayer, *Lou Henry Hoover,* 11.

11. Rapidan Guest Lists, "Guest List" Folder, Box 76, Lou Henry Hoover—Subject File, Herbert Hoover Library.

12. Eleanor Roosevelt, *Autobiography,* 167–68.

13. For an assessment of Bess Truman's concerns regarding social outreach, see Truman, *Memoirs,* 1:45.

14. Helm, *Captains and the Kings.*

15. Arnaz, *A Book,* 240–57; Holt, *Mamie Doud Eisenhower,* 107.

16. Mamie Doud Eisenhower to the Members of the National Geographic Society, *National Geographic,* January 1961, 1.

17. West, *Upstairs at the White House,* 169–85. See also Files of the Social Office (A. B. Tolley) Records, 1952–1961, White House Office, Dwight D. Eisenhower Library.

18. Dwight D. Eisenhower, *White House Years,* 262–63.

19. Mamie Doud Eisenhower, interview by Burg and Wickman. Emphasis in original.

20. Hummer, "First Ladies and American Women."

21. Chadakoff, *Eleanor Roosevelt's My Day,* 113.

22. Chadakoff, *Eleanor Roosevelt's My Day,* 112–13.

23. Bess Truman learned that attendance at events sponsored by an organization was taken as an endorsement of that organization's practices when she accepted in invitation to

tea from the DAR. Still practicing segregation in its bookings, the DAR had refused to allow African American concert pianist Hazel Scott to perform at Constitution Hall. Adding to the political complexities was the fact that Scott was the wife of Congressman Adam Clayton Powell Jr. (D-NY). Both Powell and Harry Truman made public statements in support of their wives. Truman's words were viewed as hostile to the civil rights cause, and created electoral and legislative difficulties. In the longer run, the president became known as a civil rights advocate, with an important presidential commission report and a powerful speech setting out far-reaching reforms, all of which provoked their own electoral responses in the 1948 campaigns. Telegram, Adam Clayton Powell Jr. to Mrs. Bess Truman, October 11, 1945; Telegram, Adam Clayton Powell Jr. to Harry S. Truman, October 1, 1945, and October 11, 1945; Telegram, Harry S. Truman to Representative Adam Clayton Powell Jr., October 12, 1945, all in "DAR Controversy" Folder, Box OF584, 93, Presidential Papers, Harry S. Truman Library; Memo to Files, citing Head Genealogist Belva Giest, Daughters of the American Revolution, regarding Bess W. Truman's membership status with the organization, October 21, 1993, Harry S. Truman Library. See also Gardner, *Harry Truman and Civil Rights*.

24. Baldrige, *Of Diamonds and Diplomats;* Baldrige, *A Lady, First;* Baldrige and Verdon, *In the Kennedy Style.*

25. Transcript, Bess Abell, oral history interview 1 by T. H. Baker, May 28, 1969, Lyndon B. Johnson Library.

26. Transcript, Bess Abell, oral history interview 1.

27. West, *Upstairs at the White House,* 341–42.

28. West, *Upstairs at the White House,* 343. Emphasis in original.

29. John F. Kennedy, "Campaign Speech on the Presidency," 133.

30. West, *Upstairs at the White House,* 255–57. See also Perry, *Jacqueline Kennedy,* 80–85.

31. Dickerson, *Among Those Present,* 105–6.

32. Betty Beale, "Johnson State Dinner Peppy, Provocative," *Los Angeles Times,* February 2, 1964.

33. Nan Robertson, "The First Lady Takes Huge Guest Lists in Her Stride," *New York Times,* January 4, 1964. This message was also delivered by the administration; see U.S. Information Agency, *El Weekend,* 1967, MP 148, Lyndon B. Johnson Library.

34. Ragsdale and Theis, "Institutionalization of the American Presidency," 1283.

35. Gutin, *President's Partner,* 67; Thomas, *Dateline,* 155–56; Woodward and Bernstein, *Final Days,* 166.

36. Downs, "Mostly Wine and Roses" [manuscript], 39–40, "Book, Mostly Wine and Roses" (1)-(2), (unpublished), Folder, Box 1, Maria Downs Papers, Gerald R. Ford Library.

37. Downs, "Mostly Wine and Roses," 84.

38. Gretchen Poston, exit interview conducted by Emily Soapes, January 2, 1981, Jimmy Carter Library.

CHAPTER 4

1. For a discussion of these developments with regard to White House communications operations, see Han, *Governing from Center Stage;* Heith, *Polling to Govern;* Kumar, *Managing the President's Message.* For the wider consequences for the White House Office, see Walcott and Hult, *Governing the White House;* Hult and Walcott, *Empowering the White House.*

2. For a historical survey of the frames imposed on first ladies by the press, see Winfield, "From a Sponsored Status to Satellite to Her Own Orbit."

3. This was the stance taken by Roosevelt and Truman social secretary Edith Helm. As neither President nor Mrs. Truman disagreed with this view, Helm was well chosen to serve as Bess Truman's effective press secretary—though it was a task that she disliked intensely. Beasley, "Bess Truman and the Press," 211.

4. "Shattering Precedents," *Duluth Tribune,* April 10, 1929, "Clippings, 1929, Automobile Driving," Box 37, Lou Henry Hoover Subject File, Herbert Hoover Library; Hoyt, *East Wing,* especially 192, 199.

5. Ware, *Beyond Suffrage.*

6. Harrison, *On Account of Sex.*

7. Friedan, *Feminine Mystique,* especially 33–68.

8. On this point, see Suzanne Dixon's discussion of the "first lady icon." Dixon, "Enduring Theme," 216.

9. Hummer, "First Ladies and American Women," especially 267–331.

10. On the use of private-sphere roles to justify women's public-sphere participation in the early twentieth century, the time of Hoover's political coming of age, see Skocpol, *Protecting Soldiers and Mothers,* 321–72.

11. "Bow to a Lady," *Los Angeles Times,* January 18, 1953.

12. On Bess Truman's contributions as the president's confidante and advisor, see Robbins, *Bess and Harry,* 47; Margaret Truman, *Bess W. Truman,* especially 286, 303, 310, 338, 344; Marton, *Hidden Power,* 100–101.

13. For a historical survey of first lady rhetoric, see Parry-Giles and Blair, "Rise of the Rhetorical First Lady."

14. Kumar, *Managing the President's Message,* especially xxii–xxxii, 302–3.

15. "Satellite status" was defined and developed by Lang in "Most Admired Woman," 148.

16. Margaret Truman, *Bess W. Truman,* 337–44.

17. Will Irwin, "Mrs. Hoover," *New York Herald Tribune,* October 23, 1932.

18. Hortense Saunders, "Busy Mrs. Hoover Faces New Problems Mastering Difficult Role of First Lady," *Washington Daily News,* March 13, 1929.

19. Furman, *Washington By-Line,* 56–61. Similarly, after Herbert Hoover rejected requests for photographs throughout the 1928 campaign, George Akerson arranged for a senior campaign staff member to slip into the Hoover's home and (temporarily) steal family pictures from the walls. Edward Anthony and Ester Anthony, oral history by Raymond Henle, July 12, 1970, Herbert Hoover Library.

20. Gould, "Neglected First Lady"; Rapidan Guest Lists, "Guest List" Folder, Box 76, Lou Henry Hoover—Subject File, Herbert Hoover Library.

21. "Mrs. DePriest Went to Tea as 'Duty,'" *Chicago Defender,* June 29, 1929; talking points, attached to LHH [Lou Henry Hoover] to Mr. Akerson, June 14, 1929; "Colored Question—DePriest Incident Correspondence, 1929 June 14" Folder, Box 106, Subject File, Presidential Papers, Herbert Hoover Library.

22. Harris Survey, October 1971. Sixty-seven percent of respondents respected Mamie Eisenhower "a great deal," 26 percent "somewhat," 4 percent "not at all," and 3 percent had either not heard of her or were not sure of their opinions. A Virginia Slims American Women's Poll conducted in April 1974 reported sex-specific numbers: 57 percent of women and 50 percent of men respected her a "great deal"; 34 percent of women and 37 percent of men respected her "somewhat"; 3 percent of women and 7 percent of men did not respect her at all; and 7 percent of women and 7 percent of men had either not heard of her or were unsure of their opinions. Data provided by the Roper Center for Public Opinion Research at the University of Connecticut.

23. Cook, *Eleanor Roosevelt,* 2:3.

24. Beasley, *White House Press Conferences of Eleanor Roosevelt;* Cook, *Eleanor Roosevelt,* 2:30–65.

25. Chadakoff, *Eleanor Roosevelt's My Day,* 134–35.

26. Scharf, *Eleanor Roosevelt,* 9.

27. Mrs. Roosevelt, "Women Must Learn to Play the Game as Men Do," 141.

28. Mrs. Roosevelt, *It's Up to the Women,* 202, 204.

29. On social feminism in the New Deal Era, see Ware, *Beyond Suffrage.*

30. Truman, *Bess W. Truman,* 257.

31. Frances Perkins, oral history, Columbia University.

32. Roosevelt, for her part, did not consider Perkins a suitable mentor in regard to press relations. See Eleanor Roosevelt, "Women in Politics," in Black, *What I Hope to Leave Behind,* 253.

33. Helm, *Captains and the Kings,* 253–57.

34. "Mrs. Truman—Miscellaneous Materials re.," Folder, Box 5, Raethel Odum Papers, Harry S. Truman Library.

35. "Mrs. Truman—Miscellaneous Materials re.," Folder, Box 5, Raethel Odum Papers, Harry S. Truman Library.

36. These qualities—privacy, protectiveness, and resistance—are repeatedly stressed in biographical accounts of Bess Truman. See, for example, McCullough, *Truman;* Margaret Truman, *Bess W. Truman,* 337–44. See also Louchheim, *By the Political Sea,* 117.

37. See, for example, Margaret Truman, *Bess W. Truman,* 345.

38. Margaret Truman, *Bess W. Truman,* 250–86; Harry Truman, *Dear Bess,* 528–65.

39. "Bow to a Lady," *Los Angeles Times,* January 18, 1953.

40. van Rensselaer, *Jacqueline Kennedy,* 33–34. For an example of coverage that included Jacqueline and Caroline Kennedy in John Kennedy's Senate reelection campaign, see "Kennedy Team Hard to Beat, Jackie Aids Senate Fight," *Boston American,* October 8, 1958.

41. Pam [Turnure] to Pierre [Salinger], Memo, June 22, 1961, "PP5/Kennedy, Jacqueline" Folder, Box 705, White House Central Files—Executive, John F. Kennedy Library.

42. Bradford, *America's Queen,* 117–23; Lubin, *Shooting Kennedy;* West, *Upstairs at the White House,* 232; Perry, *Jacqueline Kennedy,* 85–134; van Rensselaer, *Jacqueline Kennedy,* 284–91. On John F. Kennedy's response to the arts—his "personal tastes were very commonplace"—see Brown, *JFK,* 12–15.

43. Schlesinger, *A Thousand Days,* 671.

44. Douglas, *Where the Girls Are,* 41.

45. Baldrige, *A Lady, First,* 183.

46. Silvestri, *Becoming JFK,* 277. For a more extended study of political symbolism and substance as conveyed through Jacqueline Kennedy's fashion design, see Bowles and Schlesinger, *Jacqueline Kennedy.* Her voice tones were particularly soft and childlike in her televised tour of the White House. For text, see Wolff, *Tour of the White House.*

47. Anthony, *As We Remember Her,* 171; Louchheim, *By the Political Sea,* 136.

48. Bradford, *America's Queen,* 122.

49. As quoted from the *New York Times,* in Carpenter, *Ruffles and Flourishes,* 46.

50. All numbers calculated regarding Lady Bird Johnson's travel as first lady are developed from files kept by Liz Carpenter. See Liz Carpenter Subject Files, Lyndon B. Johnson Library.

51. Press relations in this first ladyship seemed to be as positive as those in the Roosevelt years, with both Eleanor Roosevelt and Lady Bird Johnson providing substantive information and respecting the constraints that confronted journalists, from deadlines to story length and content. See Lonelle Aikman, oral history, pp. 1–2, Lyndon B. Johnson Library.

52. As quoted in Russell, *Lady Bird.*

53. A number of biographers attribute these qualities to Lyndon B. Johnson's behavior toward his wife. The kindest description of their relationship is provided by chief usher J. B. West, who refers to the president as dominating and "at times, I felt, almost abusive." Robert Caro cites considerable evidence in support of his contention that there was psychological abuse within the relationship. West, *Upstairs at the White House,* 295; Caro, *Years of Lyndon Johnson: The Path to Power,* especially 301–5.

54. Memorandum, Douglass Cater to the President, "Here is a report on the First Lady's tour," August 18, 1964, "PP5/Johnson, Lady Bird, 7.15.64–10.1.64," Box 62, PP5/Johnson, Lady Bird, White House Central Files, Executive Files, Lyndon B. Johnson Library.

55. Carpenter, *Ruffles and Flourishes,* 18–19.

56. The work performed by members of Carpenter's press office, and others, is recorded in their memoranda and public correspondence. These materials are found in the Liz Carpenter Subject Files at the Lyndon B. Johnson Library.

57. See, for example, Carpenter, *Ruffles and Flourishes,* 119, 122.

58. Bess Abell, oral history interview 2 by T. H. Baker, June 13, 1969, pp. 8–11, Lyndon B. Johnson Library; Elizabeth Carpenter, oral history interview 1 by Joe B. Frantz, December 3, 1968, pp. 10–18; "Whistle Stop, 10.13–16.64" Folder, Box 11, Liz Carpenter Subject Files, Lyndon B. Johnson Library; Carpenter, *Ruffles and Flourishes,* 120–22.

59. Press release, "Remarks by Mrs. Lyndon B. Johnson, Alexandria, Virginia," October 6, 1964, "Press Release Copies of Mrs. Johnson's Speeches—1964 [1.11.64–10.27.64]," Box 1, Mrs. Johnson's Speeches—Service Set, Lyndon B. Johnson Library.

60. Muriel Dobbin, "Mrs. Johnson Finds Political Climate is Cooler in South," *Baltimore Sun,* October 9, 1964.

61. "The Lasting Effects," *Charleston News and Courier,* October 9, 1964.

62. Memo, Liz Carpenter to the President, February 25, 1966, "PP5/Johnson, Lady Bird 10/1/65–5/9/65" Folder, White House Central Files—Executive, Lyndon B. Johnson Library.

63. Lady Bird Johnson, "Remarks before the General Session," 128.

64. See, for example Heith, *Polling to Govern.*

65. Betty Ford's second autobiography tells her story of recovery from alcohol and drug dependency; see *Betty: A Glad Awakening.* On popular and media responses to Ford's "outspokenness," see Elizabeth Peer, Jane Whitmore, and Lisa Whitman, "Free Spirit in the White House, Woman of the Year," *Newsweek,* December 29, 1975.

66. "Traveling with Pat Nixon—A Different Type of Tour," *U.S. News and World Report,* June 30, 1969, 9; Nan Robertson, "War Protests Mar Mrs. Nixon's Tour," *New York Times,* June 17, 1969.

67. Lenore Hershey, "Compassion Power," *Ladies' Home Journal,* September 1969, 144.

68. Robertson, "War Protests Mar Mrs. Nixon's Tour."

69. Archival records of the first lady's travel are somewhat contradictory. One source claims that the first lady visited over seventy-five countries. (Mrs. Nixon's Projects and Activities as First Lady," Box 7, Susan Porter Files, Richard M. Nixon Presidential Materials.) However, her calendars indicate only thirty-seven, with several countries visited more than once. ("Official Calendars, Activities and Honorary Affiliations, 1969–1974" Folders, Box 19, Susan Porter Files, Richard M. Nixon Presidential Materials.) William R. Codus, who advanced several of the first lady's independent trips, made reference to a one-week trip around the United States, "several" one-day trips, and then independent international travel to Peru and to Africa (Liberia, Ghana, and the Ivory Coast). Codus also did advance work for the first lady when she accompanied the president to the Soviet Union. William R. Codus, exit inter-

view by Terry W. Good, November 29, 1972, Richard M. Nixon Presidential Materials. This lack of clarity is also somewhat evident in the secondary literature. Edmondson and Cohen maintain that the first lady had an "unprecedented" number of solo appearances throughout the reelection campaign, but Gutin's discussion of her travel is centered on trips taken with the president. Edmondson and Cohen, *Women of Watergate,* 216; Gutin, *President's Partner,* 67.

70. The same story critiqued the time that the first lady devoted to correspondence, stating that it was no substitute for actually seeing the first lady reach out to the public through travel and policy work. Nan Robertson, "A Starring Role Is Not for Mrs. Nixon," *New York Times,* January 26, 1970. An article that was otherwise critical of the first lady did support her correspondence practices. See Judith Viorst, "Pat Nixon is the Ultimate Good Sport," *New York Times Magazine,* September 13, 1970, 25–27.

71. Thomas, *Dateline,* 167–69; Marton, *Hidden Power,* 189; Hummer, "First Ladies and American Women," 341, nn. 640, 641.

72. Marton, *Hidden Power,* 177.

73. Flora Rheta Schreiber, "Pat Nixon Reveals for the First Time, 'I didn't want Dick to run again.'" *Good Housekeeping,* July 1968, 65.

74. Stuart was married to Charles E. Stuart, staff assistant to John D. Ehrlichman. Constance Stuart, exit interview by Susan Yowell, March 15, 1973, pp. 5–8, Richard M. Nixon Presidential Materials; Constance C. Stuart, oral history interview by Paul A. Schmidt and Frederick J. Graboske, August 15, 1988, pp. 3–6, 13, Richard M. Nixon Presidential Materials; McLendon and Smith, *Don't Quote Me,* 63–66.

75. "Nixon Depicts His Wife as Strong and Sensitive," *New York Times,* March 14, 1971.

76. Rejecting arguments that the president's aides significantly constrained the first lady's descriptive representation, communications scholar Myra Gutin maintained that Pat Nixon rejected opportunities to communicate her descriptive representation. See *President's Partner,* 61. *Washington Post* reporters Bob Woodward and Carl Bernstein are among those who, in contrast, highlight the role of the president and the president's aides in limiting the first lady. See *Final Days,* 32, 164–66.

77. Thomas, *Dateline,* 165; Edmondson and Cohen, *Women of Watergate,* 223–25. The reference to the first lady as resentful is routinely traced to a statement she made to Gloria Steinem, who was covering the 1968 campaign for *New York* magazine. Steinem, "Patricia Nixon Flying," 273.

78. Betty Ford was, however, "relatively active" as second lady. See Greene, *Betty Ford,* 31–32.

79. [Gerald R. Ford], "President's News Conference of November 26, 1975." See, for example, Myra MacPherson, "The Blooming of Betty Ford," *McCall's,* September 1975, 93.

80. The president's aides were also opposed to having an activist first lady. Given that a number of these individuals had served in the Nixon administration, this could reflect their socialization to (if not their own preference for) a marginalized first lady's staff. See Greene, *Betty Ford,* 40–42. For depictions of the first lady as advising the president, see Jane Howard, "Forward Day by Day," *New York Times,* December 8, 1974, 36.

81. For a discussion of the first lady's approval ratings and polling data, with a demographic breakdown, see Greene, *Betty Ford,* 83–84, 117–21.

82. *60 Minutes* transcript, interview with Betty Ford, CBS Television Network, 1975, pp. 8–9, Gerald R. Ford Library.

83. Borrelli, "Competing Conceptions of the First Ladyship"; Ford, *Times of My Life,* 226.

84. Gutin, *President's Partner,* 136; Greene, *Betty Ford,* 83–84, 92.

85. Thomas, *Dateline,* 273.

86. "Mrs. Ford's Remarks Before Participants in Homemaking and Identity Confer-

ence," "Homemaking and Identity Conference, White House, September 26, 1975" Folder, Box 3, Frances K. Pullen Files, Gerald R. Ford Library. Emphasis in original. For another example of Ford's prioritizing of choice in women's lives, see the interview conducted by Barbara Howar for *Family Circle*, "Spotlight on Betty Ford: A New Breed of Wife in the Nation's Capital," November 1974, 140.

87. Troy, *Affairs of State*, 207–35; Troy, *Mr. and Mrs. President*, 207–35. For cautious criticism of the first lady's descriptive and substantive representation from a member of the administration, see Anne Armstrong, oral history by David Horrocks, April 9, 1997, pp. 12–14, Gerald R. Ford Library.

88. Stroud, *How Jimmy Won*, 106–8. Douglas Brinkley noted that while the first lady was her husband's full partner, she would often "defer" to his "stubbornness." *Unfinished Presidency*, 28–29. For a discussion of the first lady's tactics in lobbying the president and her participation in presidential decision making, see Brzezinski, *Power and Principle*, 32, 105, 241, 279. Kandy Stroud, "Rosalynn Carter: The Steel Magnolia," *Cosmopolitan*, October 1979, 332.

89. A *Philadelphia Inquirer* reporter highlighted these changes in media perception in his coverage of the 1980 campaign. Christopher Bonner, "Unlike in 1976, Mrs. Carter Now Carries the Show," *Philadelphia Inquirer*, April 6, 1980. Some reporters critiqued the first lady for her complicity in the president's "Rose Garden strategy" throughout the reelection campaign. See "Rosalynn's Role," *Christian Science Monitor*, July 31, 1979.

90. "White House Study Project: Report on the Functions and Organization of the Office of the First Lady," January 6, 1977, "ADP—First Lady's Staff" Folder, Box 1, Staff Offices—Administration—Malachuk, Jimmy Carter Library. See also Hult and Walcott, *Empowering the White House*, 38, 193ff.

91. For a discussion of Carter's policy work, see Kathy Cade exit interview by Emily Soapes, January 7, 1981, Jimmy Carter Library. On the connections that Rosalynn Carter perceived among the issues of mental health-care reform, the aging, and volunteerism, see Kaufman, *Rosalynn Carter*, 42–53, 59–60, 121–130. Kaufman also examines why the press disagreed with the first lady's assessment of her agenda, finding it unclear, complicated, and confusing. Her press secretary, Mary Finch Hoyt, defends the agenda in her memoir, *East Wing*, 136.

92. Among those who felt that the first lady was not doing enough and therefore did not merit more extensive or front-page coverage was Helen Thomas. Gutin, *President's Partner*, 156. For a summary of the tensions affecting Carter's press relations, see Kaufman, *Rosalynn Carter*, 121–31.

93. For a rare positive review, see Kandy Stroud, "Rosalynn's Agenda in the White House," *New York Times*, March 20, 1977.

94. Sally Quinn, "Have You Heard What They're Not Saying about Rosalynn?" *Washington Post*, June 25, 1978.

95. Tom Morgenthau and Eleanor Clift, "National Affairs: The President's Partner," *Newsweek*, November 5, 1979.

96. See, for example, B. Drummond Ayres Jr., "The Importance of Being Rosalynn," *New York Times Magazine*, June 3, 1979, 10; "Second Most Powerful Person," *Time*, May 7, 1979, 22; "Selling True Grit—and By God She's Good at It!" *Time*, August 6, 1979, 12–13. Rare praise for the first lady's political participation came from columnist Carl T. Rowan, "The President's Wife," *Washington Star*, August 3, 1979, and from reporter Richard Cohen, "Rosalynn Carter's Role: Resolving the Mystery," *Washington Post*, July 31, 1979. For an assessment of the changes that were made in Carter's image (in the words of Democratic National Committee chair Robert Strauss, "She's more attractive physically and intellectually.

She's matured politically."), see Jill Gerston, "No Shelter from the Criticism, Rosalynn Carter Sticks to the Task at Hand," *Philadelphia Inquirer,* October 14, 1980.

97. Linda Charlton, "Rosalynn Carter: Balancing Roles," *New York Times,* November 6, 1977. This was also the frame, more generally, that Rosalynn Carter used in discussing her marriage during the presidential term. Stroud, "Rosalynn Carter," 293.

98. Hoyt, *East Wing,* 200. Emphasis in original.

99. Hoyt's own frustrations became part of the first lady's coverage. See Quinn, "Have You Heard What They're Not Saying About Rosalynn?"; Nancy Lewis, "Rosalynn Carter's Story Just Isn't Getting Across," *Atlanta Constitution,* August 1, 1978. Hoyt later acknowledged that her performance as a press secretary might have been uneven. Her son, a commercial fisherman and captain, was lost at sea in September 1978. His body was never recovered; Hoyt never learned what had happened to the boat and its crew of six. Hoyt's grief was overwhelming. She stated that working at the White House "saved" her, focusing her energies, but her actions were "very destructive" at times. Mary Finch Hoyt exit interview by Marie Allen, December 16, 1980, pp. 18–19, Jimmy Carter Library.

100. For example, Pat Nixon's first press secretary was critiqued in terms similar to those directed at Hoyt. See McLendon and Smith, *Don't Quote Me,* 59.

101. Hoyt, *East Wing,* 163. See also Hoyt exit interview, 28–29, Jimmy Carter Library.

102. Jamieson, *Beyond the Double Bind,* especially 13–21.

103. Jamieson, *Beyond the Double Bind,* 16.

104. Duerst-Lahti, "Governing Institutions, Ideologies, and Gender."

105. As quoted in Hertz and Reverby, "Gentility, Gender, and Political Protest," 596.

106. For a detailed analysis of the controversy, including study of the public mail written in response to the student petition and the first lady's speech, see Hertz and Reverby, "Gentility, Gender, and Political Protest."

107. "Radio Address by Mrs. Bush," November 17, 2001, press release. This speech was followed by a series of policy statements and meetings. See Elisabeth Bumiller, "The Politics of Plight and the Gender Gap," *New York Times,* November 19, 2001; Elisabeth Bumiller, "Afghan Women Trade Shadows for Washington's Limelight," *New York Times,* November 30, 2001. Laura Bush's 2005 comments in support of multiparty elections in Egypt generated similar debates and criticisms. See Elisabeth Bumiller, "The First Lady's Mideast Sandstorm," *New York Times,* June 6, 2005.

108. A particularly scathing presentation of Laura Bush's descriptive representation during the war is found in Tony Kushner's play, *Only We Who Guard the Mystery Shall Be Unhappy.* For a review, see *The Nation,* March 24, 2003. For a gender-focused analysis of this play, see Marso, "Feminism and the Complications of Freeing the Women of Afghanistan and Iraq."

109. King, *Woman in the White House,* 217. The 1993 task force charter initially estimated that it would cost less than $100,000.

110. Burrell, *Public Opinion, The First Ladyship, and Hillary Rodham Clinton,* 97–99.

111. Marton, *Hidden Power,* 327; Bostdorff, "Hillary Rodham Clinton and Elizabeth Dole," 222.

112. In defense of her reporting, Martha Sherrill, at the *Washington Post,* said that coverage of Rodham Clinton's "clothes and her hair" reflected the information the press corps had to convey—the first lady did not grant interviews, issue her schedule, or provide substantive materials to the press. Marton, *Hidden Power,* 326–27; Bernstein, *Woman in Charge,* 330.

113. Burrell, *Public Opinion, The First Ladyship, and Hillary Rodham Clinton,* 101.

114. Bernstein, *Woman in Charge,* 409–12.

115. Burrell, *Public Opinion, The First Ladyship, and Hillary Rodham Clinton,* 45–51.

116. Warner, *Hillary Clinton;* Oakley, *On the Make,* 3–4; press secretary Lissa Muscatine, "In the Corridors of Power," 6; Bernstein, *Woman in Charge,* 412–20, 438.

117. See, for example, Olson, *Hell to Pay.*

118. Harpaz, *Girls in the Van,* especially 278.

119. Maureen Dowd, "Dreams of Laura," *New York Times,* July 9, 2008.

120. Kessler, *Laura Bush.* Laura Bush did not attend presidential or senior staff meetings but was regularly briefed and consulted by the president's senior staff and advisors. Woodward, *State of Denial,* 349, 425; Elisabeth Bumiller, "First Lady Has Husband's Ear, Even About Staffing, She Says," *New York Times,* March 25, 2006; Elisabeth Bumiller, "Pillow-Talk Call for a Woman to Fill O'Connor Seat," *New York Times,* July 18, 2005.

121. Gerhart, *Perfect Wife,* 172.

122. Elisabeth Bumiller, "A First Lady Fiercely Loyal and Quietly Effective," *New York Times,* February 7, 2004.

123. See, for example, Marso, "Feminism and the Complications of Freeing the Women of Afghanistan and Iraq"; Ferguson, "Feminism and Security Rhetoric in the Post–September 11 Bush Administration"; Warters and Denison, "Laura Bush: The First Post-Feminist First Lady?"; Kessler, *Laura Bush,* 104.

124. That Laura Bush was caught in a crossfire of Republican expectations, while reaching out to unaffiliated voters, is a theme of Ann Gerhart's biography, *Perfect Wife.* See also Randy Kennedy, "The Not-So-Reluctant Bush Campaigner," *New York Times,* August 12, 2004.

125. There were, however, two instances when Laura Bush did move to the forefront. The first occurred following September 11th, when she conducted a media campaign and traveled extensively, counseling parents about the traumatic effects of the attacks on children. She was similarly forceful, this time speaking in support of the president's stem cell regulations, for a space of time during the 2004 campaign. This was a rare instance of her engagement in a policy debate, though her participation was characteristic in its defense of her husband. See, for example: Alex Kuczynski, "A Very Different Laura Bush," *New York Times,* September 30, 2001; Randy Kennedy, "First Lady Defends Limits on Stem Cell Research," *New York Times,* August 10, 2004; "Stem Cell Battles," *New York Times,* August 15, 2004. There were also several letters to the editor; see "Laura Bush and Stem Cells," *New York Times,* August 12, 2004.

126. Gerhart, *Perfect Wife,* 127.

127. "Laura Bush Remarks at a Victory '04 Rally in Duluth, MN," September 9, 2004, press release. This stump speech was well practiced. Laura Bush was featured at up to 167 "political occasions" during the 2004 campaigns. Patterson, *To Serve the President,* 253.

128. "Mrs. Bush's Remarks at Ron Lewis for Congress and Kentucky Victory 2006 Rally," November 1, 2006, press release. In 2006 the first lady made up to 67 political trips on behalf of Republican candidates. Patterson, *To Serve the President,* 253.

129. "Mrs. Bush's Remarks at Kilmer for Congress Luncheon," press release, March 29, 2004.

130. Susan Schindehette et al., "The First Lady Next Door," *People,* January 29, 2001, 50–59.

131. Schindehette et al., "First Lady Next Door," 52.

132. Bumiller, "A First Lady Fiercely Loyal and Quietly Effective."

133. Elisabeth Bumiller, "Go-Along First Lady Shows She Can Go It Alone," *New York Times,* July 7, 2003; Alessandra Stanley, "The First Lady's Influence Is Starting to Reveal Itself," *New York Times,* September 1, 2004.

134. For example, see Kuczynski, "A Very Different Laura Bush." For an extended discussion of Bush's descriptive and substantive representation, see Watson, "'Comforter in Chief.'"

135. Anne Kornblut, "Laura Bush Joins Hit Makeover Show as It Focuses on Storm Victims," *New York Times,* September 28, 2005.

136. On this theme in black feminism, see Collins, *Black Feminist Thought,* 97–148.

137. Jewell, *From Mammy to Miss America,* especially 36–47.

138. For a blog that provides an overview of responses to Obama's statement and Cindy McCain's countering statement, see "Cindy McCain, Michelle Obama in Patriotism Flap," *CNN PoliticalTicker,* February 19, 2008, http://www.politicalticker.blogs.cnn.com/2008/02/19/cindy-mccain-michelle-obama-in-patriotism-flap/?ibid=3EqDTW5ip5c.

139. For an example of Michelle Obama's responses to the stereotyping, see Richard Wolffe, "Barack's Rock," *Newsweek,* February 25, 2008.

140. See, for example, Maureen Dowd, "Should Michelle Cover Up?" *New York Times,* March 8, 2009.

141. [Michelle Obama], "Remarks by the First Lady at Event on Surgeon General's Report."

142. Jewell, *From Mammy to Miss America and Beyond,* 37–44; Winter, *Dangerous Frames,* 83–118; Collins, *Black Feminist Thought,* 72–84.

143. "Four Takes on the Mom in Chief," *The Root,* November 18, 2008. The blog commentaries on these reviews were, however, mixed. For a media critic's assessment of early coverage of Michelle Obama by African American women reporters, see Howard Kurtz, "Black Reporters on the Beat of Michelle Obama: Does Race Play a Role in Coverage?" *Washington Post,* July 2, 2009.

144. Lois Romano, "Michelle's Image: From Off-Putting to Spot-On," *Washington Post,* March 31, 2009. For polling results, see also "Michelle Obama's Favorability Ratings, NBC News/*Wall Street Journal* Poll," *New York Magazine,* March 23, 2009.

145. For a discussion of Hillary Rodham Clinton as an indicator of generational change, see Caroli, *First Ladies,* 288–308.

146. Andrew Feinberg, "Why Do They Pick on Nancy Reagan?" *Cosmopolitan,* May 1982, 262. For a rare qualifier on this self-presentation, see "Contest of the Queens," *Time,* August 30, 1976, 31–32; Sanbonmatsu, *Democrats, Republicans, and the Politics of Women's Place.*

147. This commitment to husband and family was delivered in a variety of ways. See Garry Clifford, "The New First Lady Is a Former Debutante, but Watch Out: 'She's a Fighter,'" *People,* November 17, 1980, 44–47; John Duka, "Notes on Fashion," *New York Times,* November 11, 1980.

148. Dugger, *On Reagan,* 122–23; Gutin, *President's Partner,* 166; Leamer, *Make-Believe,* 347; Jay Peterzell, "Designing Woman," *New Republic,* February 10, 1992, 12–13. The president defended the first lady to the press; see "Remarks and a Question-and-Answer Session at a Working Luncheon with Out-of-Town Editors," October 16, 1981, and "Interview with the President," December 23, 1981, *Public Papers of the Presidents of the United States: Ronald Reagan, 1981.* Thomas M. DeFrank and Eleanor Clift also interviewed the president about the first lady: "As Reagan Sees Her," *Newsweek,* December 21, 1981, 27. In December 1981, in the midst of this criticism, the first lady was ranked first in the Gallup poll listing of "most admired women," a public assessment that initially shocked and then pleased her. David Bird and Dorothy J. Gaiter, "Notes on People," *New York Times,* December 24, 1981. The criticisms and defenses continued through the second term. Bernard Weinraub, "Angry Reagan Calls Reports of Wife's Power 'a Fiction,'" *New York Times,* March 5, 1987.

149. Fred Barnes, "Nancy's Total Makeover," *New Republic,* September 16/23, 1985, 16.

150. In reference to the Regan firing, the press generally agreed that Nancy Reagan's strength came at the expense of Ronald Reagan's. Leslie Stahl, however, endorsed the first lady's actions and referred to her as "the president's protector in chief." Stahl, *Reporting Live,* 267, 275–76. Joseph C. Harsch agreed with Stahl that, in ousting Don Regan, Nancy Reagan had made a positive political contribution. See "In Defense of Nancy Reagan," *Christian Science Monitor,* March 17, 1987, 15.

151. Regan, *For the Record*, 290.

152. Regan, *For the Record*, 288.

153. Benze, *Nancy Reagan*, 68–86. Lou Cannon maintained that this ideological lobbying could be traced to the earliest years of the Reagan marriage, when Nancy Reagan encouraged Ronald Reagan's shift from the Democratic to the Republican party. Lou Cannon, "A Protector, Not a Policymaker," *Washington Post*, March 9, 1987, A2. *Time* reporters were interviewing Regan when the chief of staff received notice that he was fired. Their sympathetic account—which was highly critical of the first lady—was delivered by Amy Wilnetz in "Just Say Goodbye, Don," *Time*, March 9, 1987, 28–29. Schieffer and Gates, *Acting President*, 333; Thomas, *Front Row at the White House*, 272. Helene von Damm exemplifies the hostility of strong conservatives to perceived moderates within the administration; see *At Reagan's Side*.

154. Peterzell, "Designing Woman," 12–13; "Borrowed Rags," *Financial Times*, October 20, 1988.

155. On the Nancy Reagan–Barbara Bush contrasts, see Marton, *Hidden Power*, 275; Parmet, *George Bush*, 259.

156. As an example of the feminist endorsement of Barbara Bush as a gender role model for "women of a certain age," see Doris Willens, "My Kind of First Lady," *New York Times*, December 11, 1988. More generally, see Patricia Leigh Brown, "The First Lady-Elect: What She Is and Isn't," *New York Times*, December 11, 1988.

157. Troy, "'Half-Eleanor, Half-Bess,'" 453–54.

158. Somewhat ironically, it was a *Vanity Fair* article that drew attention to the issue of class in Barbara Bush's descriptive representation. See Marjorie Williams, "Barbara's Backlash," *Vanity Fair*, August 1992, 120–21.

159. Bush, "Choices and Change." Emphasis in original.

160. Troy, "'Half-Eleanor, Half-Bess,'" 457; Paul Chin, "In the Eye of the Storm," *People Weekly*, October 1, 1990, 82+.

161. Schweizer and Schweizer, *The Bushes*, 338; Fitzwater, *Call the Briefing!*, 168.

162. Grimes, *Running Mates*, 187; Williams, "Barbara's Backlash," 120–21.

163. Grimes, *Running Mates*, 202.

164. Killian, *Barbara Bush*, 199.

165. See also Parmet, *George Bush*, 425.

166. Alessandra Stanley, "Barbara Bush, The Un-Secret Weapon," *New York Times*, August 19, 1992; Alessandra Stanley, "First Lady on Abortion: Not a Platform Issue," *New York Times*, August 14, 1992.

167. For a commentary about the cookie cook-off that considers class, gender, and regional aspects of the women's identity, as well as partisan politics, see food historian Laura Shapiro's article, "The Great Bush-Kerry Bake-off," *Boston Globe*, July 11, 2004.

168. Kernell, *Going Public*.

169. Clinton's syndicated column, coauthored with press secretary Lissa Muscatine, was titled "Talking It Over." It was first published on July 23, 1995, and appeared in more than one hundred newspapers worldwide. King, *Woman in the White House*, 224; Lloyd Grove, "First Lady in the Fourth Estate," *Washington Post*, October 12, 1995, C1.

CHAPTER 5

1. On Eleanor Roosevelt's substantive representation, see Cook, *Eleanor Roosevelt*, vol. 2; Eleanor Roosevelt, *Autobiography*; Mrs. Roosevelt, *It's Up to the Women*; Goodwin, *No Ordinary Time*; Black, *Courage in a Dangerous World*. Also see Zangrando and Zangrando, "ER and

Black Civil Rights"; Perry, "Training for Public Life"; and Ware, "ER and Democratic Politics: Women in the Postsuffrage Era."

2. Margaret Truman, *Bess W. Truman,* 257, 286, 303, 310, 344.

3. Mamie Eisenhower's participation in the presidential campaigns included several television advertisements with different formats. One was a panel interview, somewhat similar to present-day talk-show dialogues with a group of women and the president; another was a more standard political commercial, and still another aired birthday parties for herself and for the president. Holt, *Mamie Doud Eisenhower,* 119.

4. Mamie Doud Eisenhower, interview by Maclyn Burg and John Wickman, July 20, 1972, Dwight D. Eisenhower Library, p. 132.

5. Mamie Doud Eisenhower, interview by Burg and Wickman, 35–38; David and David, *Ike and Mamie,* 95.

6. Mamie Doud Eisenhower, interview by Burg and Wickman, 154. On the demarcation of first lady and presidential responsibilities, see Susan Eisenhower, *Mrs. Ike,* 277–79.

7. West, *Upstairs at the White House,* 132.

8. "Mrs. Truman—Miscellaneous Materials re.," Folder, Box 5, Raethel Odum Papers, Harry S. Truman Library.

9. Margaret Truman, *Bess W. Truman,* 258–86, 303–44; West, *Upstairs at the White House,* 77, 127.

10. Neal, *Eisenhowers,* 401.

11. On the exclusion of the first lady from decision-making routines of the senior White House staff, see Eisenhower, *Mrs. Ike,* 277; Burke, *Institutional Presidency,* 62–65; Hess and Pfiffner, *Organizing the Presidency,* 56–62. For an assessment of the ways in which organizational structure reveals gender ideology, see Duerst-Lahti, "Gender Power Relations in Public Bureaucracies."

12. "Sharing the Bully Pulpit." Movement historians have debated Ford's impact. For a sense of the contrasting views, see Zones, "Profits from Pain"; Weisman, "Breast Cancer Policymaking"; Dubriwny, "Constructing Breast Cancer in the News."

13. Sargent Shriver, oral history interview by Michael L. Gillette, interview 3, July 1, 1982, pp. 15–16, and interview 4, February 7, 1986, pp. 20–21, Lyndon B. Johnson Library. For a partial documentary record of the first lady's work on behalf of Head Start, see "Head Start Volunteer Drive—Honorary Chairman (June 25, 1968)" Folder, Box 53; "Operation Head Start," Box 72, Liz Carpenter Subject File, Lyndon B. Johnson Library.

14. Penelope A. Adams, interview by Paul A. Schmidt, August 4, 1988, p. 2, Richard M. Nixon Presidential Materials.

15. Edmondson and Duer, *Women of Watergate,* 218–25.

16. Anthony, *First Ladies,* 2:177–88.

17. Nan Robertson, "Mrs. Nixon Describes Students as Idealists, 'Great Generation,'" *New York Times,* March 7, 1970.

18. Thomas, *Dateline,* 165.

19. See, for example, Nan Robertson, "A Starring Role Is Not for Mrs. Nixon," *New York Times,* January 26, 1970; Gutin, *President's Partner,* 61.

20. Martin, *Presidency and Women,* 124–27, 135–36, 157–58, 245–47, 259–69. "Women's Rights à la Pat Nixon," *U.S. News and World Report,* May 19, 1969, 18.

21. Edmondson and Duer, *Women of Watergate,* 222. See also: Steinem, "Patricia Nixon Flying."

22. "Traveling with Pat Nixon—A Different Type of Tour," *U.S. News and World Report,* June 30, 1969, 9.

23. Robertson, "Mrs. Nixon Describes Students as Idealists."

24. William R. Codus exit interview by Terry W. Good, November 29, 1972, Richard M. Nixon Presidential Materials; Anthony, *First Ladies,* 2:197.

25. Anthony, *First Ladies,* 2:186.

26. Gutin, *President's Partner,* 129.

27. Frances Spatz Leighton, "The Race for 'First Lady,'" *Family Weekly,* October 24, 1976, 4; Betty Ford, *Times of My Life.*

28. Greene, *Betty Ford,* 54–68.

29. "First Lady Betty Ford's Remarks to the International Women's Year Conference," October 25, 1975, "1975/10/25—International Women's Year Conference, Cleveland, Ohio" Folder, Box 3, Frances Kaye Pullen Files, Gerald R. Ford Library.

30. "Mrs. Ford Scored on Equality Plan," *New York Times,* February 20, 1975; "Ford, Betty, 1918–" Folder, Vertical File, Gerald R. Ford Library. See also Borrelli, "Competing Conceptions of the First Ladyship," 404; "A Fighting First Lady," *Time,* March 3, 1975, 20.

31. Richard S. Dawson Jr. to Mrs. Betty Ford, August 13, 1975, "Betty Ford's *60 Minutes* Interview, Box 443" Folder, Bulk Mail File Samples, Box 14, White House Social Files, Gerald R. Ford Library.

32. Laura Bush testified before the Senate Committee on Health, Education, Labor, and Pensions in a forum titled "Early Learning: Investing in Our Children, Investing in Our Future," 107th Cong., 2nd sess. Elisabeth Bumiller, "Mrs. Bush, Husband in Tow, Discusses Problems of Youth," *New York Times,* March 8, 2005; Gerhart, *Perfect Wife;* Kessler, *Laura Bush;* Patterson, *To Serve the President,* 243–59; Wertheimer, "Laura Bush."

33. U.S. Senate, "Forum: Early Learning: Investing in Our Children, Investing in Our Future," Committee on Health, Education, Labor, and Pensions, 107th Cong., 2nd sess., p. 12.

34. For a discussion of the multiple discourses at work in foreign policy, see Ferguson, "Feminism and Security Rhetoric in the Post–September 11 Bush Administration."

35. For an account of Laura Bush's travel and speechmaking on behalf of children's rights, see Wertheimer, "Laura Bush," 456–59.

36. Gerhart, *Perfect Wife,* 99.

37. Elisabeth Bumiller, "With Anti-war Poetry Set, Mrs. Bush Postpones Event," *New York Times,* January 31, 2003. In several previous interviews, Bush had insisted, "There's nothing political about American literature." See, for example, Elisabeth Bumiller, "Quietly, the First Lady Builds a Literary Room of Her Own," *New York Times,* October 7, 2002.

38. *Washington Post* reporter Ann Gerhart concluded that Laura Bush rejected the entrepreneurial role of a policy advocate in favor of the more circumscribed responsibilities of an "informed supporter" of the president. *Perfect Wife,* especially pp. 124, 172, 186. For a contrasting assessment that presents the first lady as far more activist in her substantive representation, see Patterson, *To Serve the President,* 243–59; Bumiller, "A First Lady Fiercely Loyal and Quietly Effective."

39. Betty Ford's speechwriter, Frances Kaye Pullen, was reportedly frustrated by the first lady's unwillingness to discuss political issues and controversies more extensively and in more detail. Pullen reportedly attributed this to the administration's lack of direction and leadership, not to competing constituencies. Casserly, *Ford White House,* 144, 225, 249–50. For a discussion of the staff's "disappointment" with the first lady's "muted" stances, see Greene, *Betty Ford,* 93–94.

40. See, for example, Neustadt, *Presidential Power and the Modern Presidents;* Stuckey, *President as Interpreter-in-Chief;* Kernell, *Going Public;* Edwards, *Strategic President.*

41. West, *Upstairs at the White House,* 194.

42. Lonnelle Aikman, "Inside the White House," *National Geographic,* January 1961,

2–41. As an indicator of Jacqueline Kennedy's success in framing her work, see "The First Lady and the White House," *Newsweek*, September 17, 1962, 71–78.

43. Wolff, *A Tour of the White House with Mrs. John F. Kennedy*, 129.

44. van Rensselaer, *Jacqueline Kennedy*, 284–89; Perry, *Jacqueline Kennedy*, 102–21.

45. Rodham Clinton, *Living History*, 449.

46. On the close coordination of the "Just Say No" program and the president's drug policies, see Leamer, *Make-Believe*, 334.

47. Klatch, *Women of the New Right*. More specifically, on the first lady's role in upholding and advancing the ideal of republican motherhood, see Parry-Giles and Blair, "Rise of the Rhetorical First Lady," 567–81; Parmet, *George Bush*, 425. For a historical study of the complex evolution of women's work in charitable and philanthropic contexts, see Ginzberg, *Women and the Work of Benevolence*.

48. Benze, *Nancy Reagan*, 154; Gutin, *The President's Partner*, 168; Deaver, *Nancy*, 91, 94.

49. The first lady was very much a part of campaign strategizing in the 1976, 1980, and 1984 campaigns. Benze, *Nancy Reagan*, 32–35; Brownstein and Easton, *Reagan's Ruling Class*, 645; Cannon, *Time and Chance*, 405; Maureen Reagan, *First Father, First Daughter*, 228; Schieffer and Gates, *Acting President*, 70; Steven R. Weisman, "Nancy Reagan's Role Grows," *New York Times*, November 11, 1984; Fitzwater, *Call the Briefing!* 157–60.

50. Benze, *Nancy Reagan*, 68–86, 122–40.

51. Thomas, *Front Row at the White House*, 272–74; von Damm, *At Reagan's Side*. On Nancy Reagan's undue influence and lack of accountability, see Regan, *For the Record*. See also Schieffer and Gates, *Acting President*; Weinraub, "Angry Reagan Calls Reports of Wife's Power 'a Fiction.'"

52. As quoted in Grimes, *Running Mates*, 44.

53. On Barbara Bush's early negatives in the 1988 campaign, see Troy, "'Half-Eleanor, Half-Bess,'" 450.

54. Radcliffe, *Simply Barbara Bush*, 183. For an example of the early coverage directed at Barbara Bush's focus on literacy, see Vivian Castleberry, "'My Choice Is to Enjoy,' Says Barbara Bush," *Dallas Times Herald*, October 30, 1979.

55. Barbara Gamarekian, "Barbara Bush Announces Formation of Literacy Foundation," *New York Times*, March 7, 1989; Benita Somerfield, Comment, in Feldman and Perotti, *Honor and Loyalty*, 475. For the findings of the National Adult Literacy Survey, see http://www.ets.org. The National Adult Education Professional Development Consortium provides a strong overview of literacy legislation and programs at http://www.naepdc.org. U.S. Department of Education, *Guidance for the William F. Goodling Even Start Family Literacy Programs*, 2–3.

56. "Stories with All the Trimmings," *Entertainment Weekly*, http://www.ew.com.

57. As quoted in Killian, *Barbara Bush*, 194.

58. As quoted in Radcliffe, *Simply Barbara Bush*, 195.

59. As quoted in Radcliffe, *Simply Barbara Bush*, 195.

60. Many first ladies, however, have publicized their correspondence. Eleanor Roosevelt frequently quoted from public letters in her *My Day* column. Though she rarely referred to the writers by name, her commentary and responses were very forthright. See also Stanley P. Friedman, "The Letters People Send Betty Ford: What They Tell Her—How She Answers," *Family Weekly*, February 29, 1976, 4–7.

61. "Accomplishments of the Administration in the First Fifteen Months" Folder, Box 14, George Akerson Papers, p. 1, Herbert Hoover Library. Emphasis in original.

62. "Re. Relief Cases & Various Pleas for Help Received by Mrs. Hoover," "Requests for Assistance—Field Investigators—Procedures" Folder, Box 82, Lou Henry Hoover Sub-

ject Files, Herbert Hoover Library; Philippi Harding (Mrs. Frederic B.) Butler, oral history by Raymond Henle, September 12, 1967, pp. 34–36; Mildred Hall Campbell, "Mrs. Hoover's Secretary," pp. 2–3; Ruth Fesler (Mrs. Robert L.) Lipman, oral history interview by Raymond Henle, September 26, 1967, pp. 33–34; Helen Hartley Greene White, oral history interview by Raymond Henle, October 27, 1966, pp. 8–11, Herbert Hoover Library. "Secretary's Work File, Form Letters (1)," Box 96, Lou Henry Hoover Subject File, Herbert Hoover Library. A penciled note indicates that this notebook was consulted throughout the post-presidential years. However, copies of these letters are found in Lou Henry Hoover's White House files.

63. D-2, "Form Letters (2), Secretary's Work File," Box 97, Lou Henry Hoover Subject File, Herbert Hoover Library.

64. "Requests for Assistance—Field Investigators—General Federation Women's Clubs—1931–32" Folder, Box 82. For Red Cross reports, see "Requests for Assistance—Field Investigators—Hassan, Natalie H.—1931–33" Folder, Box 82. Lou Henry Hoover Subject Files, Herbert Hoover Library. "A radio address by Mrs. Herbert Hoover . . . ," March 23, 1931, "Articles, Addresses, and Statements" Folder, Box 6, Lou Henry Hoover Subject File, Herbert Hoover Library. Mockler, *Citizens in Action.* "Activities of Woman's Division, The President's Emergency Committee for Employment," "Articles, Addresses, and Statements; 1931 March 23; President's Emergency Committee for Employment, Washington, DC," Folder, Box 6, Lou Henry Hoover Subject File, Herbert Hoover Library.

65. H-2, "Form Letters (2), Secretary's Work File," Box 97, Lou Henry Hoover Subject File, Herbert Hoover Library.

66. See "Requests for Assistance—Field Investigators—Heizer, Mabel—1931–39" Folder, Box 82, Lou Henry Hoover Subject Files, Herbert Hoover Library.

67. "Report Listings for Minnesota to North Carolina," "Requests for Assistance—Field Investigators—General Federation of Women's Clubs, 1931–32" Folder, Box 82, Lou Henry Hoover Subject File, Herbert Hoover Library.

68. P. H. Butler, Re. Relief Cases & Various Pleas for Help Received by Mrs. Hoover, "Requests for Assistance—Field Investigations—Procedures" Folder, Box 82, Lou Henry Hoover Subject File, Herbert Hoover Library. See also Philippi Harding Butler, interview by Raymond Henle, pp. 34–36, Herbert Hoover Library; Ruth Fesler Lipman, interview by Raymond Henle, 33–34, Herbert Hoover Library.

69. See, for example, Radio Address, Welfare and Relief Mobilization, November 27, 1932, "Articles, Addresses, and Statements" Folder, Box 6, Lou Henry Hoover Subject File, Herbert Hoover Library. These priorities were also integral to the Hoovers' post-presidential writings and statements. For example, see "Address at the Great Lakes Regional Conference Banquet," "Articles, Addresses, and Statements—1936 May 16—"My Girl Scout Family"—Chicago, Illinois" Folder, Box 8, Lou Henry Hoover Subject File, Herbert Hoover Library. Hoover, *Addresses upon the American Road.*

70. Young, *Lou Henry Hoover,* 95–110; Gould, "Neglected First Lady."

71. See, for example, Chadakoff, *Eleanor Roosevelt's My Day,* 106.

72. Black, *Courage in a Dangerous World,* 132–35. This article included Eleanor Roosevelt's response to those "who are not sure whether what they have is worth defending," speaking to those who opposed the war and who refused to serve in the military.

73. U.S. House of Representatives, "National Defense Migration Part 25, Testimony Relating to the Maintenance of Civilian Morale," Select Committee Investigating National Defense Migration, 77th Cong., 2nd sess. [January 13–15, 1942], 9766–74.

74. Doris Kearns Goodwin, detailing the divergence in their agendas as war approached, concludes that the first lady became an "agitator," the president a "politician." *No Ordinary*

Time, 104. Allida M. Black, however, sees this difference emerging much earlier in their careers, while they were in the New York state government. See "(Anna) Eleanor Roosevelt," in Gould, *American First Ladies,* 430–31.

75. As quoted in Goodwin, *No Ordinary Time,* 629. The first lady also commented on the president's initial rejection and eventual adoption of her proposals in *This I Remember* (New York: Harper and Brothers, 1949), 4.

76. Ware, *Beyond Suffrage;* Black, "(Anna) Eleanor Roosevelt," 437–39; *Congressional Record,* February 6–9, 1942; Lash, *Love, Eleanor,* 368–75. On Eleanor Roosevelt's lack of success in lobbying for a federal anti-lynching law, see Cook, *Eleanor Roosevelt,* 2:177. On her limits as a substantive representative for African Americans, see Anderson, *Eyes Off the Prize,* 11, 87, 146, 201, 275–76. On her unwillingness to address racism as an institutionalized practice, see Zangrando and Zangrando, "ER and Black Civil Rights." For a more favorable assessment of her substantive representation for African Americans, see Black, "(Anna) Eleanor Roosevelt," 441–42.

77. On the environmental initiatives of the Johnson administration, see Melosi, "Lyndon Johnson and Environmental Policy."

78. Lady Bird Johnson, "Remarks before the General Session," 128.

79. Lady Bird Johnson, "National Youth Administration," 304.

80. Gould, *Lady Bird Johnson and the Environment;* Gould, *Lady Bird Johnson: Our Environmental First Lady;* Gould, "Lady Bird Johnson and Beautification." Lasker also worked with the first lady on policies related to medical research and disease treatment. See Lasby, "War on Disease."

81. Gould, *Lady Bird Johnson and the Environment;* Gould, "Lady Bird (Claudia Alta Taylor) Johnson," in Gould, *American First Ladies,* 506–9. Reflecting on Lady Bird Johnson's lobbying on behalf of funding for the Highway Beautification Act, the *Los Angeles Times* editorial board concluded that the failure ought to be attributed to the public rather than to the first lady. "The Legacy of a First Lady," *Los Angeles Times,* January 20, 1969.

82. Not surprisingly, the press highlighted the first lady's role as a mediator between the president and the public throughout the reelection campaign, when the first lady was traveling extensively and the president was relying on a Rose Garden strategy. Praise for the first lady was often accompanied by criticism for the president. For example, see "The President's Partner," *Newsweek,* November 5, 1979; "Rosalynn's Role," *Christian Science Monitor,* July 31, 1979, 24.

83. On Rosalynn Carter's skill in retail politics, see Marton, *Hidden Power,* 26; Stroud, *How Jimmy Won;* Bourne, *Jimmy Carter,* 259–82. On the expectation that the first lady would be traveling both internationally and domestically, see Jimmy Carter's interview with executive vice president Carmelita Valdes Damron and L. C. Diaz Carlo, published in *La Luz,* October 1976, excerpted in U.S. House, *The Presidential Campaign, 1976,* vol. 1, pt. 1: *Jimmy Carter,* 892; Gart, Sidey, Cloud, and Angello, "I Look Forward to the Job," 64. This is also the interview in which the president-elect referred to his wife as "an extension of myself."

84. Susanna McBee, "Mrs. Carter's Trip Carefully Crafted to Make Policy Points," *Washington Post,* May 29, 1977; Susanna McBee, "Mrs. Carter in Jamaica," *Washington Post,* May 31, 1977; Kaufman, *Rosalynn Carter,* 61–83.

85. Jurate Kazickas, Associated Press, June 11, 1977. See Susanna McBee, "First Lady Stresses Journey Was Her Show," *Washington Post,* June 14, 1977; "Mrs. Carter on Tour," *Facts on File World News Digest,* June 18, 1977.

86. On the extensive "reassurance" meetings that were conducted by the administration, see McBee, "Mrs. Carter's Trip."

87. The first lady did continue her involvement in foreign policy making, however. See Brzezinski, *Power and Principle*, 31–32, 105, 241, 279, 349.

88. For an extended discussion of the trip and subsequent initiatives, see Kathy Cade exit interview by Emily Soapes, January 7, 1981; "Report of Mrs. Rosalynn Carter on Cambodian Relief, 8–10 November 1979," "PP5–1 11/1/79–2/29/80" Folder, Box PP-4, White House Central File—Subject File, Jimmy Carter Library. See also Kaufman, *Rosalynn Carter,* 85; Brinkley, *Unfinished Presidency,* 167.

89. Kathryn Cade in Rosenbaum and Ugrinsky, *The Presidency and Domestic Politics of Jimmy Carter,* 532–33; Kathy Cade exit interview, Jimmy Carter Library.

90. Two such setbacks were personnel related. Peter Bourne was obliged to resign from his White House position before the bill had passed, owing to questions raised about prescriptions that he had written. For a discussion of his pivotal role in establishing the commission and preparing its report, see Grob, "Public Policy and Mental Illness." Joseph Califano and the first lady had a consistently tense relationship, since the first lady was not convinced that the HEW secretary was wholly loyal to the president. She also believed that he could have worked much harder to secure passage and funding for the Mental Health Systems Act. Kaufman, *Rosalynn Carter,* 45–47; Marton, *Hidden Power,* 27–28. Funding for the act was among the first cuts made by the Reagan administration, though some reforms were sustained through agency reorganizations completed during the Carter administration. Rosalynn Carter, *First Lady from Plains,* 301.

91. Kathy Cade exit interview, Jimmy Carter Library. In her memoir, Rosalynn Carter stresses that she devoted considerable effort to seeing that mental health was perceived as a presidential concern and not merely a "'pet project'" of the first lady, in order to ensure that it was taken seriously by decision makers. Rosalynn Carter, *First Lady from Plains,* 293.

92. This framing was particularly evident in media coverage of the first lady's testimony before the Senate Subcommittee on Health and Scientific Research, chaired by Edward Kennedy. The senator challenged the president in the 1980 Democratic presidential primaries. See, for example, Marjorie Hunter, "Mrs. Carter, in Capitol Debut, Praised by Kennedy," *New York Times,* February 8, 1979.

93. Notably, however, Rodham Clinton did not participate in the political deal-making in the state capital that clinched approval for the reforms. This meant that she lacked "insider" experience and may have discounted its importance when she brought her health-care proposal before the Congress. Morris, *Partners in Power,* 318–21; Oakley, *On the Make,* 281–92; Radcliffe, *Hillary Rodham Clinton,* 202–11; Warner, *Hillary Clinton,* 102–33.

94. As quoted in Warner, *Hillary Clinton,* 102.

95. The extent to which Rodham Clinton relied on governmental versus community-based interventions was a constant issue throughout her first ladyship. *It Takes a Village* balances the two, slightly favoring community, arguably to offset presumptions about her priorities as a Democrat. For a further discussion of this issue in the context of her role as a modern jeremiad, see Jendrysik, *Modern Jeremiahs,* 153–69. The partisan character of her substantive representation was a critical issue during the 1996 reelection campaign. See Mughan and Burton, "Hillary Clinton and the President's Reelection," 111–24.

96. For an early and comparatively favorable account of Rodham Clinton's anticipated success in health-care reform, see Nina Martin, "Who Is She?" *Mother Jones,* November/December 1993.

97. Marton, *Hidden Power,* 322.

98. Bernstein, *Woman in Charge,* 395–412; Gould, "Hillary Rodham Clinton," in Gould, *American First Ladies,* 641–46; Morris, *Behind the Oval Office,* 111; Patterson, *White House Staff,* 282–87.

99. As quoted in Bernstein, *Woman in Charge,* 407.

100. More generally, presidential advisor Dick Morris conducted polls that indicated the public saw the first lady as contributing to a lack of accountability in the presidency. Morris, *Rewriting History,* 98–101. See also Bernstein, *Woman in Charge,* 476. For a contrasting view, which presents Rodham Clinton as a "master manipulator," see Olson, *Hell to Pay.*

101. Tomasky, *Hillary's Turn,* 55; Harpaz, *Girls in the Van.* For a contrasting judgment about press coverage of the Rodham Clinton 2000 campaign, which attributes its limitations more to the press, see Vavrus, *Postfeminist News,* 129–63, see especially p. 143. For a representative article covering her listening tour, see Adam Nagourney, "Hillary Clinton Begins Non-Campaign Swing," *New York Times,* April 20, 1999. See also Susan J. Carroll, "Reflections on Gender and Hillary Clinton's Presidential Campaign."

102. Harpaz, *Girls in the Van,* 10; Tomasky, *Hillary's Turn,* 7–10, 54–57, 87–94.

103. Marton, *Hidden Power,* 319.

104. Catherine Mccormick-Lelyveld, "The First Lady at the Kitchen Garden Fall Harvest," White House Blog, October 29, 2009; [Obama], "Remarks by First Lady Michelle Obama at a Garden Harvesting Event (As Released by the White House)," October 29, 2009.

105. [Obama], "Remarks by the First Lady at Fresh Food Financing Initiative," February 19, 2010, Office of the First Lady.

106. "Let's Move!" letsmove.gov; [Obama], "Remarks of First Lady Michelle Obama," February 9, 2010. See also [Obama], "Remarks by First Lady Michelle Obama at a 'Let's Move' Event (As Released by the White House)," March 3, 2010; [Obama], "Remarks by the First Lady at Event on Surgeon General's Report," January 28, 2010; White House Office of the Press Secretary, "Presidential Memorandum—Establishing a Task Force on Childhood Obesity," February 9, 2010.

107. See Martin, *Presidency and Women;* Sanbonmatsu, *Democrats, Republicans, and the Politics of Women's Place.*

108. This intersection of partisan and gender ideologies reinforces the call for continuing analyses of gender ideologies as "meta-ideologies," expressing philosophies of power that build from individual relationships to complex institutions. The close connections between partisan and gender ideologies mean that ignoring or discounting one limits understanding of the other. Accurate study of political decision making requires attention to both facets of political thought.

Selected Bibliography

Archival Collections and Materials

George H. W. Bush Library
    Firestone, Laurie. Files.
Jimmy Carter Library
    Cade, Kathy. Exit Interview.
    Hoyt, Mary Finch. Exit Interview.
    Poston, Gretchen. Exit Interview by Emily Soapes, January 2, 1981.
    Poston, Gretchen. Social Office Files.
    Staff Offices—Administration—Malachuk Files.
    White House Central Files—Subject Files.
Dwight D. Eisenhower Library
    Eisenhower, Mamie Doud. Interview by Maclyn Burg and John Wickman, July 20, 1972.
    Social Office (A. B. Tolley) Records, 1952–1961. White House Office.
Gerald R. Ford Library
    Armstrong, Anne. Oral History.
    Downs, Maria. Files, 1974–1977.
    Downs, Maria. Papers, 1975–1977.
    Pullen, Frances K. Files.
    Vertical Files.
    White House Social Files.
Herbert Hoover Library
    Akerson, George. Papers.
    Anthony, Edward, and Ester Anthony. Oral History.
    Butler, Philippi Harding (Mrs. Frederic B.). Oral History by Raymond Henle, September 12, 1967.
    Butler, Philippi Harding. Interview by Raymond Henle, November 6, 12, 1966.
    Dyer, Susan L. Interview by Raymond Henle, September 29–30, 1966.
    Hoover, Lou Henry. Papers.
    Lipman, Ruth Fesler (Mrs. Robert L.). Oral History Interview.
    Lipman, Ruth Fesler. Papers.
    Post-Presidential Papers.
    Presidential Papers.
    Social Functions Scrapbooks, Volumes 1 and 2.
    White, Helen Hartley Greene. Oral History Interview.
    White House Office of Budget and Accounting. Chief Disbursing Agent's Files.
Lyndon B. Johnson Library
    Abell, Bess. Oral History Interviews by T. H. Baker, Internet Copy.
    Abell, Bess. Files.
    Aikman, Lonelle. Oral History.
    Carpenter, Elizabeth (Liz). Oral History Interviews.

Carpenter, Liz. Subject Files.

Johnson, Mrs. [Lady Bird]. Speeches.

Miller, Dale and Virginia (Scooter). Interview by Joe B. Frantz, August 26, 1969. Interview 1, accession number AC 78–29.

Shriver, Sargent. Oral History.

White House Central Files, Executive Files.

John F. Kennedy Library

Fox, Sanford. White House Staff Files.

White House Central Files—Executive.

Richard M. Nixon Presidential Materials

Adams, Penelope A. Oral History.

Codus, William R. Exit Interview.

Porter, Susan. Files.

Stuart, Constance. Exit Interview.

Stuart, Constance C. Oral History.

Frances Perkins. Oral History. Columbia University.

Ronald Reagan Library

Brandon, Mabel (Muffie). Files, 1981–1984.

Faulkner, Linda. Files, 1981–1989.

Hodges, Gahl. Files, 1983–1984.

Franklin D. Roosevelt Library

Chief of Social Entertainments Office. Records, 1933–1945.

Hoffman, Anna Rosenberg. Interview by Thomas F. Soapes, October 13, 1977.

Harry S. Truman Library

Odum, Raethel. Papers.

Presidential Papers.

Social Functions File.

Primary Sources

Association of American Physicians and Surgeons, Inc., et al. v. Hillary Rodham Clinton, 997 F. 2d 898 (1993).

Bush, Barbara. "Choices and Change," delivered at Wellesley College, June 1, 1990.

[Bush, Laura]. "Laura Bush Remarks at a Victory '04 Rally in Duluth, MN," September 9, 2004. Press Release, Office of the First Lady, White House.

———. "Mrs. Bush's Remarks at Kilmer for Congress Luncheon," Tallahassee, FL, March 29, 2004. Press Release, Office of the First Lady, White House.

———. "Mrs. Bush's Remarks at Ron Lewis for Congress and Kentucky Victory 2006 Rally," Radcliff, KY, November 1, 2006, Press Release, Office of the First Lady, White House.

———. "Radio Address by Mrs. Bush," Crawford, TX, November 17, 2001. Press Release, Office of the First Lady, White House.

Bush, Laura. "Remarks at the 6th Regional Conference on Helping America's Youth," Portland Center for the Performing Arts, Portland, OR, February 28, 2008.

[Carter, Rosalynn]. "Remarks of the President and Mrs. Carter at the Signing Ceremony of Executive Order 11973," February 17, 1977. *Public Papers of the President of the United States: Jimmy Carter, 1977.*

[Clinton, William Jefferson]. "Remarks and an Exchange with Reporters on Health Care Reform," January 25, 1993. *Public Papers of the President of the United States: William J. Clinton, 1993.*

Clinton, Hillary Rodham. "Remarks to the U.N. 4th World Conference on Women," Plenary Session, September 5, 1995.

Congressional Record, February 6–9, 1942.

Eisenhower, Mamie Doud. Letter to the Members of the National Geographic Society. *National Geographic* 119, no. 1 (January 1961): 1.

[Ford, Gerald R.]. "President's News Conference of November 26, 1975," *Public Papers of the Presidents of the United States: Gerald R. Ford, 1975.*

———. "Remarks on Taking the Oath of Office," August 9, 1974. *Public Papers of the President of the United States: Gerald R. Ford, 1974.*

Georgia, State of, Governor's Commission to Improve Services for Mentally and Emotionally Handicapped Georgians. *Helping Troubled Georgians Solve Their Problems: A Mental Health Improvement Plan for Georgia,* October 29, 1971.

Johnson, Lady Bird. "Remarks before the General Session." In *U.S. Environmentalism since 1945: A Brief History with Documents,* ed. Steven Stoll. New York: Palgrave Macmillan, 2007.

[Johnson, Lyndon]. "Annual Message to Congress on the State of the Union," January 8, 1964. *Public Papers of the President of the United States: Lyndon Johnson, 1963–1964.*

"Let's Move!" letsmove.gov/.

[Obama, Michelle]. Office of the First Lady. "Remarks by the First Lady at Event on Surgeon General's Report," January 28, 2010.

———. "Remarks by the First Lady at Fresh Food Financing Initiative," February 19, 2010.

———. "Remarks by the First Lady at Event on Surgeon General's Report," YMCA of Alexandria, Alexandria, VA, January 28, 2010, Office of the First Lady, The White House.

———. "Remarks by First Lady Michelle Obama at a 'Let's Move' Event (As Released by the White House)," March 3, 2010.

———. "Remarks by First Lady Michelle Obama at the White House Garden Harvest Party (As Released by the White House)," June 16, 2009. Congressional Hearing Transcript Database.

Office of the First Lady, "Remarks of First Lady Michelle Obama," February 9, 2010.

[Reagan, Ronald]. "Interview with the President," December 23, 1981, *Public Papers of the Presidents of the United States: Ronald Reagan, 1981.*

———. "Remarks and a Question-and-Answer Session at a Working Luncheon with Out-of-Town Editors," October 16, 1981, *Public Papers of the Presidents of the United States: Ronald Reagan, 1981.*

U.S. Department of Education, *Guidance for the William F. Goodling Even Start Family Literacy Programs,* September 2003.

U.S. House of Representatives. "National Defense Migration Part 25, Testimony Relating to the Maintenance of Civilian Morale." Select Committee Investigating National Defense Migration. 77th Cong., 2nd sess. [January 13–15, 1942].

U.S. Information Agency, *El Weekend,* 1967, MP 148, Lyndon B. Johnson Library.

U.S. Senate. "Early Learning: Investing in Our Children, Investing in Our Future." Committee on Health, Education, Labor, and Pensions, 107th Cong., 2nd sess.

———. "Examination of the Recommendations of the President's Commission on Mental Health," Hearing of the Subcommittee on Health and Scientific Research of the Committee on Labor and Human Resources, February 7, 1979. 96th Cong., 1st sess.

White House Office of the Press Secretary, "Presidential Memorandum—Establishing a Task Force on Childhood Obesity," February 9, 2010.

Secondary Sources

Anderson, Carol. *Eyes Off the Prize: The United Nations and the African American Struggle for Human Rights, 1944–1955.* New York: Cambridge University Press, 2003.

Anderson, Christopher. *Jack and Jackie: Portrait of an American Marriage.* New York: William Morrow, 1996.

Anthony, Carl Sferrazza. *As We Remember Her: Jacqueline Kennedy Onassis in the Words of Her Family and Friends.* New York: HarperCollins, 1997.

———. *First Ladies,* vol. 2: *The Saga of the Presidents' Wives and Their Power.* New York: William Morrow, 1991.

Arnaz, Desi. *A Book.* New York: William Morrow, 1976.

Baldrige, Letitia. *A Lady, First: My Life in the Kennedy White House and the American Embassies of Paris and Rome.* New York: Viking, 2001.

———. *Of Diamonds and Diplomats.* Boston: Houghton Mifflin, 1968.

Baldrige, Letitia, and Rene Verdon. *In the Kennedy Style: Magical Evenings in the Kennedy White House.* New York: Doubleday, 1998.

Beasley, Maurine. "Bess Truman and the Press: A Case Study of a First Lady as Political Communicator." In *Harry S. Truman: The Man from Independence,* ed. William F. Levantrosser. New York: Greenwood Press, 1986.

———, ed. *The White House Press Conferences of Eleanor Roosevelt.* New York: Garland Publishing, 1983.

Benze, James G. Jr. *Nancy Reagan: On The White House Stage.* Lawrence: University of Kansas Press, 2005.

Bernstein, Carl. *A Woman in Charge.* New York: Alfred A. Knopf, 2007.

Black, Allida M., ed. *Courage in a Dangerous World: The Political Writings of Eleanor Roosevelt.* New York: Columbia University Press, 1999.

———. *What I Hope to Leave Behind: The Essential Essays of Eleanor Roosevelt.* Brooklyn, NY: Carlson Publishing, 1995.

Borrelli, MaryAnne. "Competing Conceptions of the First Ladyship: Public Responses to Betty Ford's *60 Minutes* Interview." *Presidential Studies Quarterly* 31, no. 3 (September 2001): 397–414.

———. "The First Lady as Formal Advisor to the President: When East (Wing) Meets West (Wing)." *Women and Politics* 24, no. 1 (2002): 25–45.

———. "Sharing the Bully Pulpit: Breast Cancer and First Lady Betty Ford's Leadership." In *The Presidential Companion: Readings on the Political Significance of First Ladies,* ed. Robert Watson and Anthony J. Eksterowicz. Columbia: University of South Carolina Press, 2003.

———. "Telling It Slant: Gender Roles, Power, and Narrative Style in the First Ladies' Autobiographies." *Sex Roles* 47, no. 7/8 (2002): 355–70.

Borrelli, MaryAnne, Karen Hult, and Nancy Kassop, "The White House Counsel's Office." Prepared for the 2000 Presidential Transition Team. White House 2000 Project, sponsored by the Pew Charitable Trust. Updated for the 2008 Presidential Transition.

Bostdorff, Denise M. "Hillary Rodham Clinton and Elizabeth Dole as Running 'Mates' in the 1996 Campaign: Parallels in the Rhetorical Constraints of First Ladies and Vice Presidents." In *The 1996 Presidential Campaign: A Communications Perspective.* Westport, CT: Praeger, 1998.

Bourne, Peter. *Jimmy Carter: A Comprehensive Biography from Plains to Postpresidency.* New York: Scribner's, 1997.

Bowles, Hamish, and Arthur M. Schlesinger Jr. *Jacqueline Kennedy: The White House Years.* New York: Metropolitan Museum of Art, 2001.

Bradford, Sarah. *America's Queen: The Life of Jacqueline Bouvier Kennedy.* New York: Viking, 2000.

Brinkley, Douglas. *The Unfinished Presidency: Jimmy Carter's Journey beyond the White House.* New York: Penguin Books, 1978.

Brown, Thomas. *JFK: History of an Image.* Bloomington: Indiana University Press, 1988.

Brownstein, Ronald, and Nina Easton. *Reagan's Ruling Class.* Washington, DC: Presidential Accountability Group, 1982.

Broyde, Michael J., and Robert A. Schapiro. "Impeachment and Accountability: The Case of the First Lady." *Constitutional Commentary* 15 (1998): 479–509.

Brzezinski, Zbigniew. *Power and Principle: Memoirs of the National Security Advisor, 1977–1981.* New York: Farrar, Straus, and Giroux, 1983.

Burke, John P. *The Institutional Presidency: Organizing and Managing the White House from FDR to Clinton.* 2nd ed. Baltimore: Johns Hopkins University Press, 2000.

Burrell, Barbara. *Public Opinion, The First Ladyship, and Hillary Rodham Clinton.* Rev. ed. New York: Routledge, 2001.

Bush, Barbara. *A Memoir.* New York: Scribner's, 1994.

Cannon, James. *Time and Chance: Gerald Ford's Appointment with History.* New York: Harper-Collins, 1994.

Caro, Robert A. *The Years of Lyndon Johnson: Means of Ascent.* New York: Alfred A. Knopf, 1990.

———. *The Years of Lyndon Johnson: The Path to Power.* New York: Alfred A. Knopf, 1982.

Caroli, Betty Boyd. *First Ladies.* Expanded edition. New York: Oxford University Press, 1995.

Carpenter, Liz. *Ruffles and Flourishes.* New York: Pocket Books, 1970.

Carroll, Susan J. "Reflections on Gender and Hillary Clinton's Presidential Campaign: The Good, the Bad, and the Misogynic." *Politics and Gender* 5, no. 1 (March 2009): 1–20.

Carter, Rosalynn. *First Lady from Plains.* Fayetteville: University of Arkansas Press, 1994.

Casserly, John J. *The Ford White House: Diary of a Speechwriter.* Boulder, CO: Associated University Press, 1977.

Chadakoff, Rochelle, ed. *Eleanor Roosevelt's My Day: Her Acclaimed Columns, 1936–1945.* New York: Pharos Books, 1989.

Cheshire, Maxine, with John Greenya. *Maxine Cheshire, Reporter.* Boston: Houghton Mifflin, 1978.

Clements, Kendrick A. *Hoover, Conservation, and Consumerism: Engineering the Good Life.* Lawrence: University Press of Kansas, 2000.

Clinton, Hillary Rodham. *Living History.* New York: Simon and Schuster, 2003.

Clinton, Bill. *My Life.* New York: Alfred A. Knopf, 2004.

Colacello, Bob. *Ronnie and Nancy: Their Path to the White House, 1911 to 1980.* New York: Warner Books, 2004.

Collins, Patricia Hill. *Black Feminist Thought: Knowledge, Consciousness, and the Politics of Empowerment.* New York: Routledge, 2000.

Cook, Blanche Wiesen. *Eleanor Roosevelt,* vol. 1: *1884–1933.* New York: Viking, 1992.

———. *Eleanor Roosevelt,* vol. 2: *1933–1938.* New York: Viking, 1999.

David, Lester, and Irene David. *Ike and Mamie.* New York: G. P. Putnam's Sons, 1981.

Deaver, Michael K. *Nancy: A Portrait of My Years with Nancy Reagan.* New York: William Morrow, 2000.

Dickerson, Nancy. *Among Those Present: A Reporter's View of Twenty-five Years in Washington.* New York: Random House, 1976.

Dixon, Suzanne. "The Enduring Theme—Domineering Dowagers and Scheming Concubines." In *Stereotypes of Women in Power: Historical Perspectives and Revisionist Views,* ed. Barbara Galick, Suzanne Dixon, and Pauline Allen. New York: Greenwood Press, 1992.

Douglas, Susan J. *Where the Girls Are: Growing Up Female with the Mass Media.* New York: Random House, 1995.

Dovi, Suzanne. *The Good Representative.* Malden, MA: Blackwell Publishing, 2007.

———. "Theorizing Women's Representation in the United States." In *Political Women and American Democracy,* ed. Christina Wolbrecht, Karen Beckwith, and Lisa Baldez. New York: Cambridge University Press, 2008.

Dubriwny, Tasha N. "Constructing Breast Cancer in the News: Betty Ford and the Evolution of the Breast Cancer Patient." *Journal of Communication Inquiry* 33 (2009): 104–25.

Duerst-Lahti, Georgia Jean. "Gender Power Relations in Public Bureaucracies." PhD diss., University of Wisconsin–Madison, 1987.

———. "Governing Institutions, Ideologies, and Gender: Toward the Possibility of Equal Political Representation." *Sex Roles* 47, no. 7/8 (October 2002): 371–88.

———. "Reconceiving Theories of Power: Consequences of Masculinism in the Executive Branch." In *The Other Elites: Women, Politics, and Power in the Executive Branch,* ed. Mary-Anne Borrelli and Janet M. Martin. Boulder, CO: Lynne Rienner Publishers, 1997.

———. "'Seeing What Has Always Been': Opening Study of the Presidency." *PS* 41, no. 4 (October 2008): 733–37.

Dugger, Ronnie. *On Reagan: The Man and His Presidency.* New York: McGraw-Hill, 1983.

Edmondson, Madeleine, and Alden Duer Cohen. *The Women of Watergate.* New York: Stein and Day Publishers, 1975.

Edwards, George C. III. *The Strategic President: Persuasion and Opportunity in Presidential Leadership.* Princeton, NJ: Princeton University Press, 2009.

Eisenhower, Dwight D. *The White House Years: Mandate for Change, 1953–1956.* Garden City, NY: Doubleday, 1963.

Eisenhower, Susan. *Mrs. Ike: Memories and Reflections on the Life of Mamie Eisenhower.* New York: Farrar, Straus, and Giroux, 1996.

Eksterowicz, Anthony J., and Kristen Paynter. "The Evolution of the Role and Office of the First Lady: The Movement toward Integration with the White House Office." *Social Science Journal* 27, no. 4 (2000): 547–62.

Elshtain, Jean Bethke. *Public Man, Private Woman: Women in Social and Political Thought.* Princeton, NJ: Princeton University Press, 1981.

Feldman, Leslie D., and Rosanna Perotti, eds. *Honor and Loyalty: Inside the Politics of the George H. W. Bush White House.* Westport, CT: Greenwood Press, 2002.

Ferguson, Michaele L. "Feminism and Security Rhetoric in the Post–September 11 Bush Administration." In *W Stands for Women: How the George W. Bush Presidency Shaped a New Politics of Gender,* ed. Michaele L. Ferguson and Lori J. Marso. Durham, NC: Duke University Press, 2007.

Fitzwater, Marlin. *Call the Briefing! Bush and Reagan, Sam and Helen: A Decade with Presidents and the Press.* New York: Random House, 1995.

Ford, Betty. *Betty: A Glad Awakening.* Garden City, NY: Doubleday, 1987.

———. *The Times of My Life.* New York: Ballantine Books, 1978.

Friedan, Betty. *The Feminine Mystique.* New York: W. W. Norton, 1963.

Furman, Bess. *Washington By-Line: The Personal History of a Newspaperwoman.* New York: Alfred A. Knopf, 1949.

Gardner, Michael R. *Harry Truman and Civil Rights: Moral Courage and Political Risks.* Carbondale: Southern Illinois University Press, 2002.

Gart, Murray, Hugh Sidey, Stanley Cloud, and Bonnie Angello. "I Look Forward to the Job." In *Conversations with Carter,* ed. Don Richardson. Boulder, CO: Lynne Rienner Publishers, 1998.

Gerhart, Ann. *The Perfect Wife: The Life and Choices of Laura Bush.* New York: Simon and Schuster, 2004.

Ginzberg, Lori D. *Women and the Work of Benevolence: Morality, Politics, and Class in the 19th Century United States.* New Haven, CT: Yale University Press, 1990.

Goodwin, Doris Kearns. *No Ordinary Time: Franklin and Eleanor Roosevelt: The Home Front in World War II.* New York: Simon and Schuster, 1994.

Gould, Lewis L., ed. *American First Ladies: Their Lives and Their Legacy.* New York: Garland Publishing, 1996.

Gould, Lewis L. "Lady Bird Johnson and Beautification." In *The Johnson Years,* vol. 2: *Vietnam, the Environment, and Science.* Lawrence: University Press of Kansas, 1987.

———. *Lady Bird Johnson and the Environment.* Lawrence: University Press of Kansas, 1988.

———. *Lady Bird Johnson: Our Environmental First Lady.* Lawrence: University Press of Kansas, 1999.

———. "Modern First Ladies in Historical Perspective." *Presidential Studies Quarterly* 15 (1985): 537–38.

———. "A Neglected First Lady: A Reappraisal." In *Lou Henry Hoover: Essays on a Busy Life,* ed. Dale C. Mayer. Worland, WY: High Plains Publishing Company, 1994.

Greene, John Robert. *Betty Ford: Candor and Courage in the White House.* Lawrence: University Press of Kansas, 2004.

Gregg, Gary L. II. "Dignified Authenticity: George W. Bush and the Symbolic Presidency." In *Considering the Bush Presidency,* ed. Gary L. Gregg II and Mark J. Rozell. New York: Oxford University Press, 2004.

Grimes, Ann. *Running Mates: The Making of a First Lady.* New York: William Morrow, 1990.

Grob, Gerald N. "Public Policy and Mental Illness: Jimmy Carter's Presidential Commission on Mental Health." *Milbank Quarterly* 83, no. 3 (2005): 425–56.

Gutin, Myra. *The President's Partner: The First Lady in the 20th Century.* New York: Greenwood Press, 1989.

Guy, Mary Ellen. "Hillary, Health Care, and Gender Power." In *Gender Power, Leadership, and Governance,* ed. Georgia Duerst-Lahti and Rita Mae Kelly. Ann Arbor: University of Michigan Press, 1995.

Han, Lori Cox. *Governing from Center Stage: White House Communication Strategies during the Television Age of Politics.* Cresskill, NJ: Hampton Press, 2001.

Harpaz, Beth J. *The Girls in the Van: Covering Hillary.* New York: St. Martin's Press, 2001.

Harrison, Cynthia. *On Account of Sex: The Politics of Women's Issues, 1945–1968.* Berkeley: University of California Press, 1989.

Heith, Diane J. *Polling to Govern: Public Opinion and Presidential Leadership.* Stanford, CA: Stanford University Press, 2004.

Helm, Edith Benham. *The Captains and the Kings.* New York: Putnam, 1954.

Hertz, Rosanna, and Susan M. Reverby. "Gentility, Gender, and Political Protest: The Barbara Bush Controversy at Wellesley College." *Gender and Society* 9 (October 1995): 594–611.

Hess, Stephen, with James P. Pfiffner. *Organizing the Presidency.* 3rd ed. Washington, DC: Brookings Institution Press, 2002.

Holt, Marilyn Irvin. *Mamie Doud Eisenhower: The General's First Lady.* Lawrence: University Press of Kansas, 2007.

Hoover, Herbert. *Addresses upon the American Road.* New York: Scribner's, 1938.

———. *The Memoirs of Herbert Hoover: The Cabinet and the Presidency, 1920–1933.* New York: Macmillan, 1952.

———. *The Memoirs of Herbert Hoover: Years of Adventure, 1874–1920.* New York: Macmillan, 1952.

Hoyt, Mary Finch. *East Wing: Politics, The Press, and a First Lady.* N.p.: Xlibris Corporation, 2001.

Hult, Karen M., and Charles E. Walcott. *Empowering the White House: Governance under Nixon, Ford, and Carter.* Lawrence: University Press of Kansas, 2004.

Hummer, Jill Abraham. "First Ladies and American Women: Representation in the Modern Presidency." PhD diss., University of Virginia, 2007.

Jamieson, Kathleen Hall. *Beyond the Double Bind: Women and Leadership.* New York: Oxford University Press, 1995.

Jendrysik, Mark Stephen. *Modern Jeremiahs: Contemporary Visions of American Decline.* New York: Lexington Books, 2008.

Jewell, K. Sue. *From Mammy to Miss America and Beyond: Cultural Images and the Shaping of U.S. Social Policy.* London: Routledge, 1993.

Johnson, Lady Bird. "The National Youth Administration." In *The Making of the New Deal: The Insiders Speak,* ed. Katie Louchheim. Cambridge, MA: Harvard University Press, 1983.

———. *A White House Diary.* New York: Holt, Rinehart and Winston, 1970.

Kaufman, Scott. *Rosalynn Carter: Equal Partner in the White House.* Lawrence: University of Kansas Press, 2007.

Kennedy, John F. "Campaign Speech on the Presidency." In *The Power of the Presidency, Concepts and Controversy,* ed. Robert S. Hirschfield. 3rd ed. New York: Aldine Publishing Company, 1982.

Kernell, Samuel. *Going Public: New Strategies of Presidential Leadership.* 4th ed. Washington, DC: CQ Press, 2007.

Kessler, Ronald. *Laura Bush: An Intimate Portrait of the First Lady.* New York: Doubleday, 2006.

Killian, Pamela. *Barbara Bush: Matriarch of a Dynasty.* New York: St. Martin's Press, 2002.

King, Norman. *The Woman in the White House: The Remarkable Story of Hillary Rodham Clinton.* New York: Carol Publishing Group, 1996.

Klatch, Rebecca E. *Women of the New Right.* Philadelphia: Temple University Press, 1987.

Klawiter, Maren. *The Biopolitics of Breast Cancer: Changing Cultures of Disease and Activism.* Minneapolis: University of Minnesota Press, 2008.

Klein, Edward. *All Too Human: The Love Story of Jack and Jackie Kennedy.* New York: Pocket Books, 1996.

Krausert, Sara. "From Baking Bread to Making Dough: Legal and Societal Restrictions on the Employment of First Ladies." *University of Chicago Law School Roundtable* 5 (1998): 243–76.

Kumar, Martha Joynt. *Managing the President's Message: The White House Communications Operation.* Baltimore: Johns Hopkins Press, 2007.

———. "The White House Is Like City Hall." In *The White House World: Transitions, Organization, and Office Operations,* ed. Martha Joynt Kumar and Terry Sullivan. College Station: Texas A&M University Press, 2003.

———. "The White House World: Start Up, Organization, and the Pressures of Work Life." Report Number 6, White House Interview Project, The White House 2001 Project, sponsored by the Pew Charitable Trust, 2001.

Kumar, Martha Joynt, and Terry Sullivan, eds. *The White House World: Transitions, Organization, and Office Operations.* College Station: Texas A&M University Press, 2003.

Lang, Gladys Engel. "The Most Admired Woman: Image-Making in the News." In *Hearth and Home: Images of Women in the Mass Media,* ed. Gaye Tuchman, Arlene Kaplan Daniels, and James Benét. New York: Oxford University Press, 1978.

Lasby, Clarence G. "The War on Disease." In *The Johnson Years,* vol. 2: *Vietnam, the Environment, and Science.* Lawrence: University Press of Kansas, 1987.

Lash, Joseph P. *Eleanor and Franklin.* New York: W. W. Norton, 1971.

———. *Love, Eleanor: Eleanor Roosevelt and Her Friends.* Garden City, NY: Doubleday, 1982.

Leamer, Laurence. *Make-Believe: The Story of Nancy and Ronald Reagan.* New York: Harper and Row, 1983.

Lightfoot, Elizabeth. *Michelle Obama, First Lady of Hope.* Guilford, CT: Lyons Press, 2009.

Louchheim, Katie. *By the Political Sea.* Garden City, NY: Doubleday, 1970.

Lubin, David M. *Shooting Kennedy: JFK and the Culture of Images.* Berkeley: University of California Press, 2003.

Mansbridge, Jane. "Should Blacks Represent Blacks and Women Represent Women? A Contingent 'Yes.'" *Journal of Politics* 61, no. 3 (August 1999): 628–57.

Marso, Lori J. "Feminism and the Complications of Freeing the Women of Afghanistan and Iraq." In *W Stands for Women: How the George W. Bush Presidency Shaped a New Politics of Gender,* ed. Michaele L. Ferguson and Lori Jo Marso. Durham, NC: Duke University Press, 2007.

Martin, Janet M. *The Presidency and Women: Promise, Performance, and Illusion.* College Station: Texas A&M University Press, 2003.

Marton, Kati. *Hidden Power: Presidential Marriages That Shaped Our Recent History.* New York: Pantheon Books, 2001.

McCullough, David. *Truman.* New York: Simon and Schuster, 1992.

McLendon, Winzola, and Scottie Smith. *Don't Quote Me: Washington Newswomen and the Power Society.* New York: E. P. Dutton, 1970.

Melosi, Martin V. "Lyndon Johnson and Environmental Policy." In *The Johnson Years,* vol. 2: *Vietnam, the Environment, and Science.* Lawrence: University Press of Kansas, 1987.

Mockler, Ethel. *Citizens in Action: The Girl Scout Record, 1912–1947.* New York: Girl Scouts National Organization, 1947.

Morris, Dick. *Behind the Oval Office: Winning the Presidency in the Nineties.* New York: Random House, 1997.

———. *Rewriting History.* New York: HarperCollins, 2004.

Morris, Roger. *Partners in Power: The Clintons and Their America.* New York: Henry Holt, 1996.

Mughan, Anthony, and Barry C. Burton. "Hillary Clinton and the President's Reelection." In *Reelection 1996: How Americans Voted,* ed. Herbert F. Weisberg and Janet M. Box-Steffensmeier. New York: Chatham House Publishers, 1999.

Mundy, Liza. *Michelle.* New York: Simon and Schuster, 2008.

Muscatine, Lissa, "In the Corridors of Power," *Women's Review of Books,* July 2000, 6.

Nash, George H. *The Life of Herbert Hoover: The Humanitarian, 1914–1917.* New York: W. W. Norton, 1988.

Neal, Steve. *The Eisenhowers: Reluctant Dynasty.* Garden City, NY: Doubleday, 1978.

Neustadt, Richard. *Presidential Power and the Modern Presidents: The Politics of Leadership from Roosevelt to Reagan*. New York: Free Press, 1990.

O'Connor, Karen, Bernadette Nye, and Laura van Assendelft. "Wives in the White House: The Political Influence of First Ladies." *Presidential Studies Quarterly* 26, no. 3 (Summer 1996): 835–53.

Oakley, Meredith L. *On the Make: The Rise of Bill Clinton*. Washington, DC: Regnery Publishing, 1994.

Olson, Barbara. *Hell to Pay*. Washington, DC: Regnery Publishing, 1999.

Parmet, Herbert S. *George Bush: The Life of a Lone Star Yankee*. New York: Scribner's, 1997.

Parry-Giles, Shawn J., and Diane M. Blair. "The Rise of the Rhetorical First Lady: Politics, Gender Ideology, and Women's Voice, 1789–2002." *Rhetoric and Public Affairs* 5, no. 4 (Winter 2002): 565–600.

Patel, T. Natasha. "First Lady, Last Rights? Extending Executive Immunity to the First Lady." *Hastings Constitutional Law Quarterly* 25 (Summer 1998): 585–603.

Patterson, Bradley H. *To Serve the President: Continuity and Innovation in the White House Staff*. Washington, DC: Brookings Institution Press, 2008.

———. *The White House Staff: Inside the West Wing and Beyond*. Washington, DC: Brookings Institution Press, 2000.

Perry, Barbara A. *Jacqueline Kennedy: First Lady of the New Frontier*. Lawrence: University Press of Kansas, 2004.

Perry, Elizabeth Israels. "Training for Public Life: Eleanor Roosevelt and Women's Political Networks in the 1920s." In *Without Precedent: The Life and Career of Eleanor Roosevelt*, ed. Jean Hoff-Wilson and Marjorie Lightman. Bloomington: Indiana University Press, 1984.

Pfiffner, James P. *The Character Factor: How We Judge America's Presidents*. College Station: Texas A&M University Press, 2004.

Pitkin, Hanna Fenichel. *The Concept of Representation*. Berkeley: University of California Press, 1967.

The Presidential Campaign, 1976, vol. 1, pt. 1: *Jimmy Carter*. Washington, DC: U.S. Government Printing Office, 1978.

Radcliffe, Donnie. *Hillary Rodham Clinton: A First Lady for Our Time*. New York: Time Warner Books, 1993.

Radcliffe, Donnie. *Simply Barbara Bush: A Portrait of America's Candid First Lady*. New York: Warner Books, 1989.

Ragsdale, Lyn, and John J. Theis III. "The Institutionalization of the American Presidency, 1924–1992." *American Journal of Political Science* 41, no. 4 (October 1997): 1280–1318.

Randolph, Mary. *Presidents and First Ladies*. New York: D. Appleton–Century Company, 1936.

Reagan, Maureen. *First Father, First Daughter: A Memoir*. Boston: Little, Brown, 1989.

Reagan, Nancy, with William Novak. *My Turn: The Memoirs of Nancy Reagan*. New York: Random House, 1989.

Regan, Donald T. *For the Record: From Wall Street to Washington*. New York: Harcourt Brace Jovanovich, 1988.

Ritter, Gretchen. "Gender as a Category of Analysis in American Political Development." In *Political Women and American Democracy*, ed. Christina Wolbrecht, Karen Beckwith, and Lisa Baldez. New York: Cambridge University Press, 2008.

Robbins, Jhan. *Bess and Harry: An American Love Story*. New York: William Morrow, 1973.

Roosevelt, Eleanor. *The Autobiography of Eleanor Roosevelt*. New York: Harper and Brothers, 1958.

Roosevelt, Mrs. Franklin D. *It's Up to the Women.* New York: Frederick A. Stokes Company, 1933.

————, ed. *My Days.* New York: Dodge Publishing Company, 1938.

Rosenbaum, Herbert D., and Alexej Ugrinsky, eds. *The Presidency and Domestic Politics of Jimmy Carter.* Westport, CT: Greenwood Press, 1994.

Russell, Jan Jarboe. *Lady Bird: A Biography of Mrs. Johnson.* New York: Taylor Trade Publishing, 1999.

Sanbonmatsu, Kira. *Democrats, Republicans, and the Politics of Women's Place.* Ann Arbor: University of Michigan Press, 2002.

Scharf, Lois. *Eleanor Roosevelt: First Lady of American Liberalism.* Boston: Twayne Publishers, 1987.

Scharrer, Erica, and Kim Bissell. "Overcoming Traditional Boundaries: The Role of Political Activity in Media Coverage of First Ladies." *Women and Politics* 21, no. 1 (2000): 55–83.

Schieffer, Bob, and Gary Paul Gates. *The Acting President.* New York: E. P. Dutton, 1989.

Schlafly, Phyllis. *Feminist Fantasies.* Dallas: Spence Publishing Company, 2003.

Schlesinger, Arthur M. Jr. *A Thousand Days: John F. Kennedy in the White House.* Boston: Houghton Mifflin, 1965.

Shultz, Connie. *And His Lovely Wife: A Memoir from the Woman beside the Man.* New York: Random House, 2007.

Schweizer, Peter, and Rochelle Schweizer. *The Bushes: Portrait of a Dynasty.* New York: Doubleday, 2004.

Sefton, Alice Allene. *The Women's Division, National Athletic Federation: Sixteen Years of Progress in Athletics for Girls and Women, 1923–1939.* Stanford, CA: Stanford University Press, 1941.

Silvestri, Vito N. *Becoming JFK: A Profile in Communication.* Westport, CT: Praeger, 2000.

Skocpol, Theda. *Protecting Soldiers and Mothers: The Political Origins of Social Policy in the United States.* Cambridge, MA: Harvard University Press, 1992.

Smith, Richard Norton. *An Uncommon Man: The Triumph of Herbert Hoover.* New York: Simon and Schuster, 1984.

Smith, Sally Bedell. *Grace and Power: The Private World of the Kennedy White House.* New York: Random House, 2004.

Stahl, Lesley. *Reporting Live.* New York: Simon and Schuster, 1999.

Steinem, Gloria. "Patricia Nixon Flying." In *Outrageous Acts and Everyday Rebellions.* New York: New American Library, 1983.

Stroud, Kandy. *How Jimmy Won: The Victory Campaign from Plains to the White House.* New York: William Morrow, 1977.

Stuckey, Mary E. *The President as Interpreter-in-Chief.* Chatham, NJ: Chatham House Publishers, 1991.

Templin, Charlotte. "Hillary Clinton as Threat to Gender Norms: Cartoon Images of the First Lady." *Journal of Communication Inquiry* 23, no. 1 (January 1999): 20–36.

Thomas, Helen. *Dateline: White House.* New York: Macmillan, 1975.

————. *Front Row at the White House: My Life and Times.* New York: Scribner's, 1999.

Tomasky, Michael. *Hillary's Turn: Inside Her Improbable, Victorious Senate Campaign.* New York: Free Press, 2001.

Troy, Gil. *Affairs of State: The Rise and Rejection of the Presidential Couple since World War II.* New York: Free Press, 1997.

————. "Image-Making Not Power-Sharing: How Activist First Ladies Threaten Modern Presidents." Paper presented at the 1999 Annual Meeting of the Organization of American Historians, Toronto, Canada.

————. *Mr. and Mrs. President: From the Trumans to the Clintons.* 2nd ed. Lawrence: University Press of Kansas, 2000.

————. "'Half-Eleanor, Half-Bess': Barbara Bush as 'Co-President.'" In *Honor and Loyalty: Inside the Politics of the George H. W. Bush White House,* ed. Leslie D. Feldman and Rosanna Perotti. Westport, CT: Greenwood Press, 2002.

Truman, Harry S. *Memoirs,* vol. 1: *Year of Decisions.* Garden City, NY: Doubleday, 1955.

————. *Dear Bess: The Letters from Harry to Bess Truman, 1910–1959.* New York: W. W. Norton, 1983.

Truman, Margaret. *Bess W. Truman.* New York: Macmillan, 1986.

————. *Harry S. Truman.* New York: William Morrow, 1973.

van Rensselaer, Mary. *Jacqueline Kennedy: The White House Years.* Boston: Little, Brown, 1971.

Vavrus, Mary Douglas. *Postfeminist News: Political Women in Media Culture.* Albany: State University of New York, 2002.

von Damm, Helene. *At Reagan's Side.* New York: Doubleday, 1989.

Walcott, Charles E., and Karen M. Hult. *Governing the White House: From Hoover through LBJ.* Lawrence: University Press of Kansas, 1995.

Ware, Susan. *Beyond Suffrage: Women in the New Deal.* Cambridge: Harvard University Press, 1981.

————. "ER and Democratic Politics: Women in the Postsuffrage Era." In *Without Precedent: The Life and Career of Eleanor Roosevelt,* ed. Jean Hoff-Wilson and Marjorie Lightman. Bloomington: Indiana University Press, 1984.

Warner, Judith. *Hillary Clinton: The Inside Story.* New York: Signet Books, 1993.

Warters, Tabitha Alissa, and Laura DeLorenzo Denison. "Laura Bush: The First Post-Feminist First Lady?" Paper presented at the 2002 Annual Meeting of the American Political Science Association.

Wasserman, Carl David. "Firing the First Lady: The Role and Accountability of the Presidential Spouse," *Vanderbilt Law Review* 48 (1995): 1215–60.

Watson, Robert P. "'Comforter in Chief': The Transformation of First Lady Laura Bush." In *George W. Bush: Evaluating the President at Midterm,* ed. Bryan Hilliard, Tom Lansford, and Robert P. Watson. Albany: State University of New York Press, 2004.

Weidenfeld, Sheila Rabb. *First Lady's Lady: With the Fords at the White House.* New York: Putnam, 1979.

Weisman, Carol S. "Breast Cancer Policymaking." In *Breast Cancer: Society Shapes an Epidemic,* ed. Anne S. Kasper and Susan J. Ferguson. New York: St. Martin's Press, 2000.

Weldon, S. Laurel. "Beyond Bodies: Institutional Sources of Representation for Women in Democratic Policymaking," *Journal of Politics* 64, no. 4 (2002): 1153–74.

Wertheimer, Molly Meijer, ed. "Laura Bush: Using the 'Magic of Words' to Educate and Advocate." In *Inventing a Voice: The Rhetoric of American First Ladies of the Twentieth Century.* New York: Rowman and Littlefield, 2004.

West, J. B. *Upstairs at the White House: My Life with the First Ladies.* New York: Coward, McCann and Geoghegan, 1973.

Winfield, Betty Houchin. "From a Sponsored Status to Satellite to Her Own Orbit: The First Lady News at a New Century." *White House Studies* 1, no. 1 (Winter 2001): 21–32.

Winter, Nicholas J. G. *Dangerous Frames: How Ideas about Race and Gender Shape Public Opinion.* Chicago: University of Chicago Press, 2008.

Wolff, Perry. *A Tour of the White House with Mrs. John F. Kennedy.* Garden City, NY: Doubleday, 1962.

Woodward, Bob. *State of Denial,* Pt. 3: *Bush at War.* New York: Simon and Schuster, 2006.

Woodward, Bob, and Carl Bernstein. *The Final Days.* New York: Simon and Schuster, 1976.

Young, Nancy Beck. *Lou Henry Hoover: Activist First Lady.* Lawrence: University Press of Kansas, 2004.

Zangrando, Joanna Schneider, and Robert L. Zangrando. "ER and Black Civil Rights." In *Without Precedent: The Life and Career of Eleanor Roosevelt,* ed. Jean Hoff-Wilson and Marjorie Lightman. Bloomington: Indiana University Press, 1984.

Zones, Jane S. "Profits from Pain: The Political Economy of Breast Cancer." In *Breast Cancer: Society Shapes an Epidemic,* ed. Anne S. Kasper and Susan J. Ferguson. New York: St. Martin's Press, 2000.

INDEX

The letters following a page number denote: photos(p) tables(t) endnotes(n, nn).

242

INDEX

Bush, Laura Lane Welch: approval rating of, 129; and campaign experience, 1, 50, 134, 135–37, 217n128; and independent travel, 198; and descriptive representation, 18, 130–31, 134, 137–38, 146, 216n108; as fundraiser, 51; and gender ideology, 146; and crossing of gender boundaries, 51, 164; in familial role, 5; as cultural everywoman, 131; as gender role model, 6, 130p, 130, 136; as satellite wife, 134, 136; and governing experience, 44–45, 195; and ideological activism, 51–52; and loyalty to the administration, 164; and marriage, 33, 36; as moral guardian, 6, 162; and partisan ideology, 129–30, 149, 163–64; and personal autonomy, 47; and policy-making issues, 216n107, 217nn120, 125, 221nn32, 38; as policy entrepreneur, 164, 221n38; and the press, 134, 136–37, 138, 146, 225n92; and press secretary, 163; and public/private/separate sphere roles, 5, 133—36, 137, 145, 146, 163; and the use of rhetoric, 129, 135–36, 152, 162; as state first lady (Texas), 38, 44–45, 49; and substantive representation 158, 163, 221n38; as child development advocate, 50, 151, 162–63, 164, 165; as literacy advocate, 45, 49; and Washington society, 53; and "women's issues," 50, 129, 130p, 163–64; equal rights, 134

Bush, Neil, 171
Bush, Robin, 208n53

Cade, Kathy, 183, 184
Califano, Joseph, 168, 225n90
Cambodia, 125. See also Carter, Eleanor Rosalynn Smith: Cambodian refugee crisis
Camp David, 65, 82
Cannon, Lou, 219n153
Caro, Robert, 41, 206n23, 213n53
Carpenter, Elizabeth (Liz), 110, 111, 116, 118; and gender role modeling, 112–13
Carter administration, 84, 86, 90, 96, 117, 200–201, 225n90. See also Carter, Jimmy
Carter, Eleanor Rosalynn Smith: approval rating of, 127; and Cambodian refugee crisis, 19, 125, 182, 184; and campaign experience, 6, 30, 49, 56, 117, 126–27, 181; and political promises, 30, 124, 183p, 184; travel of, 88; and Congress, 6, 151, 182; as descriptive representative, 117, 124–25, 126, 128, 184; and

gender ideology, 142; as gender role model, 117, 125–26, 184; and crossing of gender boundaries, 6, 51, 126–27; as cultural everywoman, 131; and governing experience, 44, 56, 181, 195; and human rights, 182; and marriage, 33, 36, 215n88, 216n97; and mental health-care reform, 18, 19, 30–31, 49, 50, 151, 153, 182–84, 195, 225nn90; as moral guardian, 184; and partisan ideology, 6, 184; and policy-making issues; as activist-advocate, 6, 30–31, 50, 117, 124, 128, 131, 183–84, 190; as policy entrepreneur, 19, 31, 50, 52, 56, 124, 128, 183–84; as presidential partner, 126; and the press, 92, 124–26, 215n89, 215n91; and press secretary Hoyt, 127, 182, 216n99 (see also Hoyt, Mary Finch); and public/private/separate sphere roles, 31, 126, 142, 183p; and public diplomacy, 181; staff of, 19, 96, 125; as state first lady (Georgia), 38, 44, 45, 49, 53, 195; and substantive representation, 1, 31, 86, 151; governmental, 31, 153, 175, 181, 184, 200; during international travel, 181–82; and nepotism, 16; and symbolic representation, 1; and Washington society, 31, 53; and White House Office, 125; as White House hostess, 86, 126; and diversity of guest list, 86; and funding for restoration costs, 167; and gender specific events, 86, 90; and "women's issues," 6, 50, 124, 182, 184
Carter, Jimmy, 20, 49, 88, 126–27, 131, 142. See also Carter administration
Carter, Rosalynn. See Carter, Eleanor Rosalynn Smith
Casey, William, 169
Cassini, Oleg, 109
Cater, Douglass, 112
CBS/*New York Times* poll, 132
Center(s) for Disease Control, 19, 182
Central Intelligence Agency, 47, 76
Chaney, James, 113
Chemical People (PBS documentary), 168
Cheney, Dick, 137
Children's Defense Fund, 48
civil rights movement, 3, 117, 194; Civil Rights Act (1964), 113; and Eleanor Roosevelt, 75, 175, 177; and Harry Truman, 210n23; and Lady Bird Johnson, 29, 113, 116, 131; and Mamie Eisenhower, 68
Civil Works Administration, 177

Nixon, Thelma Catherine Ryan (Pat) (*cont.*)
40, 46, 55, 159; and social outreach, 119,
199p; through personal correspondence, 119;
through volunteerism, 160–61, 165; and
staff, 96; as state first lady (California), 44,
195; and substantive representation, 159–60,
163, 171; during international travel, 2, 151,
161, 182, 213–14n69; governmental, 196;
nongovernmental, 152, 200; and symbolic
representation, 1, 83; and Washington society, 31, 53, 55; and Watergate, 158; as White
House hostess, 61; and the White House
Office, 118, 148, 159; and "women's issues,"
163–64; equal rights, 160

O'Donnell, Lawrence, 186
Obama, Barack, 139, 140
Obama, Michelle LaVaughn Robinson, 139p; as
advocate for child health and nutrition, 50,
151, 188–90; approval rating of, 139, 141;
and campaign experience, 138; and descriptive representation, 18, 138–39, 139p, 146;
fashion and style of, 139; and gender ideology, 146; in familial role, 56, 189; as gender
role model, 94, 130, 138–41; gender-race
role model, 94, 138, 141; and governing experience, 44, 195; and marriage, 33, 36–37,
138–41; and mentoring, 50; as moral guardian, 188; and partisan ideology, 6, 138; and
personal autonomy, 148; and policy-making
issues: as activist, 47, 48, 50, 51–52; agenda,
199; as policy entrepreneur, 36; and the press,
138–39, 141, 146, 148, 149; and public/
private/separate sphere roles, 6–7, 138, 146;
and the use of rhetoric, 139, 188–90; as
Senator's wife, 53–54, 195; and substantive
representation: expertise in, 56; governmental, 175, 200; and symbolic representation,
139p, 200; and Washington society, 53; and
"women's issues," 50
Odum, Reathel M., 62t, 62n1, 105
Office of Civilian Defense, 151, 176, 177
Office of Economic Opportunity, 118
Office of Legal Counsel (OLC), 16, 20
Office of Management and Budget, 19, 31
Oxfam-America, 161

partisan representation, 23, 41, 76, 89, 150, 152–
54, 191–94, 201, 226n108; and nonparti-

san representation, 116. See also first lady
entries: and partisan ideology, and substantive
representation
Pastor, Robert, 181
Pearson, Drew, 77
Pennsylvanians (choral group), 78
People, 136
Perkins, Frances, 104–105
Peru Earthquake Voluntary Assistance Group,
161
Pfiffner, James P., 39
Philadelphia race riots, 113
Phyfe, Duncan, 167
Pitkin, Hanna, 11
policy entrepreneur, 194; defined, 1. See first lady
entries: and policy-making issues; as policy
entrepreneur
policy issues. See first lady entries: and policy-
making issues
Pope Air Force Base, 139p
Poston, Gretchen, 62t
postmodern women's movement, 14–15, 94,
130–31, 199
Poulaine, Simone, 113
Powell, Adam Clayton Jr., 210n23
Powell, Jody, 181
Prendergast, James, 97, 156
President's Commission on Mental Health
(Carter), 16, 30, 151, 183p, 183
President's Emergency Committee for Employment, Women's Division (1931), 172, 174
President's Physical Fitness Challenge, 188
President's Task Force on National Health Care
Reform (Clinton), 7, 18, 131, 151, 186p,
186–87; cost of, 216n109
Presidential Records Act of 1978, 15
presidential wife (first ladies): accountability of,
8–9, 15, 21–22, 196–99; duties of first ladies:
and "orientation time," 17–18, 204n36; and
experience in state government, 42–47; and
first-lady celebrity status, 203n1; and image
making as opposed to policy making, 201n3;
and legal (statute and case law) status, 8,
16, 20–21, 22, 193, 195; and nepotism, 16,
20, 193; as policy entrepreneur, 194, 201;
as presidential partner, 2, 5, 26, 94, 99; and
public diplomacy, 199; role of: as indicator
of social change, 204n28. See also first lady
entries

Other Titles in the Joseph V. Hughes Jr. and Holly O. Hughes Series on the Presidency and Leadership